# THE
# FORTUNE
# TELLERS

## UNTOLD STORIES OF SUCCESS

## DAMON KITNEY

Published by:
Wilkinson Publishing Pty Ltd
ACN 006 042 173
PO Box 24135
Melbourne, Vic 3001
Ph: 03 9654 5446

enquiries@wilkinsonpublishing.com.au
www.wilkinsonpublishing.com.au

Title: The Fortune Tellers
ISBN: 9781922810663

A catalogue record of this book is available from the National Library of Australia.

Design by Spike Creative Pty Ltd
Ph: (03) 9427 9500
spikecreative.com.au
Printed and bound in Australia by Ligare Book Printers.

# CONTENTS

# INTRODUCTION

I was born with newspaper ink in my veins. But it took me a long time to truly recognise the amazing gift I was given.

Upon leaving school I actually studied law at the Australian National University in Canberra. I didn't really know what I wanted to do in life and luckily, I got the grades to get into law.

At the time, my father was one of the pre-eminent political journalists in the Parliament House Press Gallery. He had been for decades.

I remember our breakfast table every morning being smothered by four national – printed – newspapers, with the ABC's flagship breakfast current affairs program "*AM*" blaring from his battery powered portable wireless.

Every night when dad was home, *AM*'s evening equivalent – *PM* – was also on the radio.

No evening was complete without watching each commercial television news service, *SBS World News* and of course, the only news that really mattered: the ABC.

Yet throughout my school and university years, Dad and I barely talked about the media or journalism. Let alone me joining the profession.

I did work experience in year 10 at the Parliamentary Press Gallery, which dad helped organise, and where I was lucky enough to spend time with legends of the profession like Brian Toohey, Michelle Grattan and the late Richard Carleton.

One evening that week Richard was kind enough to let me sit next to him on the set – but off camera – while he presented an edition of the nightly *Carleton-Walsh report*, a late-night current affairs program hosted by Carleton in Canberra and Max Walsh in Sydney. Both are sadly no longer with us.

It was a great thrill to see live television up-close. I was fortunate during my final years at university to get a casual evening job at Parliament House – of course assisted by the Kitney name – as a researcher in the Financial Review bureau led by leading journalists Tom Burton, Tim Dodd and Christine Wallace.

These were the days before the internet and my job was to scour the daily printed newspapers and physically cut out the stories I felt would be relevant to the bureau staff, paste them onto blank sheets of A4 paper, label them and file them in Manila folders under a topic.

This became the treasured research library for the bureau journalists. Today it is called Google.

Another part of the role was rushing to grab press releases from the so-called "boxes" down the 100-metre-long corridor which ran through the middle of the Press Gallery, where every journalist had their own pigeon hole in which political staffers and lobbyists would plonk press releases and other paraphernalia.

At one stage I even got one of my own, which of course given my lowly stature in the gallery, was never touched.

A ring of what sounded like a fire alarm bell was a sure sign something urgent had been posted in the various pigeonholes.

Suddenly there would be a sprint race with my rival bureau researchers, who included now highly regarded ABC journalist Adam Harvey, the son of the late Nine news political veteran Peter Harvey, to get to the treasured press release for their bosses first.

Given I was then a first-grade umpire in the local ACT Australian Football League, I always relished the challenge.

The other evening task was to secure the transcripts of *Question*

*Time* from the House of Representatives and Senate from the many parliamentary offices deep in the bowels of Parliament House. I don't know how many times I lost my way in that maze.

My predecessor in the role at the *AFR* was now well-known comedian Will Anderson, a thoroughly decent and courteous bloke.

But I'll never forget his words when he handed me the baton. "I hate this place and I can't wait to get out of here." The *AFR* bureau in the Press Gallery was clearly no place for Will.

It was then that I got my first full-time job in journalism from *AFR*'s editor-in-chief Greg Hywood at the Perth Bureau of the *AFR* in 1996, the year after I'd graduated. I would be just one of two in the bureau.

Before I arrived in the West, the one-man *AFR* Perth bureau chief was distinguished veteran mining writer Mark Dixon, who became a good friend and is tragically no longer with us.

Dixon taught me plenty about the craft of journalism and also graciously allowed me to travel to places I will never go again, including North West Shelf oil and gas platforms, remote gold mining camps and pearling luggers off the Kimberley Coast.

He also detested writing about politics and industrial companies, so it was left to me to stick a tape recorder under Paul Keating and John Howard's noses as they campaigned through Perth in the 1996 Federal Election.

Or to sit down with Michael Chaney at Wesfarmers and Alan Newman at Futuris to discuss their annual profit results, or then big-talking AMP CEO, American George Trumbull, when he breezed into town.

Dixon shared the Fairfax office at 14 Kings Park Road in West Perth with another one-man bureau chief for the rival daily *The Sydney Morning Herald*. He was award winning journalist and later to be *Sydney Morning Herald* editor Paul McGeough.

When I arrived in Perth, there was nothing more exciting than watching Paul in action, especially when he was steamed up with a scoop.

You could almost feel the heat on the glass wall between our offices on some afternoons as the animated Irishman barked expletives at the Sydney news desk and then the editor as he lobbied to get his exclusive the best possible run-on page one.

He also gave me heaps of very helpful advice, which was especially kind given I was working for an in-house Fairfax competitor.

If there was one frustration of my three years in Perth with the AFR, where I also subsequently worked with esteemed WA journalists Mark Drummond and Cathy Bolt, it was the number of times figures in business and politics would ask me – very innocently – "Are you Geoff's son?"

Having worked with the *South Western Times* and *The Daily News* before his decades in Canberra, Dad was renowned and respected in Perth.

But I wanted to make my own way in the media. After a while, I would answer with the reply: "Yes, so?"

There was one bonus for me of Dad's fame. After Paul Keating lost the 1996 federal election, Kim Beazley became federal opposition leader. He had always had a close relationship with Dad, given their Perth roots and their time together in Canberra.

On a number of occasions, I had to call Kim's office to get a comment for *The AFR* on a particular story, and Kim's then PR minder Greg Turnbull would take my call.

But I'll never forget the few times another voice would suddenly come on the line and it was Kim himself. He would always ask how dad was, and then would do his best to help me with whatever the issue was at hand – on or off the record.

It certainly showed me early in my career the value of opening doors and cutting through the minders to talk directly to the subject, and that one was all thanks to Dad.

In 1999, I took the opportunity to move to Sydney to join *The AFR* as its building and construction materials writer, where I also met my wonderful wife Anna. We now have three amazing children and I have been writing about business ever since. I also have an incredible older son Johnathon, who has two special kids of his own.

I rose through the ranks at the *AFR* to eventually become a deputy editor of the newspaper under editors Colleen Ryan and then Glenn Burge, first in Sydney and then in Melbourne.

It was then Dad and I directly crossed paths for the first time in journalism, when he had returned to Canberra from stints in Europe with the *SMH* and *AFR*.

I'll never forget working one Sunday in Sydney editing the newspaper (each of the deputy editors took turns in running the Sunday book) when Dad was the sole journalist working in the Canberra bureau.

I remember him pitched me a story for page one, which I wasn't sure was worthy of such lofty placement. When the paper went to press next day and the story wasn't on page one, I received a pointed email from him suggesting I had butchered his brilliant scoop.

Over the years since, unlike the early years, we have often talked about journalism.

Dad also played a fundamentally important role in editing my first book, the biography of James Packer titled *The Price of Fortune*. I am eternally grateful for his help.

I would never say being a Kitney has opened many doors in business for me because after my early years in Perth, we operated in completely different worlds over our careers.

But I think just having the credibility of the Kitney name has always been important.

I think when people see it in print, they know what it stands for.

I am often asked what are the most difficult interviews I have done over my career and what are the toughest topics to discuss with subjects.

I have to say that talking about children is always very difficult, as are occasions when there has been an illness or a tragedy that has impacted someone. Divorces are usually a no-go zone, but not always.

With some subjects, you obviously need to discuss those difficult issues – when you are aware of them – beforehand to get them comfortable to talk about them on the record. But there have been occasions when their revelation has come by complete chance.

I have also learned over a long career that deeply private high net worth people rarely grant you an interview unless they want publicity for something they are doing – whether it is buying or selling an asset, raising capital or launching an initiative. But that comes with the territory.

Once you are in the door, I find many are happy to talk more expansively about their lives, even if they carry a famous name.

I have also often been asked about the difference between Sydney and Melbourne when it comes to private wealth. From my observation, I would say Sydney can be more transactional. In Melbourne, the networks are harder to crack, but when you do, they run deeper.

But a downside of the latter is that some of its older-world networks are inevitably "clubby" and as a result, frustratingly shallow.

One question that I find stumps most in any interview I have conducted is "What is your greatest weakness." The responses are always telling.

In any big interview, listening is key. But to really get people to explore their inner demons and trials, trust is fundamental. People need to be comfortable and feel implicitly that you will handle their revelations fairly.

Minders or advisors to the subject are generally present on a zoom or in person for a big media interview – sometimes, somewhat unbelievably, there can be three or four on a call or in the room.

Some of those have been incredibly important and helpful just to reassure the subject that everything is going to be okay. Some of the classiest simply listen and say nothing. Others, sadly, have been more of a hindrance.

Over nearly 30 years in journalism, I don't think there is any subject who has come to me after an interview and claimed that I treated them unfairly.

I think there were quite a few people who were a bit stunned by how graphic their story was or how open they were. But never were they unhappy.

I think they respected the way that I presented them, even if it was warts and all.

I have great pride in the fact that as difficult as some of these stories are for the subject to have them out in the public domain, people have respected the way that I told them.

I think that too often, we get obsessed in business journalism with share prices, numbers and strategies and forget there are human beings that run our companies.

Sometimes those human beings do the wrong thing and when they do, they should be absolutely held to account to the full force of the law or by their shareholders.

But too often I fear there is not a proper appreciation of the amazing journeys of those in business and what they have done for the country. Especially in private business.

From a journalistic perspective, from my experiences private company CEO's and founders are inevitably more open than their public counterparts.

A public company CEO is usually incredibly scripted because they answer to a sharemarket, and continuous disclosure rules, which are more stringent than they have ever been.

They often employ an army of minders to look after them.

But private interviewees are not bound by the same rules – they often answer only to themselves and their families.

Often because those people rarely talk in public, it is almost always a privilege for them to sit down and talk to a journalist that they can trust. Many then embrace the opportunity.

Some of them who have their stories told in this book will do it only once in their life. For me that is truly exciting and what keeps me in this industry, nearly 30 years on.

Finally I would like to sincerely thank *The Australian* newspaper and its team of editors and staff, the home of my published journalistic work for the past 13 years, for all their incredible support.

I also want to thank the fine editorial team at The Institute of Company Directors magazine and previously in my career, the editors and staff from whom I learned so much at *The Australian Financial Review*. Their mentoring and opportunities they gave me at a young age were absolutely priceless.

I would also like to sincerely thank Wilkinson Publishing for bringing this book to life, and all the assistance and support of Michael, Jane and their team.

# JOHN ALLEN

*John Allen would have to be one of the best-connected people I have ever met. We stumbled across each other at a corporate function many years ago and have stayed in touch ever since. Over many years we would meet for coffee at or near the discrete suite of John Allen & Associates inside 530 Collins Street to discuss our shared passions of cricket, people and networking. John was always happy to make an introduction for me, and even helped facilitate the odd interview over the years.*

*But he is also one of the most discrete people I have ever met – never once did he talk about clients or appointments, even though he was responsible for filling some of the biggest executive and board roles in the country over many decades.*

*Given I was one of the only journalists he ever befriended and trusted, he very kindly granted me his only media interview when he decided to close the doors of his business in 2022. It was one of my best-read stories that year.*

John Allen has worked with Prime Ministers, Premiers, top bureaucrats, chief executives and big-name company directors.

Over the past 30 years, literally as a one-man-band, John Allen has been the head-hunter of choice for some of the most powerful figures in the land as his Melbourne-based executive search firm completed over 500 top level executive and board appointments.

One-third were for Commonwealth and State government entities in Victoria, New South Wales, Tasmania and South Australia.

300 in the private and not-for-profit sectors were for 40 different client organisations.

In more recent years, from its discrete suite number 908 inside 530 Collins Street, John Allen & Associates has also completed 40 appointments of listed company directors, most of whom have been leading businesswomen.

In the sporting field the firm has advised on CEO appointments for the Western Bulldogs AFL club, the Melbourne Racing Club and made a key executive appointment for Cricket Australia after the 2011 Argus Report.

But as he celebrated his 75th birthday on April 30, 2022, the man who was also renowned for his impeccable Liberal Party political connections as a foundation member of its 500 Club and the Higgins 200 Club decided that it was finally time to go enjoying his passions for travel and watching cricket around the world.

The doors of John Allen & Associates are now officially closed, the trigger being two life-changing health crises suffered by its sole principal during the COVID pandemic: the first led to heart surgery in March 2020, and the second, on February 27 2021, was a sudden stomach upset that became life-threatening and John was in hospital for four days.

If the ambulance that eventually attended to him that night after dinner at a friend's house in Dromana had been 30 minutes later, his doctors believe he would not have made it.

In the only media interview of his life to mark his retirement, Allen is reflective.

He's conscious of what he describes as "myths" about his legacy, especially being regularly labelled a "well-connected Liberal Party Melbourne head-hunter".

To disprove them, he points to his confidential meetings with five of the past eight Victorian Premiers and being privy to conversations with six of the past nine Prime Ministers, including one – Malcolm Fraser – as a client.

While he was appointed by the Howard government in 2000 as the inaugural chair of the Australian Government Solicitor Advisory Board and in 2002 as a member of the Commonwealth Remuneration Tribunal, re-appointments came from both the subsequent Rudd and Gillard Labor governments.

"Almost every quarter since 1982 I have sent an invoice to a Victorian government entity." he says.

"Nowadays I find myself feeling more of a centrist. I am saddened by the thought that somehow that makes me a Liberal Party wet."

Allen also recalls an anecdote from 2002 when at 5:15 on a Friday afternoon Ian Little, the then Secretary of the Victorian Department of Treasury and Finance and the first client of Allen & Associates, helpfully called him to say: "I can see that your firm has not responded to a tender. That will mean you can no longer be a preferred supplier to this Department. The tender closes at 5:30 PM, so I need an email from you now."

Allen still feels embarrassed about the incident, given Little gave him an introduction to State Finance Minister, Lynne Kosky, days earlier. Allen got to know her quite well in subsequent years.

## EARLY YEARS

Over the decades Allen has sometimes been labelled a "ten-pound Pom", largely the creation of old arch-rivals in his ultra-competitive profession.

He was in fact born and raised for 17 years in South India by his English tea planter father and third-generation Adelaide-born mother.

His memories of happy childhood years in India with regular ship voyages to Australia are reinforced by his father's 8mm cine films and other mementos he still has, including a 1.96m King Cobra perfect skin caught and poisoned by his father in 1929.

Allen's semi-regal English accent draws from his school education in Sussex and Devonshire in England and university in London before starting his business career there (he is now an honorary life member of the Australian British Chamber of Commerce).

After securing an MBA from INSEAD in France in 1976, he moved to Sydney in 1979 and in 1982 was hired by Spencer Stuart & Associates in Melbourne.

At one point during his years in the UK and Europe, Allen spent an "unforgettable" 45 minutes with Dr Egon Zehnder in the Zurich offices of his global firm. The interview questions came in English, French and German, to test Allen's tri-lingual claim.

In May 1984 Allen was also interviewed by the founders of Korn/ Ferry – Lester Korn and Dick Ferry – in Los Angeles, then in April 1987 he met Russell Reynolds himself in London.

He says the learnings from these one-on-one interviews with four of the legendary names in international executive search were "utterly invaluable".

Perhaps Allen's most often quoted piece of advice about spotting leaders borrows from the words uttered to him privately by former US President Bill Clinton after a lunch in Melbourne in 2001.

"Are they real and who is around them. Then can they see round corners and do they get back on the horse?" Allen says Clinton told him.

Known as an independent thinker with an eccentric streak, Allen feels bound by confidentiality understandings that prevent him from naming political and corporate clients.

But he is prepared to name some that are now deceased, including one powerful ally who opened many important doors.

"I was fortunate to get an early introduction to John Elliott through my tennis-playing friend, James Lee's invitation to Chemical Bank's July 1983 Melbourne introductory Cocktail Party. This first encounter with John lead to my becoming a Foundation member of the 500 Club and numerous encounters with him in the subsequent 20 years in social life, in politics and playing cricket. He gave me great support, though never as a direct client, in business," Allen says.

The late packaging magnate Richard Pratt also became a valued connection, both in business and with invitations to what he terms "singalongs at Sunday night Chinese" at the billionaire's Raheen mansion.

Among the many friendships he has made in politics, Allen has particularly fond memories of the late former National Party leader Tim Fischer, whom he first met in 1966.

During their last exchange over lunch at the 2016 Boxing Day cricket Test in Melbourne, Fischer exclaimed. "John, you have been the Where's Wally of my life!"

1989 marked the zenith of Allen's career as an international firm executive search consultant after moving to Russell Reynolds, assisted through earlier advice by the late Bill Flintoft.

In February that year he walked into the office of James Strong, the chief executive of Trans Australian Airlines, to stimulate his candidacy to run Melbourne based law firm Corrs as part of a mega merger to create Corrs Chambers Westgarth.

"James said he would not be a candidate without a guarantee of the merger going through as he was still running an airline. But the merger partners would not commit to the deal without a high-profile CEO. There was also a strong London-based candidate that would not commit to be in the process if there was any other candidate," Allen recalls.

History now shows Strong's appointment was later splashed across the print and electronic media, the first time one of Allen's appointees achieved genuine celebrity status.

The news broke the same day that "Russ" Reynolds himself was making his first visit to Melbourne, and within a few months Allen was promoted to be managing director in the firm and head of the Melbourne office.

He left the firm early in 1993 after 75 search assignments before John Allen & Associates opened its doors in August that year. In recent years Reynolds has become Allen's most valued friend and mentor.

## RULES OF THUMB

The Strong experience taught Allen an important lesson, one of many he is willing to share to shed some light on what many still see as the dark art of top level political and corporate head-hunting.

"That is my most tight squeeze illustration of how important it is to keep the process ahead of the noise. I just had to worry about the logistics and had two candidates. I would never have got the outcome if I worried about the conditions laid down by both sides," Allen says. "At all stages of dialogue with clients and candidates, do not necessarily give full updates of progress as regards decision-making and other people involved, though ensure that every word uttered is the truth."

In handling a workload of frequently more than a dozen open assignments at a time, Allen regards other guidelines that he has refined as "lastingly vital".

"Be often disappointed, though never surprised. Also, in working with clients and candidates aim to be as transparent as possible and on the basis of 'Please don't try to manage my thinking and I will not try to manage yours'," he says.

Allen has always been constantly aware of the reality that head-hunter's reputations are forged as much through dialogues with unsuccessful candidates as with appointees.

"Understand that people you invite inside the loop of confidentiality around an appointment do not talk, but those that are outside the loop – especially having been inside – do talk and thus the risk of the appointment being devalued in the marketplace becomes a reality," he says.

Other rules of thumb he highlights are:

- There are very few people who are more than 90 per cent happy with their career, so I started from the premise that I could potentially turn that 10 per cent of unhappiness into a career move.

- Allow a maximum of 15 hours for a message requesting contact to be acknowledged; then if not returned as a sign of possible interest in further dialogue about an appointment, move on to other contacts.

- Attempt to picture the scene you are interrupting, through virtually seeing with your ears on the phone.

- Never be seen talking to a non-client CEO at a function attended by a client CEO.

- Always be open to meeting and advising close relatives of a client CEO or Chair, free of any accountability on both sides.

- Always back the person first and the organisation second.

- Always take market soundings to calibrate potential deal-breaking issues before presenting a candidate and do not rely only on their nominated referees.

Allen believes being forced to personally make all the first calls to potential candidates and leave voicemails with high profile people he had never met gave him an edge on his rivals, who often left them to underlings.

"These had to be well prepared and perfectly delivered in a voice that would distinguish between a salesman and a professional confidant yet would arouse sufficient curiosity to generate a quick response," he says.

In 1996 Allen was able to take stock of his firm's competitive positioning by attending a seminar by the US-based guru on service firms, David Maister.

Many learnings he noted either for the first time or were reinforced by his then 20 years in management consulting.

"Revenue follows reputation; Never send an unexpected invoice to client; and 'You reap as you sow, but not necessarily in the same place, highlighting the benefit of business development time and effort'," Allen recalls.

"Also appreciate the significance of any career decision being second in significance only to choosing a life partner and choosing a new home, with both an intellectual and emotional journey needing to be sensitively managed by the head-hunter."

He believes that having no recognised international brand to cover his missteps meant he had to be extremely attentive to signals before they became "possible tight squeezes".

"Though at the same time I have always remembered the motto of Jack Nicklaus in golf," he says.

"The key to achieving perfection is to understand that you can only aim to minimise the degree by which you miss. Because there is no such thing as the perfect shot."

# WARREN ANDERSON

*With my Western Australian heritage, I was well acquainted with the legend of Perth entrepreneur Warren Anderson, even though I never met the man himself until years after he had faded from the corporate limelight. In 2022 I was given a chance introduction to him from an old WA journalistic colleague. After a brief phone conversation with Anderson, I flew up to Sydney from my Melbourne home to meet the man himself at his favourite morning coffee spot in Potts Point. He looked a shadow of the corporate titan that once commanded the attention of billionaires and Prime Ministers. But over a two-and-a-half hour off the record chat, he was still his gruff old self and in fighting spirits.*

*He eventually agreed to do an interview, and we met again a few weeks later at a cafe down the road in Rushcutters Bay. What he didn't tell me that day was that he was bringing along two of his daughters. But it was an unexpected bonus. They helped keep him focussed when he veered off into rants and even provided their own unique, on-the-record perspectives on his amazing life. I admire Anderson for having the courage to finally tell his story. And for all the difficult times they shared together, his daughters were immensely proud of their dad.*

The Toppi family's Italian cuisine is the stuff of legend in the Sydney restaurant scene. For almost three decades family matriarch Giovanna Toppi was the owner of Machiavelli Ristorante in Clarence Street, a treasured haven for titans of arts, business and politics. In 2018 her daughter Paola started its offshoot, Bar Machiavelli in Rushcutters Bay. Now known as Bar M, it played host to a very special celebration one Saturday evening in mid-October 2021: the 80th birthday party of Warren Perry Anderson.

"It was a good night. I was very happy," the man himself said of the event, where fine food and wine was consumed by everyone except the guest of honour, who has been a teetotaller for decades. Among the guests were his ex-wife Cheryl and his four children – who gave him an elegant, bound album of family photos from his colourful life – as well as veteran Sydney racing writer Max Presnell, his wife Colleena and members of the Sanderson family, famed for the Mercedes-Benz dealership one block away. But this birthday milestone was unlike any other in Warren Anderson's life.

It was now over a decade since the tycoon, once worth a reported $190m, was declared bankrupt. Anderson blames his bankruptcy on losing control of his finances after receivers took over nearly $380m of family trust assets following his messy public divorce in 2009. But he also borrowed heavily to fund property developments.

The final personal bankruptcy blow was actually dealt by Perth builder Warren Sizer the same year over an unpaid debt worth more than $1m.

He now borrows money from his children and mates to get by, and rents an apartment not far from Bar M. In the turmoil of the past decade, he's lost some friends including former prime minister Paul Keating. It's a far cry from the heady days of the 1980s and 90s when his connections with senior politicians and businesspeople including Keating, Kerry Packer, Graham Richardson, Alan Bond and Brian Burke set him apart from other entrepreneurs.

They helped him build landmark property developments in Melbourne, Perth and Darwin. But he was also called a thug, a bully and worse.

In his prime, Anderson boasted a personal portfolio featuring

Boomerang in Elizabeth Bay, one of Sydney's most famous mansions, as well as ski lodges in Perisher Valley, a luxury country estate called Fernhill at the foot of the Blue Mountains and the spectacular Tipperary cattle station in the Northern Territory. He and Cheryl accumulated what was called the "Owston collection", named after Anderson's family company, comprising fine art and antiquities purchased around the world. It was said to be the largest sale of fine art and antiquities in Australia when it was put on the block in 2010 after their 42 years of marriage ended in a bitter legal stoush. The fire sale by receivers KordaMentha, which also sold Fernhill, enraged Anderson and prompted him six years ago to launch legal action against the firm and the Adelaide mortgage fund Angas Securities, one of his financiers. He lost round one. "They struck me out and it's going to cost me $1.5-2 million to get it back into court," he says.

Even after decades of courtroom drama – both as plaintiff and defendant – Anderson isn't giving up on getting the money together for his last great fight. It is one of the reasons that after years of despising the media and publicity, he has agreed to give the first sit-down interview of his life.

We meet to talk over coffee at Cafe Maybach, attached to the Sanderson Motor Group's Mercedes-Benz dealership at Rushcutters Bay. With tired-looking eyes, a gruff, raspy voice and wispy, greying hair that was once brilliant blond, he seems a shadow of the high-flying entrepreneur the world once knew and many feared. But he is still smiling. Joining him for coffee are two of his beloved daughters, Cath and Shauna.

When I ask if he is happy, the old street fighter momentarily comes out swinging. "I'm busy running around trying to get the funds to sue these bastards down in Adelaide," he snaps. "But I'm doing all right thanks." Putting the legal case aside, I ask what else has motivated him to talk now. "I'm 81 in a month's time," he whispers, staring out the window as the rain tumbles down outside. "I have kept my head down over all these years. Now I just want to leave some legacy."

## FAMILY ROOTS

To understand what shaped Anderson's entrepreneurial character, his foul mouth and fighting spirit, you need to go back deep in his past to examine events that have never previously been in the public domain. He was close to his mother, so much so that his brother and sister called him "mummy's boy". On his first day of kindergarten in Perth, he refused to go, so his mother dragged him to the school yard and promptly left him. "I was furious! I was swearing so much they locked me in the outhouse toilet," Anderson recalls. A teacher later said to his mum, "Mrs Anderson, where on Earth did he learn to swear like that?"

"I got it off my old man," Anderson says now. "He was a mad bugger. He would take his teeth out and put them in his pocket when he was arguing with someone and then bang." But Anderson says that he, his siblings and mother were always spared and that his father taught him the importance of defending family. "My dad was a tough bastard. But he protected us kids and mum. They stuck together for 50 years."

When Anderson was just eight years old, his father gave him a single-shot Lithgow rifle. He eventually amassed a collection of 279 antique, collectible and modern guns.

His father's passion for defending family manifested itself when Anderson was a teenager. Sent to Christian Brothers College in Perth he was picked on by his fellow students and the brothers, being one of only three non-Catholics in the school (he still believes there is no God). One day he got revenge when a brother took the strap to him for no reason. "I said, 'Don't hit me, I haven't done anything.' But he just yelled at me and hit me again. So, I clocked him." Upon hearing about this, his father raced down to the school to confront the brothers. "The headmaster told dad, 'Mr Anderson, you have an uncontrollable son.' Dad said, 'What did you just say?' And the silly bastard repeated it! Dad reached across, grabbed him by the clergy collar, went to hit him but the collar came off in Dad's hand and the brother fell back in his seat. It was the only thing that saved him," he recalls with laughter.

After his expulsion from school, Anderson wanted to work in the country. His father bought a block of land near Bindoon, 85km north of Perth, and promised his son he could have it if he cleared it. But after Anderson had duly finished the backbreaking work and blown out the tree stumps with gelignite, his father reneged on the deal. "You know Dad, you can stick it up your backside," he told his father before travelling a further 150km north to the small town of Latham, where he worked clearing scrub with a bulldozer on a 3000-acre (1200ha) property owned by his uncle.

In 1965, at 24, he had earned enough to buy his first property, a 3300-acre (1335ha) parcel of land at Dandaragan in the WA Wheatbelt region. To this day he carries a faded copy of the original title contract in his wallet to remind him of where it all started. A year later he married Cheryl and they began leasing the nearby Cataby Roadhouse, the last petrol station where the Brand Highway stopped. (It was later connected to Geraldton.) Cheryl used to cook kangaroo for lunch under the trees while their dog, Prince Rupert, guarded the fuel supplies. She hated the place.

Anderson got his start as a serious developer of shopping centres in the early 1970s with the help of Bill Wyllie, a wealthy Australian living in Hong Kong. Together they built 25 shopping centres for GJ Coles & Co in Western Australia before Anderson moved to Sydney and his company New World Developments built more centres with the retailer's financial support.

The relationship faltered by the mid-1980s when he moved on to CBD developments, backed by the Japanese company Kumagai Gumi. Today Anderson also carries in his wallet a list of the locations of the 56 shopping centres, scrawled in pencil on a scrawny piece of lined paper. I ask why. "It just reminds me of how many shopping centres I built. I'm 81 years old very shortly and my memory is not what it used to be," he replies. He still sees them as his greatest contribution to Perth and Sydney suburbia. "I built 55 shopping centres and a big distribution centre in Perth between 1972 and 1984. They were all rezoned. Today you would be lucky to get a rezoning in five years."

## PROPERTY MAGNATE

Anderson was later associated with some of Australia's largest property developments, including at least six major office blocks in Melbourne's CBD and the refurbishment of the Windsor Hotel site opposite Victoria's Parliament House. He also built the Northern Territory Parliament complex in Darwin.

The biggest deal was the $1 billion-plus Westralia Square skyscraper in Perth's CBD, partially developed in partnership with Kerry Packer and John Roberts of the construction giant Multiplex. Anderson will never forget the day he met Packer. "I went to his office and he said, 'I want to build office towers in all the major capital cities of Australia and then put them in a trust and flog them off," he recalls. Anderson soon agreed to be Packer's business partner and they invested $270 million in the Westralia Square project in 1988. When the deal soured, it sparked a punch-up between Packer and Anderson in the former's office in Park Street, Sydney, during which Packer reportedly declared: "All West Australians are crooks."

"That was far from the truth," Anderson says. "Westralia Square cost my family $150 million. I never went to the public to raise funds, unlike the modern-day billionaires. I was a bit angry about Kerry saying that to me." But Anderson will not comment on the punch-up.

He also claims the reported $200 million loss Packer booked on Westralia Square was offset by gains they made on other projects. "I made him $40 million on Latrobe Street in Melbourne, $20 million on Spring Street and another $40 million without laying a brick on the site next to BHP, which I sold to National Mutual Life. Then I made another $40 million out of Westralia Square. That's $140 million," he declares.

Anderson also built Packer's lavish Ellerston property in the NSW Hunter Valley, where the billionaire is now buried. He says it cost him $40 million, from which he "never made a cent". The pair never reconciled. "Meeting Kerry was the worst thing that ever happened to me in my life," Anderson says. "But it was an experience. I'll just leave it there. I did Kerry quite a lot of favours. [His widow] Ros is a very good friend of mine. She would acknowledge they would not have had Ellerston but for me. When I took over Tipperary, I also got the TV station in Darwin that I virtually gave to Kerry for $10 million because I had too many other things on my plate at the time."

Anderson made headlines in 1985 when he paid $15 million for a huge parcel of land 100km south of Darwin and created a 1200ha sanctuary at Tipperary Station, where he amassed about 1900 exotic animals for breeding. Some were extinct in the wild, such as the scimitar-horned oryx, or critically endangered, such as the addax. Hundreds of rare birds were also brought to the property by Lord Alistair McAlpine, developer of Broome's Cable Beach Club Resort, when he closed his Pearl Coast Zoo in the town.

Tipperary Station featured a 3m-high fence to keep out predators and had its own school, post office, equestrian centre, indoor tennis court and pool, a sealed runway long enough to accommodate a

Boeing 727 and single men's quarters decked out in brass and jarrah. The staff, numbering more than 100, were reportedly allowed six cans of beer a day. "There was absolutely nothing there when I started. I spent $80 million at Tipperary, including the bitumen airstrip … Paul Keating and Kerry Packer both went up there."

Anderson's daughter Cath remembers the wet season at Tipperary when the mud was thick and deep outside the homestead and the family played cards inside to pass the time. "Dad sees something and sees what it can be, not what it is. Dad did all the hard work there," she says.

Anderson eventually sold half of Tipperary to an Indonesian group, and in 2003 offloaded the remainder to Melbourne barrister Allan Myers in a deal that allowed Anderson to keep the rare and endangered animals in the wildlife sanctuary. But controversy struck when the NT Government was forced to pick up a $13,000 tab for animal feed after wildlife sanctuary manager Kevin Freeman complained that the food supply had run out. Freeman then accused his tycoon boss of planning to kill all of his beasts. It forced the Territory government to apply to the Supreme Court for an injunction prohibiting Anderson from shooting, killing or disposing of a single animal on the station.

Anderson's version of events, reported at the time, was that Freeman had in one hit rolled out months' worth of hay, which was quickly eaten by deer. He says he then secured approval to fly from WA to the station with a powerful rifle so he could shoot the deer himself. Yet when he arrived at Darwin Airport with the gun slung over his shoulder, he walked into a frenzied media scrum. When asked by a reporter if he planned to shoot his collection, he angrily replied "Go away," before adding, "I'll f–king shoot you."

"It was a throwaway line," Anderson says now with just a tinge of remorse. "Kevin Freeman said that I was coming up to shoot the rare and endangered animals, which is just bullshit. I mean, why would I shoot animals worth $2 million? When I got halfway between the airport and Darwin I was surrounded by cops. A female cop had a pistol shoved in my ribs. They took the serial number of my rifle, checked that it was registered and let me go. The police eventually went to the property to search it but they didn't find anything."

The court case, which focused only on two southern white rhinos, collapsed after Freeman admitted he'd overfed the animals and sold some, banking the proceeds. Anderson also repaid the government for the feed bill.

Anderson today is still horrified that some of the rare and endangered animals he acquired wound up at a safari park for trophy hunters at Mary River in the NT. But asked if he misses Tipperary, his reply is matter of fact. "No. It was just a development. Yes, it was a passion when I first went there, the animals were dear to my heart," he says. "Its purpose was twofold. It was a passion, but it also had its tax benefits."

It wouldn't be the end of his troubles. He was back in the headlines after the collapse of a listed technology company called Firepower, which claimed it had developed a magic pill to improve vehicle fuel efficiency. It was backed by some of the nation's best-known sports and business figures. In 2008, an investigation by the corporate regulator led to Federal Court action against companies associated with Anderson and others alleged to have profited from sale of Firepower shares. Anderson was never named as a defendant.

He now recalls Firepower's principal, Tim Johnston, inviting him along to some "dodgy countries" to help sell the company's wares, including Pakistan, South Africa and Russia. "He paid me with 40 million shares. I went to Russia on three occasions with him. I met the oligarchs and Putin's men from the KGB. They were good blokes, dodgy as buggery, but good fellas," Anderson recalls.

But he stresses he was not involved in the activity that led to the ASIC action. After their falling out, in January 2010 Johnston claimed in court that he had been personally threatened with death by Anderson. "He got up in court and said I used to take people up into the mountains in the boot of my car and give them a shovel to dig their grave, which is absolute nonsense," Anderson says. "I spent four years with him, I sold my shares and I made $24 million which was fair enough for the time I spent in it. I put the money straight into the family trust."

## TRUST FIGHT

It was a family trust established for the benefit of Anderson's children that became central to an acrimonious two-year legal battle with his now ex-wife, which also saw him found guilty of assaulting her by grabbing her arm at their former Perth home. He was given a six-month conditional release order and a spent conviction, meaning he escaped a criminal record.

Now, looking back on his life, he says the only thing he would change was "my wife walking into the court and demanding $100 million. That was just ridiculous. No company has $100 million they can write a cheque for. They need time to sell assets," he says, noting that almost $400 million of assets were instead subject to fire sales. Yet they remain civil to each other and are not divorced. "I don't hold it against my wife. She went for a property settlement. But the problem is, she got manipulated by dubious characters and I was unable to stop it. We only see one another every now and then these days but we are still reasonably amicable," he says.

Anderson stresses he has always respected Cheryl's relationship with their children. Shauna, a naturopath, has two young children.

Anderson tears up momentarily and his voice drops to a whisper as he speaks of the challenges of his grandson, who was diagnosed with autism in 2015. In addition to Shauna, Cath and their elder sister Madelienne, Anderson and Cheryl adopted a son, Daniel, in the mid-1970s. After three daughters, he was determined to have a boy, but says he treats them all equally. "I love my daughters and my son. There is no difference for me," he says.

"It makes me feel quite proud that Dad has gone from basically nothing, given the hard times in his own family. He has managed to pick up the ball and run with it," Cath says. "He has made a difference in Australian life by building infrastructure. It was always improving something, it was never degrading something. He built shopping centres, law courts, apartments that people use and take for granted. Dad had a journey of learning and he taught us to teach ourselves." He has also given millions of dollars to philanthropic causes, she adds, including $400,000 towards saving the bilby, numbat and rufous hare-wallaby.

Shauna says that her parents' separation was "very difficult" but they are a lot happier now. "I've got a good relationship with both of them," she says. "Yes, it is hard to look back and think, 'Oh, that's what we could have had'. But at the same time, this is what we are and we are a close family still. That's what matters more than the money."

Says Anderson: "I put my wife in the best houses in Australia, I had apartments in London, ski lodges in Colorado, ranches here and overseas ... Jesus Christ, I had things everywhere. But family has always been important to me.

"It took me 60 years to build up that fortune," he adds. "But given where I came from, wealth hasn't meant anything to me. I accept things as they come because they are just material items."

Anderson is still determined to fight Korda Mentha and Angas in the courts, claiming they acted inappropriately in selling up his assets after his separation from Cheryl, forcing him into bankruptcy. The other parties deny the claim and in October 2016 the Anderson family failed in its bid to stop the sale of Fernhill Estate. Anderson blames his bankruptcy on losing control of his finances after receivers took over nearly $380 million of family trust assets following his messy divorce in 2009. The final blow was delivered by Perth builder Warren Sizer the same year over an unpaid debt worth more than $1 million.

Asked if he has lost friends through the years, he replies simply: "Not really. Only a few. Cheryl and I knew Barry Humphries, for example. We were very close at one point. He just went away, he never got in touch. I had a blue with Paul Keating after Cheryl got control of the family trust. Paul Keating was very upset about my situation with Cheryl. We were really close. He used to come around to Boomerang with his Federal Police escort. I went quiet on him for a while. I even asked him to see Cheryl to try to patch things up." He last saw Keating three years ago. "I still have friends now," Anderson says. "But the way things worked out, it is a bit embarrassing for me."

Three hours have passed and our interview is drawing to a close. Anderson's eyes are bloodshot and he seems a tad weary. But he looks satisfied to have finally told something of his story. Asked what he would like his legacy to be, he pauses for a sip of tea. "I haven't given it much thought," he eventually muses in reply. "I just don't want my family to think I wasted my life. That is about it. And I didn't."

# DEBBY BLAKEY

Debby Blakey could not take her eyes off the television. The year was 1992 and the South African cricket team was playing in its first international tournament, the World Cup in Australia, after 30 years in the cricket wilderness.

"I was living in Cape Town at the time. I really had not grown up on cricket but I became so passionate about it. I didn't know the rules so I wanted to learn them," says the now chief executive of HESTA, the $70bn industry super fund for health and community services workers.

Blakey has previously spoken of the trials and treasures of growing up in South Africa but never has she publicly spoken of an experience in the country that helped shaped her life. It started in 1993 when she returned to Durban on South Africa's east coast, the city of her birth.

"My interest in cricket started me on a journey where I ended up being an umpire in first division cricket. It was one of the most life changing experiences for me because it was all men on the field. It was very unusual to have a woman in the middle and it gave me lessons," she reveals.

"I'll be honest, it was hard. I can remember my heart thumping when I had to make some tough decisions on the field, decisions that I knew would not be popular. It was beating so loudly, you almost felt the whole field could hear it. So, it was tough. But I just learned so much: Hold your ground, trust yourself and back yourself in a very difficult environment."

During 18 months of umpiring, Blakey met some star South African and ex-international players.

But she will never forget one, the late West Indian star fast bowler Malcolm Marshall, who finished his career playing for South African provincial team KwaZulu-Natal after retiring from national duties. Tragically he passed away in 1999 after a battle with colon cancer. He was only 41.

"He was amazing. He was funny, sharp and as tough as anything," Blakey recalls.

"But he was also very respectful of me as a female."

After Blakey broke the mould in cricket she carried that spirit into business, firstly in South Africa, when she set up her own employee benefit consulting practice before emigrating to Australia in 2000. She joined HESTA in 2008 and became chief executive seven years later.

She never set out to be a CEO. She's used a personal coach extensively through her corporate career to unlock her self belief.

Where at university and in her early career she admits she was "extremely conscious" of her gender, she wasn't bothered by the unwelcome critiques of her advancement.

"There was some very unfortunate comments at times. While I was there as a female, I had done well in my studies and I was confident in terms of my capability, so I let everything just wash off me. I never focused on that," she says.

"But later in life I've had experiences where I actually have wanted to challenge the status quo. I've seen other people call it out in a very assertive way and I think sometimes that is needed. I think my style is possibly more understated, but I'm think I'm also very clear."

## LIFE LESSONS

Growing up in South Africa was at times confronting for Blakey and her two sisters.

Her father Richard was a shirt manufacturer and her mother Lorraine was involved with the local community and arts scene but really devoted her life to her three daughters.

Her father, in particular, was passionate about social justice issues.

"I saw in my dad the opportunity for impact. He was a small business owner who was intent on bringing about change. He was very connected with the international community and my parents made our home very open to people from abroad," she says.

"Near where we lived outside Durban, there was a local underprivileged community and my parents also became involved in that through the Methodist Church. My father mentored some of the young men in that community and we used to joke about how often they would pop into our home at dinner time to have a good meal where they might not have had one otherwise."

There are bad things she saw growing up – not terrible things, she stresses – but incidents that she would rather not highlight.

"Growing up in a society where there was no democracy is incredibly confronting. It is one of the reasons why I am so passionate now about diversity, but very much about the inclusion that you want to see. It is something we believe so deeply in at HESTA. It is not only having diversity at the table, but it is how you cultivate a culture of inclusion. I do think that comes from my youth," she says.

But the end of the apartheid era and the election of Nelson Mandela as president in 1994 also had a profoundly positive impact on Blakey, who earned a Bachelor of Science from the University of Natal where she was the recipient of an IBM scholarship.

"Coming through that time of democracy and the celebration of democracy was a phenomenal thing to experience firsthand. Hopefully you never forget how important democracy is," she says.

That appreciation led her to spend a year in the US studying psychology and biblical literature after completing her science degree. Yet she stresses she isn't religious per se.

"I'm always happy to say that I've got deep core beliefs. But being classified as a religious person, that doesn't sit well with me," she says.

After setting up her consulting practice back in South Africa, she returned to university to study maths, computer science and two pension fund qualifications following the birth of her two children.

"My mother was the most phenomenal support to me and the children, I had lots of exams and she was just there for me," she says.

After a decade of running the practice and with her son and daughter becoming teenagers, she and her husband Lawry sought a better life abroad. She sold the business and the family moved the Melbourne. The family dog, named Kirby, did seven months in quarantine.

She took a year off to settle the family in their new homeland before taking up a business development role for an industry superannuation fund, which paved the way for her to join HESTA.

Four years later her parents, who were then in their early 70s, also moved to Australia where they lived happily and made many friends before her mother became unwell for several years.

"She died last year," she says.

"It was an amazing time for us as a family to be able to be there for her and also actually to experience firsthand the amazing, incredible people who work in health and community services. That is always a privilege, given my role, but to really experience that in terms of the caring for my mum was just amazing."

Blakey's father still lives in Melbourne and while he has been blind for the last decade after suffering macular degeneration of his eyes, he is still going strong at 91 years of age.

"He is amazing. I see him a few times a week. He is still very inspirational in our lives," Blakey says.

"I now have a sister in Melbourne and between the two of us we obviously give my dad all the support we can. But he is a very independent gentleman, even though he's blind."

## MENTORS AND FRIENDS

HESTA is chaired by Nicola Roxon, who was the first female Federal Attorney-General and a former minister of health and ageing, with whom Blakey enjoys a "phenomenal" relationship.

"She is so smart and so clear in terms of prioritisation of the things that really matter," the latter says.

"She's a very influential chair, yet she brings the board completely on her journey. There is a gutsiness that she has taught me. We are all on a journey of further development."

Blakey's greatest passion has long been developing a fairer and more equitable super system for women.

While she welcomes the government's decision to cut back super tax concessions for account balances over $3m, she wants it to prioritise paying super on the Commonwealth Parental Leave Pay scheme and other important equity measures that will help close the gender super gap.

HESTA believes it sees women retire with, on average, about a third less super than their male counterparts.

"People are now aware that these are poor system issues that are up to us to solve. This is the period we have to do it. This is the decade we have to significantly change things," she says.

"Coming out of Covid, the care economy and those who work in health communities have carried us through this incredible three-year period. This is the time we have to firmly deal with equity issues for them. There needs to be a different value in the super system put on unpaid caring work."

She also supports Treasurer Jim Chalmers' call to tap the sector's vast pool of capital for nation building in areas such as affordable housing, climate, health and aged care, and the digital economy.

In 2022 HESTA committed $240m to support the launch of a specialist affordable housing fund manager, Super Housing

Partnerships (SHP), to focus on developing build-to-rent (BTR) apartment projects in Victoria.

"My number one objective is investing for long-term returns for members. But there is an opportunity to invest in ways that have a positive impact in things like affordable housing," she says.

HESTA has also developed a reputation as an activist investor and took a vocal stand in 2020 against mining giant Rio Tinto after its destruction of the Juukan Gorge rock shelters in WA.

It has also taken vocal positions against financial services giant AMP and in June 2021 Blakey herself criticised the Sydney gentleman's club The Australia Club for its vote against allowing women to join.

"I have had to be more comfortable in being in the limelight than I expected," she says with a smile before adding that HESTA must "lead by example" on behalf of its members.

"We invest $70bn of our members' money so how do we do that with influence and with impact?"

Specifically, HESTA has also warned AGL Energy, Origin, Santos and Woodside that it may dump its shareholdings unless they get serious about limiting global warming to 1.5 degrees. HESTA has about $720m invested across the four companies.

"We need to be in these conversations. This is our approach to active ownership and if we are going to invest in companies, we do have a seat at the table as an investor," Blakey says.

"We really want to support a global transition to a low carbon economy, and to do that we need to remain invested and seek to influence the transition that those companies make."

Blakey, who is also the president of the powerful Australian Council of Superannuation Investors whose members manage about $1 trillion, might have been HESTA CEO for eight years but she still sees plenty of unfinished business.

"I can't see the end yet and I think that is very important. I feel I'm in the sweet spot," she says.

"You never know what the end looks like. But right now, I'm the middle. I've done so much yet there is still so much more I want to achieve."

# JOHN BOWEN

John Bowen was only 23 when in 1994, his father sent him to work in America.

Only 12 months earlier and less than a year out of university, John had started working at his family's century-old Bowens timber and hardware business, which had been established by his great grandfather, Richard Bowen.

In 1894 Bowen and Redmond Pomeroy began selling timber products from a small yard in North Melbourne under the name Bowen & Pomeroy, Timber Merchants. Both tragically passed away in the same year, 1924, before Richard's son, John senior, became managing director in 1931.

John senior's son, Jack, took over the business in 1971. Fast forward 23 years and Jack was looking to the future, sending his eldest son abroad to work at three timber companies on the US West Coast for six months.

When his US tour of duty had ended, John junior will never forget returning to Melbourne's Tullamarine Airport on a brisk Sunday morning, being picked up by his father and the stunning conversation that ensued.

"Dad said, 'Do you feel like starting at our Rowville store tomorrow? I said 'Sure'. He said, 'Well you are the manager! I said 'What?!'," Bowen junior now recalls of his stunned reaction to his unexpected promotion, conscious of the responsibility of carrying on the family's extraordinary legacy.

"I couldn't use our prehistoric computer system. I didn't know the staff very well and I certainly had never managed people. I was literally thrown in the deep end. But I loved it and have continued loving it since."

John has now been CEO of Bowens since his father handed him the reins in 2005. His younger brother Andy re-joined the family business seven years ago as chief investment officer after working as an investment banker in New York.

The fourth-generation family-owned Bowens is a market leader in supplying quality timber and building supplies throughout Melbourne and regional Victoria.

For the past 12 years Bowens has also owned Timbertruss, one of the nation's largest prefabrication timber manufacturers which employs staff in Victoria and Queensland.

The Bowens story is also a textbook example of how to achieve a successful succession across generations in a family business and provides lessons for the family-owned firms managing the biggest generational wealth transfer in the nation's history.

PwC has estimated $4 trillion is projected to be transitioned between generations over the next 20 years.

John Bowen says his father, who these days is Bowens chair, got the "mix exactly right" in passing the baton to his sons when he was in his early 60s. Jack's two daughters are not involved in the business.

"I was calling him five times a day early on. Now I won't ring him unless I have something good to tell him. He has had this great mix to exit the business and be completely positive with what I'm doing," John says.

"He backs me in every opportunity. In fact, there are times I've got to ask him just to settle it down a little bit. There are other families where owners will move away and completely disappear or move away but continually interfere. Dad doesn't do either of those things. He's been great. My uncle David, who is also a shareholder in the businesses, has been equally supportive of me. So, I've been very fortunate."

## FAMILY LESSONS

He says his greatest learning from his father, who in his heyday famously knew the names of every staff member, was "to be honest and to engage with people beyond just the work they are doing."

When John Bowen senior passed away in 1971, ownership of the business passed to his wife Betty, his two sons, and his daughters Carole Hart and Diana Lowe.

Two decades ago the sons purchased their sister's shares in the business, while Betty Bowen transitioned her shares to her grandchildren.

"My dad and his sisters and brother were able to have meals and get on and speak to each other before and they haven't missed a day of that ever since. So, it's a great lesson to understand there are other priorities apart from the family business," Bowen says.

"I think my aunties gave a bit. But at times, the business gave a bit as well. There's been just a different balance over time. A good transition relies on good personalities and good people who are willing to give and listen."

The smooth transition was assisted by a board of directors established by Jack Bowen, which still meets once a month. A member of the Hart family, Peter Hart, sits on the board.

Another external director is former Reece executive Neil Cathie, who had a 27-year career at the nation's most successful plumbing and bathroom distributor.

"I've been fascinated by the Reece story. I think Reece were and still are just amazing. They are an unsung Australian business, one that not enough people know the story of. They are the best in the world in what they do," John Bowen says. "Neil left that business over 10 years ago and we were fortunate to fall across him."

There are no plans to float Bowens as its turnover this financial year

– expected to be over $460m – makes it too small to be a significant public company.

"We are not super wealthy, we enjoy what the business gives us. Private ownership is important to the staff – there are plenty that have been there for 20 years plus," Bowen says. "I'm fiercely independent. It is a shame how many businesses are being swallowed up by big box players."

While his brother Andy is 12 years younger, John says he has enjoyed working with him in management because they are "literally a generation apart".

Andy Bowen's focus has been establishing an e-commerce function for the business. Principally for the trade, but also increasingly for retail customers.

Bowens' 16 stores across Victoria and its range of delivery options were repurposed by creating a digital front end, allowing it to make promises to customers around tight delivery times, especially for large and often fragile products needed by builders on work sites.

"We have stores that are set up in an industrial manner which works perfectly for distribution when it comes to an online offer," John Bowen says.

## FUTURE PROOFING

The e-commerce site was launched as a retail service in December 2020 and has generated a sharp increase in website traffic.

Bowens also thrived through the depths of the pandemic, being declared an essential industry and allowing it to remain open under strict Covid protocols.

Bowens has benefitted from an unexpected lift in demand for new construction and renovations, driving record volumes through the business.

Supply shortages have also led to unprecedented price increases for timber products and more recently, associated hardware.

"It started with timber. That has flattened out now. I really don't see it jumping much again. For some of the other products, they have really only got some (price) momentum at the moment," Bowen says.

Imported timber products have also been impacted by global supply chain issues, which have flowed through to price increases for engineered wood products, vital for beams and other structural timbers in buildings.

While Bowens uses largely Australian products, others in the market rely on imports.

"The market across Australia relies a lot on what's happening overseas and North America has virtually cut itself off from Australia. So those importers have had to move to other markets. It's very difficult and then very expensive," Bowen says.

During the pandemic Bowens continued to invest in its operations, including in a new prefabrication plant, showroom and a new timber yard in Geelong.

"You've got to keep investing. Independent businesses can't just stand up and say, 'We are family owned and independent so therefore people should walk in and buy from us'," Bowen says.

"We need to keep rebuilding our stores, investing in them and making sure the product that they stock is relevant, rather than just resting on the laurels of 127 years."

Going forward he says the firm will stick to its knitting, increasing its site footprint with new facilities and innovative products.

He believes the Timbertruss plant at Geelong – which specialises in producing roof trusses and wall frames – is the most technically advanced in Australia.

"So we are doing a few really exciting projects, not just walls, roof trusses or floor systems. We are doing some prefinished panels for customers. Our version of next stage prefabrication we're calling it," Bowen says.

He also wants more women in what continues to be a male-dominated business. The firm last year had its first ever women in trade event at its Port Melbourne showroom.

Bowen has no expectation his four children – two are still at school – carry on the family name in the business.

"My wife and I are very keen for our children to find their own way outside of the business.

"We will give them opportunities at some point, but at this stage, we want them to start outside and see if I can find another path first."

He will continue to live by the motto – which has served four generations of his family – that "We can't be anything unless we are the best at the basics."

"That's something that I reiterate to our team again and again. Having the right product, serving people the right way, getting it out onto site on time and accurately, continues to be our first priority," he says.

# ELIZABETH BRYAN

*Elizabeth Bryan and I passed like ships in a night over two decades
of corporate history until March 2016 when I met her in a corner of
Virgin's top shelf, invitation-only lounge at Sydney airport then known
simply as "The Club". Our paths finally crossed because she had
become chairman of Virgin Australia. She was impeccably dressed in
a red suit with matching rings and earrings. As we dined on a lunch of
lobster rolls, grilled calamari and freshly shucked oysters, she let fly in
trademark Bryan style about the bickering between Virgin's big-name
shareholders. The story that resulted made headlines, just as she had
wanted. Fast forward to October 2021, and she granted me what would
be her final interview to round off her long career in the corporate
world. While Elizabeth always presented a hard edge in public, that day
I learned more about her softer side and the personal challenges in her
life which until then had largely remained out of the spotlight. She will
always be a country girl at heart and rightly respected as a pioneer that
paved the way for more women to enter the nation's boardrooms.*

May 9, 2004, will always live long in the memory of Elizabeth Bryan.

That day her husband Bill Gee, Australia's chief veterinary officer for
15 years who was awarded an Order of Australia in 2000 for his services
to quarantine, died peacefully in Sydney after a tortuous health battle.

"It is a long and terrible experience for anyone with prostate cancer.
I nursed him, I looked after him. It is a great privilege to look after and
care for people who are close to you when they are going through a
terminal illness," Bryan says.

"It does change you. It does stop you and make you think about things that in our busy day-to-day lives we just don't go near."

But Gee's death would only begin a decade of pain for Bryan, as her new partner, her mother and father all subsequently contracted debilitating terminal illnesses.

Just as she was forging her boardroom career with chairmanships at oil refiner Caltex and industry super giant UniSuper and a directorship at Westpac, Bryan was locked into a cycle of caring, dying and death.

In 2014, the death of her greatest hero, her father John Bull – a farmer from the town of Tooraweenah on the lower western slopes of the Warrumbungle Ranges in central NSW – proved a turning point in her life.

The previous decade – during which she now muses she was "deathed out" – showed her the very real caring burden that can fall on women during their careers, which she says has made her more "alert and careful" in caring for women – and men – facing similar stresses.

Hours of sombre reflection on the veranda at the homestead of her family property known as Boonery – which her father had given to her a few years before he died – also steeled Bryan for the final phase of her corporate career, which came to an end in late October 2021 when she stepped down from the chair of insurance giant IAG.

It was also just over a year to the day that she resigned as chair of Virgin Australia after the airline's disastrous plunge into voluntary administration and subsequent sale to private equity firm Bain Capital.

"I was old enough to justify retiring before I took on IAG and Virgin. But after my father died I had lost all the structure in my life," she says. "I was not keen to suddenly dump the structure that my career and my working life had given me. It was very helpful for me to continue to work and continue in a rhythm that I had run with all my life."

## TOUGH TIMES

In 2016 she succeeded Brian Schwartz as IAG chair but in the final years of her reign, with the onset of the pandemic, the insurer hit sharp headwinds.

In July 2021, IAG posted a shock $427m loss after it booked $1.5bn worth of provisions, largely for potential business interruption claims associated with Covid.

A month later Bryan now famously laid out the failures of the IAG board and management in her annual letter to shareholders. She apologised for "organisational and risk management failures within the company".

She disputes suggestions it was a "bombshell letter".

"I have always thought that openness is the best way to go," she says.

"All through that royal commission era we went through, we learned the lessons of boards not getting on the front foot, not really knowing what had gone wrong, and not coming out and talking about it clearly. Any public company board now, you need to get on the front foot."

It was asserted the provisioning gave IAG an inglorious entry to "Australia's risk failure club", alongside the likes of the big four banks, AMP, Allco, Babcock & Brown and Centro Properties.

But in response Bryan reiterates the comments in her letter that IAG failed to price its insurance policies properly because of shortcomings in contractual exclusions for pandemics, resulting from a failure to update references to legislation and poorly integrated IT systems.

"So, you can see how these problems can sit there and then if something goes wrong that pulls them out, you look like idiots. It shouldn't happen," she says.

"But is it a matter of joining a club of bad behaviours? No, it's a risk system issue that is an issue across all complex organisations."

Asked if her corporate legacy has been tarnished at IAG (its 2020 cash profit was also the lowest since 2012 and its reported insurance margin was the lowest since 2011), Bryan bristles before pointing to the feedback from those that really count.

"I think I've done the right thing," she says. "If people want to judge me in a way that tarnishes my reputation, I just don't think they are right. In fact, there's been very little of that. Making the comments I did in the shareholder letter was the right thing to do and that is shown by the fact that the shareholders have thanked me for clarity and for frankness."

## CRASH LANDING

In terms of the headlines generated, IAG's challenges during Bryan's reign might seem insignificant compared to the demise of Virgin Australia, which she and her board put into voluntary administration in April 2020 with debts of $6.8bn. Five months later, creditors voted in favour of a sale to Bain Capital.

Bryan and her fellow directors were praised for the way they handled the dying days of the airline, ensuring it could be sold as a viable entity. "The fact it is flying again and in private hands and is still here, that is a great victory for all of us involved. That is an amazing thing," she says.

But she still feels great pain for the staff who were let go, describing it as "a personal loss" for the many who had worked for 15 years to build a serious rival to Qantas.

Another casualty was CEO Paul Scurrah, the popular leader ousted by Bain after just 20 months in the job, replaced by former Bain partner and Jetstar CEO Jayne Hrdlicka.

"Paul did a really good job. One of my regrets was that Paul wasn't given an opportunity to show what he could do with that airline," Bryan says.

"It was a brutal demise. He was used through the difficult part of the process and the tables turned on him at the last moment."

Scurrah had in March 2019 replaced John Borghetti, the man who with the backing of deep pocketed foreign airlines as shareholders had transformed Virgin into a fierce rival to Qantas.

But eventually they would give no more, triggering Virgin's eventual collapse as the Covid storm hit.

Borghetti has said he first flagged leaving Virgin in 2016 after six years in the role, but stayed on for another three years at the request of Bryan and the board.

"I always had a good working relationship with John," Bryan says of Borghetti. "We successfully managed many difficult issues over the years. We solved a lot of problems together. He was a man who was passionately committed to building the second airline.

"This job of building a second airline, having real competition, was part and parcel of his make-up. It must have been terrible for John when the airline had to go to administration. He retired and was given a good send-off by all of us."

The comments appear to contradict what was reported as a "withering broadside" Bryan issued Borghetti in June 2020 in an interview with the ABC's Four Corners, where she claimed the Virgin board didn't like the way he was running the company.

"That was my first time on television. I was terrified," she says upon reflection.

"If I got the wording slightly wrong, I was just very thankful I didn't get it completely messed up. But it was not my intention in that program to give that impression."

While she never heard from Borghetti, she understands he "wasn't that impressed" with her comments.

Has she spoken to him since? She pauses and sighs. "When things are emotional and you are going through these big corporate changes, all of us, we react," she says. "I just think you let that stuff dissipate. Most of it goes away after a while. Time heals and gives perspective."

## BOARDROOM TRAILBLAZER

Bryan's third public company chair at Virgin cemented her status as a trailblazer. She has paved the way for other women to follow at the helm of some of the nation's top board tables. But she had broken the mould much earlier when in 1992 she was hired as general manager of $25bn superannuation fund manager NSW State Super, becoming the first woman appointed to run a large financial institution in Australia.

Now three decades on, she has pride in the latest AICD data showing women hold more than 33 per cent of ASX 200 directorships, and she downplays concerns the progression has stalled.

"What really matters in a boardroom is that you have some numbers in there," she says. "What we are developing now is experience and skill among women in boardrooms. It is an influencing role. You have to argue a case. These are quite subtle roles. We are developing more women who know how to do that.

"The really important thing is women getting into the top executive layers. Women must populate those. That is where we are still pretty thin on the ground. That really is the next wave of what we have to get done."

At NSW State Super, Bryan also became known as an activist investor, challenging several underperforming boards including teaming up with AMP and Bankers Trust to question the board composition at Coles Myer.

Again, she was before her time. In recent years super fund activism, especially from powerful industry funds, has transformed the dynamic between boards and investors. More recently, environment social and governance (ESG) issues have also come to the fore.

Bryan is a strong supporter of ESG, stressing that maximising profits for shareholders "no longer cuts it" in an era where corporations have so many touch points on people's lives and where the value of intangibles make up a greater proportion of the value of a business beyond a balance sheet.

"The push that's going to come from all the climate change warriors is going to be a real issue for companies over the next few years. That is immediate and here," she says. "So, it won't be good enough to have a light greenwash over everything. You must have a serious understanding of what you can do, what you can't do, and how you can play a constructive role."

Bryan says she will leave corporate life with no regrets, conscious that she took a path that was before her time and different to the "traditional life for women", even if it worried the life out of her parents at times.

Now living on Sydney's lower north shore, she will always miss the country life and brilliance of the stars above the Warrumbungle Ranges on a clear night.

When she was in her 30s she bought a small block of land next to her father's property. But in 2016, tired of the commute from Sydney, she decided to sell all of the family holdings she inherited and her own. "The country has always been quite important for me. But once that part of the family died out, I really lost both my family and my rural connections. It was tough," she says softly.

"To just go up there by myself – 7½ hours in the car – you put the chairs on the veranda, you sweep the mouse droppings out of the house, you sit down and have a beer and you think, 'Oh, this is wonderful.' Then you think, 'What now?' All things come to a close."

After staying six years longer than she expected in the corporate world, Bryan is now enjoying retirement.

"This extra six years has given me time to recalibrate," she says.

"To think of myself not as part of a family and a country girl, but a Sydneysider who's looking forward to enjoying the life Sydney has."

# BRUCE AND ELIZABETH BUCHANAN

*It was former journalist-turned renowned PR advisor Simon Westaway who first introduced me to Bruce Buchanan in 2010. Bruce had just taken over from Alan Joyce as CEO of Qantas's budget carrier, Jetstar, and Simon was doing the PR for the airline. Bruce and I immediately struck a chord and would subsequently catch up for lunch a few times a year. He is one of the most intelligent people I have ever met. When Bruce decided to leave Jetstar ahead of starting a fledgling digital marketing business he called Rokt that had a string of big name backers, he gave me his only exit interview. I then followed the Rokt story from the outset, watching its amazing growth.*

*But over the years Bruce also made me aware of the struggles of his stepdaughter Sophie. Occasionally he would call me from hospital wards when Sophie had been rushed for emergency surgery. I always respected his wishes to keep her story private. But in 2022, Bruce convinced Sophie's mother and his second wife Elizabeth that the day had come to share her inspiring story with the world. It was hard not to get emotional listening to a father and mother reflecting upon the darkest moments in their lives dealing with the life and death struggle of their beloved daughter. But thankfully, the story had a happy ending.*

The ten days before Christmas 2021 were set to be a time of celebration in the New York household of the Buchanan family.

Bruce Buchanan's technology unicorn known as Rokt, whose long-term shareholders include the James Packer-backed Square Peg Capital and media mogul Lachlan Murdoch, had just signed off one of the largest single-venture capital fund raisings in Australian history.

Secretive American financial powerhouse Tiger Global had helped Rokt bank a cool $458m, valuing the e-commerce business founded by the Australian born and bred Buchanan – who in his former life spent a decade building Jetstar into the nation's first low-cost airline – at $2.75bn.

Yet as the ink was still drying on the deal and Bruce and his marketing team were lining up publicity for the biggest moment in Rokt's nine-year history, his 14-year-old stepdaughter Sophie Joyce was preparing to fight for her life in the heart surgery unit of Boston Children's hospital.

Born with an unusual condition known as Heterotaxy syndrome, when the heart and other organs are in the wrong place in the chest and abdomen, it was her eighth major heart procedure.

What was supposed to be a routine cardio check-up for Sophie in the same week as Rokt's monster deal was finalised discovered her condition had suddenly become life-threatening.

Bruce's wife Elizabeth, who had been visiting a Californian health retreat and had never missed a doctor's appointment for her daughter – except this one – immediately flew across the country to be by her side.

For much of the flight, she was in tears. When she saw Sophie smiling in the recovery ward after the operation, her feelings of fear and dread had turned to joy.

It was from there after the operation that Bruce did a host of media zoom calls around the world for the record Rokt raising, still wearing his ward visitor's name badge.

"The Boston Children's Hospital team did an awesome job once again. It's incredible. They put a stent in to clear the obstruction. They were also saying, 'She's going to be bedridden and won't be able to do anything after the surgery.' But typical Sophie, a week later, she was in Telluride with her sisters in the snow up in the mountains. Literally within 24-48 hours after the operation, she was back on her feet," Bruce says.

Her mother bought Sophie a puppy named "Milo" when she was in surgery, which has since been a hit for her daughter.

"It was me trying to make sure the universe knew she needed to get through it because she had someone to look after. We went to pick Milo up the day she was discharged, directly from the hospital," she says.

"He has quickly become Sophie's number-one fan and is magical support for her emotionally."

Elizabeth found out about Sophie's medical challenges at her 20-week scan during her pregnancy and went through her daughter's first two open-heart surgeries on her own before she met Bruce.

Her congenital heart issue saw Sophie born with a cleft lip and palate, and other medical conditions, including hearing loss and arthritis.

"I have slept hundreds of hours (or perhaps more accurately, tried to sleep) in plastic fold-out beds beside hers in ICU wards in Australia and now also in America, listening to the monitors beep away reassuringly when they do stay consistent," Elizabeth says.

"It feels just impossible to explain what each of those moments have truly been like. Each one of them has felt like the world paused and made time slower and harder."

In a bid to insulate the immune-compromised Sophie from the Covid-19 virus and to be closer to Boston Children's Hospital, the family moved in February 2020 from their home in Brooklyn to a beach house on the shores of Plymouth Bay, a coastal town in Massachusetts, south of Boston.

They even found a local Montessori school for Sophie and her younger brother, Baxter, to attend face-to-face during the pandemic.

But on December 2 of that year, Sophie went through the most traumatic surgery of her life, a six-hour procedure her specialists warned was serious and unusually complicated.

The head of cardiology at Boston Children's Hospital ensured one of the world's best cardiac surgeons managed Sophie's case due to the level of complexity and risk.

The operation was a success and Elizabeth says her daughter was "given another 15 years of runway on her heart".

"She has had such a tough journey. It has been exhausting. But she is the one that suffers the most and has the toughest time," she says.

The family moved back to Brooklyn in September 2021 and Sophie returned to doing her schooling there. Bruce and Elizabeth loved the home in Plymouth so much that they decided to buy it as a weekend retreat and a base for Sophie's check-ups in Boston every three months.

The former says in recent years, in the face of all the adversity she has faced, Sophie has got "stronger and stronger". Two decades ago her condition was viewed as untreatable.

"I think the real fear now is just the fear of the unknown," her father says.

Elizabeth, who is a former director of the Luke Batty Foundation – established for the 11-year-old boy tragically murdered by his father in 2014 – has put countless hours into raising money for the cardiac unit at Sydney's Westmead Children's Hospital.

"It wasn't until we got to Boston and they had more advanced medicine that they were actually able to define Sophie's condition," Bruce says.

"That money is about giving kids like Sophie a chance."

## BALANCED SKILL SET

Sophie was one of the two children Elizabeth brought to her "Brady Bunch" marriage to Bruce, celebrated on the beach in Phuket in October 2011. Her husband brought two of his own and together they now also have a nine-year-old son.

They had met two years earlier at a function at Sydney's ANZ Stadium ahead of a Bledisloe Cup rugby union match. The next night, they went on their first date.

"I remember Bruce saying to me 'What adversity have you been through in your life which has made you so amazing?' So, I told him about Sophie. And he started crying and said how amazing it was what I had done," Elizabeth recalls.

"This extraordinary man chose me and Sophie and that says so much about him and continues to. He not only took on the challenges but has been my partner through the thick of it and the tears."

In 2012 they went into business together when Bruce founded Rokt and Elizabeth became an inaugural executive director of the firm. Before joining Rokt she had started and built The White Agency, a digital advertising firm, before selling it to STW Communications.

When the family moved to America in 2016, Elizabeth quit Rokt and did a year of consulting to global media and marketing giant Omnicom before joining the firm full-time as OMD Worldwide's chief marketing officer.

"When we moved to the US I was very conscious of being Bruce's wife. So, I worked for Omnicom for two years where I regained my sense of self in the market and I built a big network of connections," she says.

She returned to Rokt in June 2018 as chief commercial officer, where she now leads the strategy and execution for the firm's marketing, people, and new business departments.

"We are very Yin and Yang in our skills-sets which is why it works," she says.

"He is a generalist but where he spikes is in vision and product strategy, organisational structures and the what and [the] how. What I am good at is how to operationalise a vision and how to take it to market," she says.

There have been times when they have wondered whether it was the right thing for themselves and the family to be working together, especially given Sophie's ongoing challenges.

But Bruce says the board members and executive staff at Rokt have been determined to have his wife in the business.

In early 2022 Elizabeth cut down her workload to three days a week to help manage Sophie's ongoing post-operation issues.

She is now completely open with her team about her life and challenges, a far cry from when she started with Rokt when she was deeply protective of her privacy.

"The team feel that I am real and human and they can approach me about things going on and can bring their own-selves to work," she says.

Each evening at 6pm when they are in Brooklyn, Bruce and Elizabeth spend at least an hour over dinner with their children – their three elder girls are named Sarah, Hannah and Charlotte.

They also play board games. By design there is no television in the living area of the Buchanan's homes in Brooklyn and Plymouth.

Square Peg co-founder Paul Bassat, a foundation investor in Rokt, describes Bruce and Elizabeth as "remarkable parents".

"Bruce is a really special founder and person. I have known him for 15 years," Bassat says.

"We have a number of life partner, co-founder couples in our portfolio or where a partner is in the business. Bruce and Elizabeth have made it work incredibly well and she is a very seasoned operator."

Bruce says the experiences of Sophie and of the family over the past 14 years have helped put all of their lives – at work and at home – in perspective.

"I think we often get carried away with what we're dealing with, with a people issue or a business issue or shareholder issue or whatever. There's always issues when you're growing a business, there's never a shortage of them," he says.

"But I think your perspective on how big the problem is, everything gets put in a new light when you're dealing with life and death of children and serious medical issues."

He also believes the family's struggles have helped him in the running of the Rokt business, which has patented technology that connects advertisers through partners' websites to new digital online and mobile consumers.

"I think you also learn a sense of compassion and understanding that life is not a straightforward thing," he says.

"It doesn't take your focus off big ambitious objectives that you want to conquer. But I think it puts a softer edge around the way you deal with people and the human issues that we all face on a regular basis. So, I think it makes you more human."

## TRANSPARENCY AND FAIRNESS

Sophie's struggles were not the first in Bruce's life.

His parents separated when he was young and he lost his mother, Linda, when he was only 16.

The former nuclear-medicine university researcher stoically battled leukaemia for five years as her son and daughter watched on. Bruce was forced to care for his sister at their home on the Central Coast of NSW as his mother grew weaker and weaker.

"There was a whole journey there that was quite tough, I think, as a child to go through. To see your mother, a key person, who's been very strong, very smart and very successful and seeing her waste away as the disease took over her," he says softly.

"I almost dropped out of school and decided it was time for me to go and do something else. The hardest thing was staying somewhat normal after that and trying to finish school and pretend you put something like that behind you. With all that adversity, I grew up very young and learned to deal with problems at a very young age."

Bruce will always have regrets about the last time he saw his mother. He had booked a holiday with his father, who he only saw on weekends and holidays, to the NSW Snowy Mountains.

He said goodbye to her on the Friday afternoon, took off to the mountains and by the next Tuesday she was gone.

"It was always one of those weird feelings like despite all the years of supporting her and being there, not been there at the end," he says.

"So, it's one of those things of guilt – it makes me even emotional now – that you carry around with you afterwards."

His mother left him with a piece of advice he has never forgotten: Always ask questions.

"My mum taught me that and it's held me in great stead my whole life," he says.

At Bruce's wedding, his father Denis – who is still alive, running a farm in Tasmania – told a story of Bruce's school years when they were living for a time in New York.

His son was in serious trouble for refusing to stand and sing the national anthem when the American flag was raised in the courtyard during morning assembly.

It highlighted, early on in his life, Bruce's devotion to principles. That now carries on at Rokt in a quarterly publication called the *Career Guide*, which publishes every role, salary and benefit awarded across the business for all to see.

"We see so many businesses that give different people a better opportunity and better remuneration, because they're better at negotiating or they've got a boss that advocates for them more or they come from a gender or a race or a group that is better at negotiating. We just feel like that's wrong. It's just not fair," he says.

"Things like transparency go to the heart of who I am, because of where I came from. A very rough public school and feeling like the system wasn't fair and wasn't transparent. And so I always strive to get people with backgrounds that are less fortunate, a chance."

Rokt has been using the funding provided by Tiger Global, Square Peg and other backers TDM Growth Partners and industry super fund giants AustralianSuper and Hostplus to invest in research and development, international expansion and strategic acquisitions ahead of one day pursuing an initial public offering.

Bruce does not have fond memories of working in a public-company environment.

After graduating from university with a civil-engineering degree he built an engineering technology business, and with the Boston Consulting Group he wrote a business case for a start-up airline that would later be named Jetstar.

He spent 10 years building Jetstar into the leading low-cost airline in the Asia-Pacific region, where he led a team of over 7000 people and managed revenue in excess of $3 billion. But as a subsidiary of Qantas, Jetstar was always part of the bigger airline machine.

"That experience for me, I never found positive. I always found it as something that, from an entrepreneurial perspective, distracted you from your core mission and vision. I felt like there was a lot of politics and a lot of time-managing messaging as opposed to delivering and building a business," he says. It is one of the reasons Rokt has remained private.

It Is also why he readily acknowledges the day will eventually come, when Rokt is in public ownership, that there will be a better person to run the company. But he says there is plenty still to achieve before then.

A Rokt float could crystallise incredible wealth for the Buchanans. Yet Bruce and Elizabeth have made the decision to give all of their wealth away to charity in the future.

Beyond their education, their children will not receive any other financial assistance.

"It was something that really connected Bruce and I when we first met. Bringing two girls each to our marriage, we had similar views that we didn't want them growing up to be brats. We had both grown up in backgrounds of struggle financially," Elizabeth says.

"We are here to support them, but we want them to fund their own paths."

Bruce says his children have been told their parent's wishes and accept them.

"I think they're all also very keen to make their own way in the world. Part of the fun of life is the adventure of actually struggling a little bit and finding your own path and not having your parents set your path," he says.

Bruce will never forget the words of his former Qantas chairman, Margaret Jackson, who once told him that once you get to a position of having wealth in life, what does another $10m or $30m really matter?

"I don't know what the right number is. But I think the point is very valid," he says.

"Once you get to a certain amount of income to be comfortable in life and don't have to worry about money, the rest of it doesn't actually make you any happier. It doesn't help you achieve anything."

# MICHAEL BUXTON

A ruddy-faced Michael Buxton, fresh from two days of playing golf with his brother on King Island in Bass Strait, is all smiles as he greets me at the gates of his Portsea mansion on Victoria's Mornington Peninsula.

The address is unmistakable.

It's on the famed Point Nepean Road – home to the seaside mansions of the Fox family and many others – and recognisable for the towering palm trees that adorn the spacious front yard, some of which Buxton specially imported from China.

On a warm Friday afternoon in late summer 2021, the Melbourne property developer, art collector and philanthropist is dressed in board shorts and T-shirt and wearing a bright red cap bearing the logo of one of the charities he supports.

He's eager to show me around the spectacular Arabic front garden he designed and built with the help of his landscape architecture consultant, Mike Stokes.

"What do you do with a piece of land that was a tennis court, and how do you want to live your life in this house? The Arab garden, to me, is part of paradise. It is something that is very beautiful but also very practical," Buxton says proudly.

The centrepiece of any Arab garden is a fountain or sculpture and Buxton has carried on the tradition: a giant water feature urn topped with luscious fruit – all ceramic and built by a young craftsman from Ballarat – rises from the narrow, cool canals that take the sting off the surrounding sandstone. The garden walls are adorned with trellises laden with pears, apples and figs, plus a seemingly out-of-place mango tree, thousands of miles from its Queensland home. Buxton reckons it produces perfect, sweet fruit.

"This place gave us lots of things to do," he says, beaming, as he turns his gaze to the two storey-home that boasts stunning views over Port Philip Bay beyond an expansive backyard, complete with a butler's kitchen (where he cleans the seafood he regularly catches in the bay), lush buffalo grass, and deck. Buxton and his wife Janet bought the property in 1982 and retained one-third of the original timber building. The rest they made contemporary. "And it is profitable because we grow our own fruit and vegetables," he adds.

He says Portsea became their sanctuary during the covid pandemic and symbolic of where he is in life. He and Janet barely left during lockdown and have since continued the ritual. For Christmas he bought his wife an electronic piano to go with his suave traditional version in the downstairs study. They are now learning to play together.

Buxton remains an executive director of MAB Corporation, the property development giant he founded with his brother Andrew – who is six years younger – in 1995. Decades earlier he co-founded Becton Property Group with fellow member of The List and close friend Max Beck, and together they built some of Melbourne's most famed office towers, including 333 Collins Street.

"I have been an executive director of MAB for quite a long time," Buxton says. "I'm on the board. Andy and I talk about whether we buy something or we don't buy it. And we have outstanding staff. He is the MD, he runs the business. I was the visionary in the beginning, instrumental in solving problems, finding finance, and then eventually I became a board member. We have a good relationship; we get on socially. But we have never worried about wealth, and I think that is probably the key to the sustainability of what we have because we have enough. If we do better than that, so be it. We watch the numbers just to make a profit."

Indeed Michael Buxton, who received an AM in the Australia Day honours in 2021, is less focused on the ins and outs of MAB and more on the future of his children and enjoying his good health and happiness.

We venture to the downstairs pool room, where during last year's lockdown he and Janet played what they christened The COVID Cup. "We played 260 games, three games a night with our cocktails. I had a whisky and soda, she had a gin and tonic. I won by eight," he says, holding up a pencilled scorecard on a dog-eared piece of paper. The ritual has continued after lockdown. "We are now playing the Easter Cup," he says.

On the wall is a photo of Buxton's late father Richard, who played 10,000 rounds of golf in his life and was still playing competitively at 94. He died only three months after his last round. One of six children, Buxton inherited his father's love of golf, becoming a life member at the suave Victoria Golf Club in Melbourne's sand-belt precinct. These days he prefers to play at Sorrento Golf Club, just up the road from his Portsea home. In the expansive garage outside the pool room sits a high-tech golf simulator he bought in 2017 that let him play 43 of the world's best courses through lockdown without taking a step beyond the tee.

He's played bridge twice a week for the past five years, and during covid it was all over Zoom.

"I plan the future," he says. "You have to stay active mentally and physically. That is why I do yoga, swim and play golf. I see people who live a long time because they use their mind. That is why my wife and I have taken up the piano. These are age-resistant activities, so if you end up not being able to move very far, you are still very active."

## BUILDING WEALTH

Half of Buxton's wealth is tied up in MAB, the rest he controls with his immediate family. "Wealth has given me freedom," he says.

"Freedom is probably the most important thing, because then you have time to do other things." In 2014, he gave $26 million to the University of Melbourne, including $10 million worth of works by major contemporary artists including Bill Henson, Howard Arkley and Patricia Piccinini, and $16 million towards the construction of a gallery dubbed the Michael Buxton Centre of Contemporary Arts (MBCOCA). He and Janet have also established a philanthropic foundation known as the Michael and Janet Buxton Foundation, which he says is "part of what we are giving to the kids".

In 2015, with the assistance of the Baillieu family-backed Mutual Trust, they established a family office known as the Michael Buxton Family Office. In January 2021 it appointed its first external chief executive, former MAB boss Mick Brennan.

"I've really got a very good relationship with my kids," Buxton says. "They have all been successful, so they don't necessarily need to have a lot of money from me when I die. So I said, let's preserve it. You get some, the majority of it stays invested, is managed and goes all the way through. That money is education, foundation and support when you need it. Plus you all get a nice dividend. But it should go on. That's not to say it will, but it would be great if they did. Our wealth is there to help each other. This is a multi-generation business. My constitution for the family office is for seven generations. That was based on research in Europe, America and China. We have already done seven generations in the Buxton family [In 1871 his great-grandfather, J.R. Buxton, founded an estate agency in Melbourne] so why not do another seven?"

In late 2020 Buxton moved to extend his decades of success in property development into the non-bank lending arena, joining forces with MaxCap co-founder Michael Fowler. The firm, known as Corsair Investment Management, is now providing property loans and equity for residential, commercial and industrial projects. Buxton's son Steve is a director of Corsair.

"Corsair Capital I created because I used to fund all my kids in their development, and other people," Buxton says. "It was about formalising that process and it is fantastic. I put my own capital in and my kids are running it.

"Michael Fowler came to us and we are now developing the external capital, and that has been pretty successful. It is a tough business at the moment. We have a lot of inquiries and it is just a matter of whether the deals are any good. I said to Steve 'It doesn't matter if we don't make any money but don't lose the capital', and it has been a great exercise for my children."

Buxton is also working with Smorgon family scion, and adviser to some of the richest families in the nation, David Smorgon, on further development of his family office and succession planning for the transition of his wealth to the next generation. He believes COVID and last year's short, sharp recession in Australia was a good time for his children to think 'It doesn't go on forever'.

"They had 25 years of no recessions. Max Beck and I, when we started in 1974, we used to have a recession every four years," he says. "We have been having discussions on the succession thing for the past 10 years. As long as I can keep doing all the other things I will keep going as long as I can. Everything we do is beautifully creative, it is exciting."

So is the family's succession plan sorted? "No," he answers nonchalantly. So when will it be? "I don't know," he replies with a wry smile. "And that is the difficult thing, because none of my kids are in the MAB business. It is definitely work in progress. Is it a big worry? Probably not. We are wealthier than we ever thought we would be and we are self-sufficient. I guess the succession will either be sorted, or I die. And then someone else has the problem!"

# PETER AND SUPARNA COOPER

*I'll be forever indebted to Michael Wilkinson for introducing me to Peter Cooper in late 2019. I'd long known of the legend of Cooper in Australian funds management, yet never had the privilege of meeting the man himself. At our initial meeting I was immediately captured by Peter's passion, his curiosity about my story and – despite his low profile – his fascination with the media. Over the next two years I had the pleasure of meeting Peter's now wife Suparna, and developed a friendship with them both. I know it took both of them right out of their comfort zone to do their first ever media interview together with me in 2022, for which I am greatly appreciative. Their personal story is truly unique and inspiring.*

The Art of Living International Centre is spread over 65 acres of flowering foliage, a peaceful lake and winding footpaths, just over 20km southwest of the bustling Indian city of Bangalore. Its stunning, lotus-shaped central building, a five-storey architectural masterpiece with 81 pillars known as Vishalakshi Mantap, draws more than 1.2 million visitors every year for yoga and meditation programs.

It is named after the mother of spiritual teacher Gurudev Sri Sri Ravi Shankar, who is to Vedic knowledge what the Dalai Lama is to Buddhism. Gurudev founded The Art of Living (AOL) in 1981 as an international educational and humanitarian organisation to revive, preserve and grow ancient Vedic knowledge traditions based on the oldest scriptures of Hinduism. On August 4 2022, he presided over a very special ceremony at the Bangalore Ashram: the marriage of Peter Cooper and Suparna Bhasin.

Cooper, the founder of famed funds management group Cooper

Investors, rode into the ceremony on an elephant. His wife-to-be was dressed in a traditional red Indian sari. There were 85 guests, including Peter's 90-year-old mother Fran and his 89-year-old father – also named Peter – plus his son from his first marriage, Dylan. He also has two daughters from that marriage, Bronte and Paris.

"It was very special to have somebody of Gurudev's stature and achievements," Cooper says. "He's been able to pull off an incredible feat around something that I've thought endlessly about. He has found the sweet spot that intersects the secular, the spiritual and philosophical worlds, so that they can operate in harmony and not in conflict. No small accomplishment in today's world.

"I have always been drawn to the pursuit of greater freedom and liberty. And a big part of that is the freedom of the mind, which is what attracted me to Sri Sri Ravi Shankar's teachings. The Art of Living is about fostering human values, and is dedicated to creating a stress-free, violence-free society. And what I love is Sri Sri backs it up with do do, not just talky talky."

For Cooper, the day capped a decade-long personal transformation that began when Bhasin introduced him to meditation, and the calmness and peace that can be found in a life that honours mind, body and spirit. They now spend around two hours together every morning from 6am, walking, swimming, practising yoga and meditation – including the Sudarshan Kriya, a rhythmic breathing technique that leads to a state of alert calmness and is the backbone of the Art of Living Happiness Program.

Cooper says that after more than two decades of building Cooper Investors (CI) and transitioning the firm to its next generation of leaders – a process he calls the CI Way 2.0 – the Art of Living has brought a centred, calm focus to his work life that had long been missing.

"My issues with work were around too much intensity, and expectations of myself," he says. "That led me to being impatient, overbearing at times, stressed, with poor sleep patterns and self-limiting behaviour. So I think Suparna has brought true equanimity into my life, and that makes the work of an investor much more effective and sustainable.

"That's been a huge help for me in terms of discerning what is important and what is not, making me a better business owner, investor, leader, father and husband.

CI now manages $10 billion and for the past two decades has been one of the best-performing fund managers in the nation. Its trademark has long been its so-called VoF investment process, which focuses on value latency and carefully evaluating operating industry/strategic trends and focused management behaviour in making investments.

"What excites me about Cooper Investors is that after 21 years in business, we have all the people and the pieces of the jigsaw puzzle on the table for a multi-generational investor organisation. That is no mean feat in a Darwinian sport like investment management. But that's still not good enough. I'm seriously excited about taking the CI Way 2.0 to the next level, which means the transfer of our tacit knowledge in a systematic way for the benefit of our clients and employees. The results, by which we live or die, will tell the story over the coming years, for which I can't wait."

## FIRST MEETING

Cooper and Bhasin met a few months before the September 11 terrorist attacks of 2001 – the year he started CI – on a stunning 100-acre pastoral campus nestled in the beautiful Berkshires of western Massachusetts. Over the decade their friendship developed, and in May 2013, she invited Cooper to a dinner with 15 friends at an apartment in the hip neighbourhood of Williamsburg in Brooklyn, New York, that would change his life.

On his many trips to New York, as he built CI into a firm that now values his wealth at $541 million, Cooper had been used to drinking beers and visiting wine bars and the occasional cigar den. Indeed, many outings in his life – from school fetes to boat trips and Friday night drinks – had involved alcohol as the lubricant for celebration.

This evening in New York felt very different. There was no alcohol or meat. On the menu were light snacks of vegetarian Indian food, fresh fruit and non-alcoholic drinks, including green tea. The entertainment was Indian Vedic music and chanting in an event known as a Satsang. He recalls it as an "incredible, memorable evening."

"I remember the sweetness of it," he says. "I was home in bed at 10pm. I just remember thinking in the cab ride home that it was one of those moments. I have never experienced such an enjoyable night out. I had a warm inner glow."

The couple got together romantically a year later and Cooper proposed to Bhasin on the sidelines of one of the outer courts of Melbourne Park at the Australian Open tennis tournament in early February 2021. They don't eat meat or drink alcohol and they still love their tennis.

"The biggest change that I see in his whole life, especially at work but in general, is Peter finding his voice," Bhasin says. "He now says: 'This is what I stand for. These are my values – curiosity, humility, authenticity', but behaves and sets boundaries in a way that honours those values. He's found his voice and an ability to stand up for himself in a non-angry way. I've seen that at home with very intensely challenging family dynamics, but also at work, where he says 'This is actually who I am and this is acceptable or unacceptable according to my values'.

"His love has been incredibly healing for me," she adds. "His love for me has made me feel very safe – both emotionally and financially – in a way that I can build myself up, go out in the world and give my greatest gifts. Let me really tell you why I married him. Not for his good looks, not for his money, even though those are good things. Those would not be anywhere close to enough if he did not have the commitment he has to becoming the best version of himself."

Suparna Bhasin was born in Cleveland, Ohio, on August 18, 1971. After an arranged marriage in India, her parents – Anand and Ranjana Bhasin – had moved to America in the 1960s. Bhasin jokes that there is actually a name for people like her: ABCDs, or American Born Confused Desis. A Desi is an Indian/South Asian person.

Her undergraduate education began at Emory University in Georgia. She progressed to Johns Hopkins University in Baltimore, where she graduated with a Bachelor of Arts in International Relations. She then worked as a trainer and manager for a large regional bank in Baltimore, Legg Mason, where she had the opportunity to explore what she was good at and for a time loved the inside of a very traditional firm.

But the breakdown of her first relationship in 1996 turned her world upside down. She cried for two months.

In September 1996, she was accepted into a Masters in Arts in Organisational Psychology program at Columbia University but delayed going there for a year when she was diagnosed with a mental health condition, hospitalised at John Hopkins Hospital and put on antidepressants.

To this day she believes she was misdiagnosed and it led her to seek alternative remedies, including SKY breathing and mantra-based meditation, as well as yoga and regular silence retreats – all led by The Art of Living.

She took a two-month leave of absence from work – just before the 9-11 attacks – to visit the Option Institute in Massachusetts, a training centre for personal growth and happiness. Being trained in the tools and technologies of The Option Process is intense. The course is six hours a day, five days a week for eight weeks straight. In June 2001, 50 people had enrolled: 40 women and 10 men, including Peter Cooper, whom Bhasin met for the first time. They were just passing acquaintances in the group but in the following years came to establish a significant spiritual connection.

While Cooper is best known for starting his investing career at NSW State Super before moving to BNP Paribas, Mercury Asset Management and Merrill Lynch, then starting Paradice Cooper with fellow investment legend David Paradice – part of which became Cooper Investors – little is known about his early years. He was born on August 25, 1959, and for three and a half years his family lived in the working class inner-city suburb of Brunswick in Melbourne, while his father worked as a prison guard at Pentridge jail. To this day CI's flagship fund is known as the Brunswick Fund. At Pentridge, Peter senior got to know warder George Hodson, who was famously was shot dead outside the jail by inmate Ronald Ryan on December 19, 1965.

The family moved to Darwin for a time and then Pine Creek, a boom-to-bust outback town of 150 people known as the gold mining capital of the Northern Territory, where Peter senior ran a wild outback pub for many years. His son, who has one sister named Karen, later did his secondary schooling on the Gold Coast, and went to university in Toowoomba and UNE in Armidale.

Peter senior had come to Australia from New Zealand with nothing after his family's fortune had evaporated with the demise of a firm started by his great great grandfather called F. Cooper Seeds, once a world leader in the production of seed peas and a supplier of agricultural chemicals to commercial and household growers.

"There's that saying that the first generation makes it, the second generation enjoys it and then the third generation blows it," Cooper says. "Cooper Seeds started in 1860. By 1970, it had 110 years of building incredible global businesses. But nepotism and poor financial management saw it eventually sold in 1974 to archrival Arthur Yates & Co for a pittance and there was basically no money left."

That tragic downfall has driven Cooper's financial conservatism and a burning desire to preserve wealth for the future, leading to the establishment of a Cooper family office. "We have the chance to innovate and explore ways to build an enduring stewardship family model," he says.

"I have been working my arse off for 40 years, without much of a break, nor boats, planes, Ferraris or Range Rovers. I still feel like Sisyphus pushing that boulder up the hill.

"I'm looking forward to the next 200 years of building a sustainable family business that incorporates social enterprise, not for profit philanthropy and ensuring that we – my children, Suparna and I – are responsible custodians and managers of the family assets and its activities. I am convinced we can make a valuable contribution, and if that doesn't work, give it away to people who can do a better job."

## PHILANTHROPIC PASSIONS

Cooper's passion for freedom and liberty has manifested in the focus of the family philanthropic vehicle he has established with Bhasin known as the MaiTri Foundation. MaiTri is a Sanskrit word meaning loving kindness.

"We are going to be doing more philanthropy together aimed at leaving this world better than we found it," Bhasin says. "I never wanted to have children, but I do feel I'm here to mother the next generation so that we create a completely different world from the one we have right now. Because I think that's going to be required."

The $20 million MaiTri Foundation has a dual focus: helping to solve the mental health crisis in the world; and spreading the philosophy of individual liberty and freedom. One of the most exciting projects it is supporting is The Art of Living's Intuition Process on brain activation, which teaches children and teenagers simple and powerful techniques to delve into the sixth sense known as intuition.

"There is a good quote that underpins my philosophy, and it really has come from many conversations with a good friend of mine, Dr. Evian Gordon," Cooper says. "If you can't align your thinking, rational mind with your non-conscious emotional brain, you are just walking around in the dark. You will continually be making the same mistakes that end in suffering. The intuition process is bringing a different type of intelligence to the way we live, the way we problem solve, the way we think. It is another type of intelligence. The freedom of mind not only solves problems, but it is also at the heart of creativity and innovation."

Cooper first saw the Intuition Process at work at a school in India at the Art of Living Ashram. "I saw children who were able to replicate drawings and read books with fully covered and blindfolded eyes. That deserves real attention and research to understand this phenomenon," he says.

Through The Art of Living, the Intuition Process was launched in 2015 for children who lived in the Bangalore Ashram where Cooper and Bhasin were married. The group is now working with several reputable scientific research institutions to explore how the Intuition Process affects anxiety, depression, academic performance and emotional regulation among school-aged children.

"Let's run the experiments in a rigorous way to fully understand what is happening here," Cooper says. "Then we can assess the educational infrastructure required to ensure it goes on a pathway of good and is not just seen as a magic bullet, which it is not." With support from the Cooper family office, led by Bhasin, The Art of Living also supported the teaching of Intuition Process courses in Sydney and Melbourne in 2023. They were run by Mala Sundareshan, the Global Head of the Children teacher's program.

"We've got a lot of families whose kids are being introduced to this and we are looking to get an entree into some top schools in Melbourne," Bhasin says. "A documentary film is also being made.

"It is the unconscious mind, the rotting mind and the angry mind that is creating hell in the world. If we raise a generation of kids that have ultra-high integrity who would never think to hurt themselves, each other or the planet, that's the opportunity. They will be the future leaders of governments and corporations. The way they would imagine a world can be very different from the one we are living in."

# SHIRLEY AND FRANK COSTA

*One thing you could always count on with Frank Costa was that he would answer his phone. Any time of the day or night you could call his mobile, and you would hear the raspy but impeccably polite words on the end of the line: "Hello, this is Frank..." In the lead-up to the sharemarket float of his family's Costa Group produce empire in 2015, I made one of those calls and snared an interview with Frank that is now part of Costa corporate folklore. In it he admitted he had lamented floating Costa Group, and almost decried the group's bankers for talking him into it. The next morning when the story was published, all hell broke loose. But that was Frank. Always honest, whatever the consequences. He did the same when he gave me what would prove to be his final media interview in mid 2019, sounding off at one of his brothers. Yet no-one ever questioned Frank's passion and sincerity. That came through again in 2023, two years after his passing, when SecondBite founder Ian Carson kindly organised for me to interview his widow and two of his daughters to discuss the family's $1 million donation to the famed food rescue charity. Their respect for Frank's legacy was utmost. It has always been a pleasure to know and write about such an amazing Australian business family.*

Frank Costa called it "A gift from above". The fruit and vegetable industry king, former legendary president of the Geelong Football Club and patriarch of the Costa family passed away on Sunday, May 2nd, 2021, surrounded by his loving family and comforted by his faith.

The deeply religious Italian-born father of eight daughters died a fortnight after he and wife Shirley celebrated their 61st wedding anniversary.

Frank, one of the nation's most successful businessmen, had been battling ill-health for about a year. He was 83.

He also lived a life of service to the community. His passionate advocacy for the welfare of others now lives on through a $1 million donation to SecondBite, the national community food program backed by retail giant Coles and food behemoth Mondelez.

"He found the idea that his gift was ongoing really attractive, which is why he wanted it to be called "A gift from above," Frank's second eldest daughter Laurelle Cecic, who maintains a strong association with SecondBite, says of the family's bequest. "It showed that he had a strong Catholic faith, but also that he wanted to be able to keep on giving after he had gone."

Today Laurelle is sitting with her mother and one of her sisters, Edwina Arto. None of them have done a media interview before.

One million dollars is the largest single donation ever made to SecondBite by an individual, matched only once in the past by Geoff Handbury, Rupert Murdoch's philanthropist brother-in-law who was also a long term supporter of the food charity.

Shirley, Laurelle and Edwina now want to reflect publicly for the first time about how Frank Costa's tireless philanthropy impacted their lives and many others. As they speak of their beloved late husband and father, you sense a part of each of them still can't believe he is gone.

"I'm still meeting everybody on the street or wherever and they all want to know how I'm going. They all ask how I am managing," Shirley whispers.

"He's still talked about all the time in Geelong."

She still lives in the luxury penthouse she and Frank purchased on the Geelong Waterfront in 2008 after leaving their five-bedroom, four-bathroom family home in the inner Western Geelong suburb of Newtown, where they brought up all their children over more than a quarter of a century. Laurelle says her mother had to twist Frank's arm to move there as he struggled to give up their family home.

"He was, however, quick to admit it was the right move for them. It gives her a strong sense of home and security as it was their last place together," she says.

In the apartment's main living room, a grand piano has long taken pride of place surrounded along the walls by antique vases and ornaments. Frank's favourite features 10 birds – a striking red one sits atop the other nine.

"There are my eight girls," Frank told me in 2016 during a guided tour of the apartment for a story on the property.

"Shirley and I are the bird on top."

Shirley will never leave Geelong, the city she will always love. In late 2023 the life and achievements of her husband were publicly recognised with a permanent bronze statue of him in the centre of town.

"Geelong is home. It is my world now. I still love to go back to Warrnambool. (The nearby town of) Killarney is where I am really from. I still have a few cousins there. My parents were both from an Irish background but they were born here," she says.

In 2019, after Frank stepped down from the board of the listed Costa Group, he took Shirley on a tour of 10 European countries in eight weeks. It was an exhilarating but exhausting experience, the longest period Frank had spent away from the country of his birth.

"When we went over to Ireland, it felt like home," Shirley says of her Irish heritage before she met Frank. "Then I had to adapt to the Italians," she adds with a smile.

She doesn't go to the football anymore, but Laurelle still has seats at

Kardinia Park, home of the Geelong Cats.

When they were growing up Frank used to take Laurelle and her eldest sister Rona to Melbourne to watch VFL matches whenever Geelong was playing away from home.

He'd leave them at the entrance to the rowdy outer before heading into the grandstands to watch the match (where he never drank alcohol – he was always a non-drinker) and then he would pick them up after the game. They loved every minute of it.

Frank almost single-handedly saved Geelong from financial collapse in the late 1990s after being asked to take over the presidency in a time of crisis.

So I pop the question to Shirley that so many friends and strangers still ask her. What occupies her time, two years after losing her soulmate?

After a pause, she smiles proudly and utters a single word in reply. "Kids."

She has 24 grandchildren and 12 great grandchildren. She excitedly reveals number 13, "God willing", was born in November 2023.

"I've also still got certain friends that you just keep," she adds. They include trucking magnate Lindsay Fox and his wife Paula.

Frank was always good friends with the former. Edwina's youngest child is coincidentally named Fox, and one of her most treasured photographs is of her tiny baby in the giant arms of the Fox family patriarch.

"The sad part lately is funerals, too many of them," Shirley continues with a sigh, as for a moment her eyes go watery behind thickly-clad black eye-shadow.

"I had a call today before I left to come here that another one was gone. That is just happening all the time. We are just at that age."

## GEELONG LEGACY

Frank Costa's legacy in Geelong was so much more than football. He was a generous philanthropist and fierce advocate for the local community.

Even into his late 70s he maintained a formal role as patron of up to 25 different organisations and charities. One of his greatest passions was giving to St Mary's Church where his parents, he and Shirley, and seven of his eight daughters were married.

"We started off fairly poor. I was staggered when I found out we were paying five pound rent to his father when we got married and we were living above the shop. So, I got out of there as soon as I could," Shirley recalls. "When he made money, Frank spread it around a bit. But we were never over the top. Because he worked so hard."

She says the biggest change in their lives came when Frank joined the Young President's Organisation, better known as YPO.

The secretive group has long described itself as a global leadership community of extraordinary chief executives. Its network includes chapters in Melbourne, Sydney, Adelaide, Brisbane and Perth, part of a global community of more than 29,000 chief executives in 130 countries.

"He always said that was his university, his education. He went to a technical school but he only knew how to change a light globe," Shirley jokes.

"YPO was wonderful for him and for me. You sought your friends out there. I just had a call yesterday from Connie Kimberley (co-founder of the Just Jeans retail group) to say, 'It is a long time since I have seen you'. So, I have committed to going to a Christmas function with them."

She says Frank was a long-term supporter of SecondBite by donating food and supporting events because he understood the value of fresh nutritious food for those in need.

The charity was founded a decade ago by Tanarra Restructuring

Partners Executive Chair and former Victorian Liberal Party president Ian Carson and his wife Simone.

Its long-time ambassador is Penny Fowler, Rupert Murdoch's niece and chairman of the Herald and Weekly Times.

She hosted a special luncheon in August 2023 to acknowledge the Costa family's generous bequest.

"Whenever I asked Frank for anything, within reason, he was always there to support us. Whether it was coming to a function or giving a donation or food, he was always there," Carson now says.

With his $1 million gift, Frank will become one of the foundation members of SecondBite's Feed the Future program.

Carson says all bequests made to SecondBite become part of the program and are invested in the SecondBite Future Trust, a segregated and professionally invested fund established in 2008 following Geoff Handbury's generous donation.

"The money gets put into a trust and then that gives the income so SecondBite staff, who work so hard, don't have to spend all their time fundraising. They can focus on what they do best," he says.

Importantly the trust has diversified SecondBite's funding to ensure that its goals of ending food waste are supported in perpetuity.

SecondBite is also establishing the new role of a Gift in Wills Officer, whose salary will be paid from the Future Trust annual dispersal. This position will be named after Frank Costa.

Simone Carson notes that Frank took a risk in backing the group in its infancy.

"When he first met SecondBite we were still quite young. It was a big leap of faith from him to get involved in our organisation in its early days," she says.

"All the people that are involved in food, and we hear this again and again, they just understand. There is so much that goes into the production of food, in growing and moving it, and they always believe that to waste it is just terrible."

Edwina Arto says the greatest lesson her father taught her about giving was "If you can, do."

"We will bump into people we don't know and they will say 'I'll tell you a little story about how I bumped into your dad years ago' and they needed some help or their son needed help with something. Dad went over to see them, he gave them advice and he kept in touch. There were a million little things he did that impacted, that just showed he cared," she says.

"SecondBite is a perfect example of the stuff that he cared about, the community that he lived in and his passion for food not being wasted."

She says the family's philanthropy will remain focussed on the late patriarch and her mother's passions.

"As far as Laurelle and I are concerned, we are always looking to do things that we think dad would have wanted," she says.

"So we don't want to branch out into crazy new areas. We are trying to stay mindful of what mum and dad get fired up about and what interests them. SecondBite is central to that."

## FAMILY FEUD

Frank Costa was the eldest of five brothers, born of Sicilian parents.

In 1959, aged just 21, he and his brother, Adrian, purchased their father's fresh fruit business, "The Covent Garden", which was established in 1888 by Frank's great uncle on his mother's side on Moorabool Street, Geelong.

With Frank and his brothers in charge of the business, it was renamed Costa Group and expanded into wholesale, becoming the largest supplier of fruit and vegetables in the country.

It is now perhaps best known for its Driscoll's brand of premium berries.

After steadfastly keeping Costa Group private since its birth, Frank said he felt no excitement about seeing the family name on the ASX bourse when the group floated in July 2005.

It has had a volatile history since, with a number of profit downgrades and a roller coaster share price ride.

When he retired from the Costa Group board in July 2019, Frank granted me what would be his final media interview. It was at his Melbourne home, a converted church with rendered bluestone walls in the shadows of the Melbourne Cricket Ground.

During a wide-ranging discussion, he revealed to the world for the first time his anger at the way the broader Costa family had dealt with the family's shareholding in Costa Group.

For a moment I saw the steely Frank Costa that took on the Melbourne's underworld in the 1970s and cleaned up the wholesale markets, in particular the corrupt supply of fruit and vegetables to Coles and Woolworths.

For his efforts he earned a contract on his life, courtesy of the Calabrian mafia, which was eventually withdrawn.

The public never knew it at the time but the Costa family's shock decision in November 2017 to sell more than $100 million worth of shares in Costa Group opened a rift between Frank and his younger brother, Robert, who chairs the Costa's family office, Costa Asset Management.

The sale was triggered by the sudden death in February that year of their younger brother with a shareholding in the business, Anthony Costa, who worked on the wholesale market floor of Costa Group until the day he died.

His son, Stuart, is still general manager of Costa's domestic berries business.

"I was very close with Anthony and his family. So, it wasn't easy.

It was a bloody shock actually," Frank told me in his first public comments on the loss of his brother.

"He went in to have two knee replacements done. A day later he had this massive stroke and it killed him. I have kept close to his wife and his kids, and they seem to be managing pretty well."

Robert Costa made the decision to sell half the family's shareholding in Costa Group to deal with estate planning issues flowing from his younger brother's death. His older brother was livid.

"I was very upset about it but I couldn't do anything because I was locked in," Frank told me.

When I asked him to describe his present relationship with Robert, there was a long sigh before he eventually replied: "Probably not as warm as I would like it. He made the decision to sell shares really without any discussion with me at all. I found out when he was selling them.

"That didn't please me, so I personally haven't had much to do with Robert since then. Anthony, of course, has gone to heaven. But he would not do anything himself, he would always ask the others."

Frank said nothing more on the issue. While Robert no longer holds any shares in Costa Group, he said after Frank's passing that his brother was an inspiring figure who would go out of his way to help people and demonstrated his steely resolve in times of crisis.

Shirley Costa now retains a 1 per cent holding in the company, which in early July 2023 received a takeover offer from its largest shareholder, New York private equity firm Paine Schwartz Partners.

But Shirley and her daughters don't follow its fortunes closely.

"My husband John does more than I do because he worked there for a long time," Laurelle says.

John Cecic previously ran Costa Group's export fruit and vegetables business.

"Of course we want it to do well. But I don't follow it."

Frank long lamented that none of his daughters had a career in the business. But not once did he ever insist they considered it. Or even ask.

"There was never a discussion about the girls in Costa," Shirley declares. 'They just did their own thing."

Laurelle worked for a time in the business supplying fruit and vegetables to hotels and restaurants in the Geelong area before she had children.

"I really enjoyed it while I was there," she says.

Edwina worked in the Costa shop after school when she was just 11 years old, peeling carrots for the Geelong hospital.

But she never had any interest in the business.

"You know what, it didn't matter. You didn't feel like a massive disappointment, because Dad didn't want you to go that way," she says proudly.

"He and mum were always very conscious of us doing our own thing. Of course, Dad would have loved it if we went into the business because he was very proud of it. But we didn't feel like we could not follow our own path."

For decades the Costa family has owned a huge holiday compound set on rugged cliffs overlooking the Southern Ocean at Aireys Inlet on Victoria's Great Ocean Road.

Over the last decade of his life Frank tried to spend most of his weekends with the family there.

All of his children and some of the grandchildren have homes and apartments on the site.

When they are all in residence, they still gather each afternoon at a rustic children's in-ground trampoline Frank installed on a grassy patch within the compound, after he failed to get the approval of local residents to put a tennis court on the spot.

Frank and Shirley's eldest grand-daughter was married overlooking the ocean there last December, exchanging vows with her husband amid the stunning backdrop of the soft late-afternoon light striking a cliff face above the roaring sea.

While Airey's Inlet remains a favourite of the grandchildren, visits there have not been the same for Shirley and her daughters since they lost Frank.

Another family legacy is a property development business Frank created on the side when he was 21. After being advised to put all his spare money into property, he bought one every year with cash the Costa business did not need.

Today Costa Property Group targets mainly residential subdivisions. Two of his other daughters – and busy mums – Rona (formerly her father's personal assistant) and Kate have helped out with its administration over the years.

Asked about learnings for life from her father, Edwina repeats one of his trademark sayings: "If it is to be, it is up to me."

"That was his favourite. Plus 'Attitude, not aptitude, decides your altitude'. All these things I now find myself saying to my kids. Dad got those sayings from his mother," she says. "I can also still recite parts of the Desiderata that hung framed in the billiards room (in the Newtown family home), given the number of times I was sent there," she says of the famed early 1920s prose poem by the American writer Max Ehrmann.

"That was sort of my naughty corner. Dad used to point out to me one particular line, saying 'This one is for you. Avoid loud and aggressive persons, they are vexations to the spirit!'."

Laurelle says her father's greatest teaching was simply "to be caring, to care about everybody."

Her mother concurs. Shirley says her husband's greatest gift was giving. Not just of money, but of himself.

"When he was Geelong president, he would often see these people who just lived for football, and had little else. They looked down and out. But they would call out to Frank and he would give them the time. That has been passed onto our kids," she says softly.

"Many times we would be sitting on the side of the road in the car after a game, sometimes for an hour, waiting for him to finish sorting someone out. We'd always ask 'Who was that'. He would reply 'Oh, I don't know. But they needed my help'."

# MINDY ESPIDIO-GARCIA

*This was one of the most difficult interviews of my life. Having a son of my own of a similar age, listening to Mindy tell the story of her daughter Alana was at times deeply distressing. Mindy broke down several times during the discussion, which – unfortunately in covering such an emotional topic – was done over zoom. But to her great credit, she got through it.*

*When the interview was over, I was completely drained. I sat in silence for a good 10 minutes just staring at my computer screen, finding it difficult to move. I thought of my own children, and tried to comprehend the enormity of the story I had just been told. When I sat down later to compose the piece, I felt an incredible responsibility to tell Mindy's story accurately and sensitively. But I also knew I had something very special and rare. That proved to be the case – the story became one of the best-read pieces I have produced in my entire career.*

*There was to be, thankfully, a happy ending.*

*Several weeks after the interview, I was one of several journalists to attend billionaire packaging magnate Anthony Pratt's annual dinner for customers in Sydney.*

*Amazon is one of his Visy Group's biggest customers and by pure coincidence, Mindy was there. I was introduced to her first thing in the evening. I'll never forget the long hug she gave me and her words of thanks.*

*It is moments like those that you appreciate how privileged you are to be entrusted to tell such stories.*

Saturday March 17, 2018 is forever forged in the memory of Mindy Espidio-Garcia.

It was the day she kissed her precious 10-year-old daughter, Alana, goodbye.

Alana was known to her family and friends as "Prancer" because she regularly ran around on the tips of her toes and loved to dance.

She enjoyed throwing tea parties, or any occasion which she could get dressed up for. She collected stuffed animals and loved unicorns.

Her diagnosis of incurable leukaemia in 2017 rocked her mother's world.

"At that moment, we just dropped everything and tried to take account of what it meant and what we wanted to do," Mindy now says of listening to the doctor's confronting words, while holding the hand of her second husband and Alana's father, Rafael Espidio-Garcia.

"We told Alana, 'This is your time. If you want to fight, we will go and find every way to fight this. If you want to take your time and spend it with your family and doing fun things, we can do that too'."

Mindy, now director of operations in Australia for online retail juggernaut Amazon, has told the story of her daughter's passing many times to her family, friends and Amazon staff.

But today, sitting in a nondescript meeting room at Amazon's Sydney headquarters, it becomes too much. She breaks down.

"I'm so sorry," she eventually says after a long pause, wiping away tears.

"I don't tell it this way all the time … I'm not so good to get deep."

After her media manager brings her a box of tissues, she composes herself.

"Alana wanted to fight it. She wanted to do everything that she could to try to get through it," Mindy continues in a pained tone after a deep breath.

She and Rafael found an experimental drug program that was willing to accept Alana, at Seattle Children's Hospital on the other side of the US from the family home in Tampa, Florida.

She stayed with her daughter as she was treated there between November 2017 and February 2018.

"In early March she picked up a fungal infection on her lungs. There came a point where we just knew there was no turning back and that she would ultimately succumb to this fungal infection, unfortunately, so she wanted to go home. We found this medical flight to get her home that was hugely expensive. But you know, in all honesty at that moment, who cares about that. It's just about her," she says slowly.

"So we got her home. I think it was five or six days later that she ended up passing away."

There is another long pause, and more tears. "I'm sorry," she says again. But I tell her there is no reason to apologise. She is a mother who lost a daughter.

After joining Amazon in June 2014, Mindy worked her through the ranks and took on the leadership role of director of operations in Australia midway through 2021, moving to Sydney with Rafael.

I ask her why she has put herself through the pain of sharing her deeply personal story with the wider world for the first time.

"It really forces you to think about your life and how you are living life, and how you are prioritising things in your life. I think the big thing for me is that by sharing my story, it allows others to see that it is possible to live through it, even though it sucks," the now 38-year-old says resolutely.

"It was hard as hell. I don't wish it on anyone else. I just know that there are other people out there who are dealing with the same things. "I want them to know it is okay to deal with things in your life. You can still find your way through them, even though sometimes things are terrible."

## YOUNG SINGLE MOTHER

Mindy had the world at her feet in 2005 when she secured a scholarship out of high school in Florida to go to college.

She wanted to study medicine, loved helping people and volunteered for work at the local hospital.

But just before she started university, her life took a very different turn when she decided instead to get married and have children.

"As a young mum I didn't have the best of luck in my first marriage. I was a victim of domestic abuse and left in the middle of the night, essentially, with my two dogs and two very young daughters," she says, without flinching.

As a single mother with two young girls in her early 20s, Mindy was working two jobs while struggling to make ends meet. She eventually met Rafael and they were married in 2009 after the birth of Alana.

Trying to earn more money, she went to college as an adult; it took her five years to graduate. She was recruited by Amazon to join as a junior manager on the fulfilment centre floor after the family moved from Tampa to New Jersey when her mother was diagnosed with cervical cancer.

When they eventually returned to Tampa and Mindy took on a senior managerial role, they discovered Alana had leukaemia. She started chemotherapy treatment at John Allen Hopkins Hospital – an hour's drive away from the family home.

Suddenly the Amazon fulfilment centre staff that Mindy managed, became her family.

"My general manager was super supportive. He said, 'Listen, we'll do anything that you need. We're here to support you. You take whatever time you need; it's not a big deal, your pay cheque will continue to come'," she recalls.

"So I had meals delivered to my house basically every night. People were coming over to watch the kids. Just that outpouring of community and love was overwhelmingly unexpected.

"You don't expect that from people that you work with."

Alana received a bone-marrow transplant and improved to the point where Mindy could return to work.

"I would pop over to the hospital in the evenings and in the mornings, and go to work in between. We had this really great routine going," she says.

"We got her cancer free and we thought, 'This is our path, we are headed in a good spot'. About three months later, we had a spinal tap and her cancer had returned.

"My Amazon team was there for the whole time. They were bringing gifts, checking in and just doing everything that they could.

"One of the things I've always kept from that is: this isn't just a team, it isn't just humans who come in to get a pay cheque and check out at the end of the night. This is truly a family, a community that leans on each other when we really need it."

During Alana's final months, the Ryan Callahan Foundation – the charity of former American pro hockey player Ryan Callahan – offered Mindy and her family a week-long trip to the TradeWinds Island Resort on St Pete Beach, so they could cherish some final moments together.

They threw Alana a tea party and made her feel like a queen.

During the party at the resort restaurant whose centrepiece was a giant fish tank, a diver appeared carrying a sign that read: "Hi, Alana! There is nowhere you could go that we won't be with you. We love you!"

Alana's funeral was held on Friday March 23, 2018 at the Sylvan Abbey Funeral Home in Clearwater.

The family requested that in lieu of flowers, donations be made in her name to the Ryan Callahan Foundation.

"Her funeral was filled with Amazonians. Not just the leaders, but the associates who I led years ago or who had heard about it, and had kids or family members who were impacted by cancer and wanted to be there. It was just really cool to see everybody come together in that moment," Mindy says.

To honour Alana's love of unicorns, the team at Tampa's Amazon fulfilment centre created unicorn pins to be awarded to associates who go above and beyond.

Mindy says Alana's passing was confronting for her older sisters, Caterina and Isabella. But they got through it.

"Something like this changes the family dynamic. I think they were very nervous about 'How do I express my emotions without making mum and dad sad'. Which is tough," she says.

Now aged 18 and 20, they are both at university.

"The two of them have done phenomenally well. They've done well in school and they are super resilient young ladies."

## LEADERSHIP STYLE

Mindy took just a month off after Alana's passing before she returned to be general manager of Amazon's Orlando distribution facility.

She ran another six Amazon facilities in the southeast of America before moving to Australia last year – a market vastly different in population density to the US and other areas of the world Amazon operates in.

A key part of Mindy's role now is navigating a complex logistical land mass, while still being able to meet Amazon's delivery promises.

Amazon Australia offers more than 200 million products across 31 different categories.

The business more than doubled its operational footprint in 2021 and now has more than seven million cubic feet of storage space across six fulfilment centres nationwide.

But it is also experiencing growing pains.

In January 2023, the Seattle-based company revealed plans to cut 18,000 jobs worldwide – the biggest set of lay-offs in its history – representing about 6 per cent of the retailer's overall corporate workforce of 300,000 people.

Amazon is responding to threats of a recession and a decline in consumer spending in America after its shares lost half their value in 2022, which was the worst year for shareholders since the dotcom crash in 2000.

Waves of redundancies across the tech sector by companies such as Salesforce, PayPal, Google and Facebook have been widely criticised as most were announced via email.

But in Australia, Mindy says she is working to drive cultural change with a leadership style defined by the way her team corralled around her in the face of adversity.

She believes that as a result of her experience, the company made significant changes to its care leave and benefits policies globally. It also set up a an organisation called "Amazon Goes Gold" to support children with cancer.

"When I started with Amazon in 2014, there weren't any general managers who were women," she says.

"We now want to provide mentorship opportunities for female leaders to be able to see what their path is and how they can get there.

"For the single mums who are dealing with the pressures of daycare and domestic violence and some of these other things."

She wants the business to give back to the community in which it operates and she wants to build a workplace that is "safe, inclusive and connected".

She recalls the story of a male executive in Sydney who recently lost their child to a miscarriage and how she tried to help.

"I think having somebody on the outside to talk through it, who went through it, is just sometimes helpful when you're not sure how to get through it at home," she says.

After having surgery, Mindy's mother is now cancer free and living a healthy life in California with her step-father.

She says the tragedy of her daughter's passing has given her a new awareness of the curve-balls life can throw at anyone.

"Work is much more about the people than it is necessarily about the end result of producing business numbers or metrics," she says.

"There's certainly also a theme of resilience and how you take a really tough situation – whether it was my first divorce, my daughter or some of these other challenges – and not give up. How can I help others go through these same types of problems and offer up my experience to just remain positive and keep going."

# PAULA FOX

The Fox family mansion on Irving Road in Toorak looks imposing as you stand before its grand front gates. On a cool, sunny morning in March 2023 they opened before me and I walked up a grand front path to be greeted at the front door by a hobbling but smiling Paula Fox, who shook my hand and ushered me into a sitting room for her first ever media interview.

Paula looked a tad nervous but was eager to get into the discussion. After only 30 minutes we were done. One of the most significant interviews of my career had taken just a half an hour. But Paula wasn't one to waffle – her answers were direct to the point and honest.

After the interview she took me on a tour of the spectacular gardens, including showing me a bunch of stunning roses behind the tennis court that were specially named after her.

She let me take photos, just for my private collection. One of her staff even offered me a cookie or two that had been freshly made that morning with a cup of coffee.

Many people have asked me how I got Paula to talk, and for that I have to thank one of her three sons, Andy, who I have known for many years.

I had called him a few months earlier to ask him to do an interview for The Australian's Richest 250 magazine. He politely declined and instead suggested I interview his mother. Which, after some months of waiting, I duly did.

But I was also lucky to have built trust over more than a decade with the Fox family. In 2010 I interviewed Andy's brother David, his first and – to this day – only media interview.

*I've also interviewed Lindsay over the years, as well as having an unforgettable 90-minute off-the-record coffee with him in late 2019 where he mused endlessly about family, fortune and the meaning of life. Not a word of that discussion was published because he asked me not to. My word is my bond. Which was immensely frustrating at the time. But my vow would pay handsome dividends four years later.*

*Paula left me a very polite voicemail thanking me for the piece after it was published. Lindsay, I am told, was excited and proud that his beloved wife had finally told her story to the world.*

Paula Fox was at Sydney Airport about to board a commercial flight to America with five of her children many years ago when she spotted a solitary male figure not far from her across the terminal.

For a few moments she stared. Then something inside willed her to walk towards the man, who was waving off a departing flight. She then took a deep breath and steeled herself for a conversation that had been decades in the making.

"I just looked at him and thought, 'God, I know that face.' So, I went up to him and said 'Are you Raymond Peele? He said yes and asked me who I was. I replied, 'I'm your daughter, Paula!'," she recalls. For a moment there was a poignant silence.

"He just got tears in his eyes and didn't say anything."

Paula Fox, the matriarch of the billionaire Fox family and wife of trucking magnate Lindsay Fox, has always spoken her mind.

She did just that this day to her long-absent father. Raymond Peele was a former navy officer who had walked out on Paula and her six siblings when she was just eight years old and living in Mackay on the Central Queensland Coast.

Her mother Edith was left to raise the family on her own.

"Then I said to him, 'But I can't talk to you because my children are all boarding the plane," she adds of the fateful airport exchange.

"So we just left it at that. I never saw him again. It was an amazing coincidence that he was there that day."

Sitting in the front room of her $50m arts and crafts heritage-listed Melbourne mansion known as "Eulinya" on Toorak's Irving Road and surrounded by stunning gardens, Paula shows few nerves in the first wide-ranging media interview of her life.

Before we sit down she has hobbled to greet me at the front door, a legacy of complications from knee surgery late last year. But she is in fine spirits. And sharp as a tack.

She and Lindsay, who has long spoken of his wife as his "one and only" and a "marvellous lady", bought Eulinya in 1978 for $570,000 from the lady mayoress, Lady Lilian Coles, wife of Sir Arthur Coles of the supermarket family.

The home is littered with photographs of Paula, Lindsay and her children with Prime Ministers, princes, popes, celebrities and sports stars. Photos of her grandchildren and great grandkids adorn the refrigerator in the homely-looking kitchen.

To Paula Grace Fox, family is everything.

Her mother Edith, one of 12 children herself who was born in America and came to Australia on a steamship, moved her family from Mackay to Melbourne to be closer to her sister. Paula later became skilled at making her own dresses.

Edith worked three jobs just to keep the family together before she met a single father named Frank Gillies, who lived in a boarding house in St Kilda nearby.

They became friends and he often told Edith of his sadness of missing his two boys, who he wasn't allowed to see by decree of their mother. One of them was named Max, now better known as one of Australia's most famed comedians.

"I've since met Max and told him quite a bit about his father, this most wonderful man. He was so gentle and handsome," Paula says.

"Frank and my mother weren't in a relationship. But they became really good friends. Frank and I were very close, I used to call him Figgy. He was really like a father figure to me. He actually gave me away when I got married to Lindsay. So I was very fortunate that I met him."

Edith Peele lived a long life and spent her final years in an apartment Lindsay bought for her on St Kilda Road.

"My mother died 10 years ago. She was an amazing lady. She was the most generous person and everything she had she gave away," Paula says.

"So I really instil into my children that the most important thing in life is to give."

## PHILANTHROPIC PASSIONS

The Fox family, owners of the Linfox trucking empire, have long been one of Melbourne's most generous philanthropists.

Their multimillion-dollar donation in 2022 to The Alfred Hospital for the Paula Fox Melanoma and Cancer Centre followed a $100m gift a few months earlier to the National Gallery of Victoria for the construction of the NGV Contemporary as part of the new $1.7 billion Melbourne Arts Precinct.

The name of the $152.4 million specialist facility at The Alfred was revealed in June 2022 during an event at the site attended by Paula, Prime Minister Anthony Albanese and the then Victorian Premier Daniel Andrews and his wife Catherine. The five-storey centre will have the capacity to care for close to 300 patients a day and is set to be completed in early-2024, thanks to support from the Victorian and Commonwealth Governments, the Fox Family, billionaire Andrew Forrest's Minderoo Foundation and Monash University.

In the basement of the new development will be a cutting-edge $US12 million high-tech scanner that has revolutionised cancer patient care in America by producing faster and higher-quality clinical whole-body scans compared with currently available scanners. It will be the first in any public hospital facility in Australia.

Paula was first told about the device over lunch in Melbourne with her good friend Larry Ruvo, the American drinks entrepreneur and philanthropist who started the Cleveland Clinic for Brain Health in Las Vegas in 2010.

"Larry raved about this machine," she says. "He said it would do the work in two minutes where a normal scan can take up to 40 minutes, and it scans every part of the body and is so much safer. It is the new way forward."

Paula had every one of her six children – four boys and two girls – at The Alfred.

"When I had them it was a private maternity ward," she says. "Any time any of the children had a problem, especially with four boys, they always took good care of us.. Her granddaughter Bella, Andrew's daughter, is now an intensive care nurse at the hospital.

Paula also owes her life to Dr Frank Bruscino-Raiola, now the director of the Plastics and Reconstructive Unit at Alfred Health and one of the leading surgeons in the nation for melanoma surgery, who removed a cancerous growth on her back seven years ago.

It required two operations and 45 stitches. "I never asked the doctors how bad it was; I was too nervous," she says.

Since the surgery she has remained cancer free, and that has driven her passion for providing financial support for the new cancer centre.

She also underwent emergency heart surgery at The Alfred in 2020, where she had a coronary stent put in place. Her husband now has six.

"The doctor said one more day and I would have been dead. So how lucky was I? So here I am still here and I'm a very positive person," she says.

Paula now gets her greatest satisfaction in life from giving, and is glad her children are following in her footsteps.

"Our children are going to be very wealthy one day. They are now but they will be very wealthy. The Linfox business has just grown and it's worth so much money," she says.

"But we are now giving away as much as we can, because I think that's important. You get so much pleasure out of giving to other people."

## LOVE STORY

Lindsay and Paula Fox have been married for nearly 64 years.

They first met when they were teenagers – Lindsay was aged 16 and Paula 15 – at the old St Moritz ice skating rink in St Kilda.

It was 12 months before the former acquired his first truck when he bought trucking company E.V. Timms in Collingwood. Today, Linfox Logistics has more than 8000 trucks, employs 30,000 people in 12 countries and is run by Lindsay and Paula's eldest son Peter.

His younger brothers Andrew and David also run arms of the family business, which owns Avalon Airport and the giant Essendon Fields development at Essendon Airport in Melbourne.

The Fox Family Foundation, which manages the family's charitable donations and activities, is the responsibility of Lindsay and Paula's daughters, Melbourne-based Katrina Fox and Lisa Fox, who lives in New York.

But tragedy has also rocked the family. Six months after David Fox celebrated his 21st birthday, the big brother he nicknamed "Skinny" killed himself.

David and his younger sister Katrina found the body of their 23-year-old brother Michael on the floor of his Kooyong home in Melbourne in

January 1991. He is buried in the same cemetery as his father's parents in Melbourne.

"I think it is good to talk about Michael because he was part of our life. I've got friends that have lost children and they won't talk about it. But he was part of our life and he will never go away," Paula says without flinching.

"The truth is he was too young to get married. He was only 21 and his wife was only 20 … They separated after only about 18 months and he was devastated. So, he just made a decision and took his life. It is very sad."

Michael Fox was tasked by his parents each December to buy the family Christmas tree that would take pride of place in the front room at Eulinya.

"That was his job," his mother adds solemnly.

"So, every year I buy a little Christmas tree and put it on his grave, with a Christmas card."

Following his son's passing Lindsay Fox advised the Federal and Victorian governments on youth suicide and joined the board of the National Advisory Council on Suicide Prevention.

He once said he thought he was invincible until one of his beloved sons took his own life.

"I think it made him a lot more protective of his children," he wife now says of the impact of the tragedy on her husband.

"If one of them is down, the others all rally around, which is pretty good. Lindsay just loves his children. They are his whole life."

She reveals the family fortune will remain intact and be shared equally among the children under a succession plan she and Lindsay have finalised with their advisers.

They include former ACTU Secretary Bill Kelty and Peter Yates, a former CEO of the Packer family's Publishing and Broadcasting. Both are Linfox board members.

The Fox family also has a close relationship with Sayers Group founder, Carlton Football Club President and former PwC Australia CEO Luke Sayers.

Given alleged tensions over the years between some of the Fox siblings, sharing the fortune equally could be a recipe for disaster. But Paula and her husband believe it is the only fair way.

"We've done it (the succession) that everything is equal. It's got to be equal, because we don't want any of the children arguing about finance. But I have to say, my kids don't care about the money, really. They do care a little but they don't care about who gets what. Like this house. I said to Lindsay the other day, 'If I sell this house, I'll give all the money away'. My children don't need it. What could they do with all that money?

We have looked after the grandchildren by paying for their education but now our children can afford to do that themselves too … They've all got their own homes, they've got good lifestyles and are comfortable."

The Fox family in 2022 took delivery of a new Global Express 6500 private jet. But even that is shared equally.

"We've got a plane and we let them have X amount of hours on it. But we don't say 'Take the plane whenever you want'. They haven't got their own planes," Paula says.

"I've seen so many of our friends with the arguments. I've got some that are still in court arguing about the finances and it's tragic. So that's really important that we sorted that out."

Lindsay Fox has previously described "dividing up the pie" for his children as "just a natural process of life".

"There is only one way to do it. Cover the thing on the basis of there is no such thing as entitlement, there should be nothing in the form of expectation," he told me in 2019.

"What comes out of it – whether it is $10, $100 or $1000 – the only difference is noughts."

## LUCKY LIFE

The close relationship between Victorian Premier Daniel Andrews and the Fox family has long been the subject of media speculation and opinion.

Paula proudly declares she is fond of the Premier and his wife Catherine.

"Dan I think is amazing. I'm also very fond of Catherine. We are very supportive of everything she does. She does a lot of things behind the scenes and she is so involved with different charities. But people don't know about her. I like Dan, I like her and we've become friends, which is nice. He's very relaxed when he's here (at the Fox mansions in Toorak or Portsea). He and Andrew (Fox) are good friends," she says.

In January it was revealed in the media that the Premier attended a five-hour barbecue at the Fox Portsea mansion.

In response to the story Andrews declared that he had not discussed the Fox family's business interests during the visit and claimed nothing inappropriate had occurred at the private event, which Prime Minister Anthony Albanese also attended.

"Dan is a bit nervous because with the media, as soon as they know he is with the Fox's, they write about it. That's sad that he can't just come here, have a drink or have lunch. I hate it, its awful," Paula says.

The Fox family was also the subject of media speculation relating to its alleged involvement in the holiday home accident that left Mr Andrews with a broken back and off work for more than three months in 2020.

"He never ever fell down our stairs, I can assure you," Paula declares.

"I knew where he was in the house down at Portsea which he rented … People hate Dan so I'm always protecting him. A lot of my friends don't like him. But they are all loving Anthony Albanese, they can't believe it. They are all Liberal supporters, but they're loving him."

She defends the family's relationship with the Prime Minster, who she describes as "incredible" and who she believes is "doing a great job".

"In January when Anthony came down to Portsea, he was in Melbourne and he rang Lindsay and said, 'Look, I'd love to come down to see you'. Lindsay has known Anthony for 25 years, because he was the Minister for Transport. So Lindsay had quite a bit to do with him. But the fact that he went down on the beach and had a swim, they write all about that. It's really sad. I feel sorry for Anthony and Dan. They've got no privacy."

Paula turned 85 on July 12 2023 but unlike her husband – who in 2022 celebrated the same milestone with a cruise on their 650-foot yacht to Montreal with the entire Fox family and a number of leading business people in tow – the Fox family matriarch was sailing in Greece with just her immediate family.

"Lindsay's parents both died in their early 60s. So he keeps thinking, 'Well, I'll have another party," she says.

"I don't have parties. I had one year when I turned 80, which was in Italy. But I'm not into big parties. That's not me."

Paula says the secret of her and Lindsay staying together for more than six decades has been the age-old art of compromise.

"We always say 'compromise, compromise'. We're very fortunate that we've never really had a major problem and we've got wonderful children that are all there for us. So we've just been very fortunate," she says.

So does Lindsay have a temper? The Fox family has long been known as tough negotiators and Lindsay has intimidated many a unionist or politician over the decades.

"He did but now he forgets very quickly," Paula replies instantly.

"He gets angry and then he forgets. He's mellowed so much over the years."

His greatest passion remains his trucks. For decades his business card has simply read: Lindsay E. Fox – truck driver.

"And his trucks have to be immaculate," his wife adds.

"The moment he sees a dirty truck on the road, he gets its number, rings up and reports it. That's why his trucks stand out so much."

In February 2023 the family patriarch took all of his blood relative males on a once-in-a-lifetime experience, a two week expedition to Antarctica.

He even fulfilled a lifelong dream to jump in the freezing waters near the South Pole and reportedly turned blue before being pulled out by his sons.

He was there on Valentines Day, so called his wife on a satellite phone to sing her a love song.

She continues to worry about him, especially his health. But Lindsay Fox never thought he would reach 80 years of age, let alone 85.

He and his wife now make everyday count.

"He forgets a lot. When they left for Antarctica, I told the boys and the grandchildren to make sure he takes his medicines. But they all really look after each other and he's very loved by his family," she says.

"I am very fortunate I married such a wonderful man. He is a great father, a great husband and he is always there for us."

# CHRIS GARNAUT

The Ukrainian city of Bucha near Kyiv has become a tragic symbol of the brutality of the war against the Russian invaders.

In March 2022, 458 bodies were found in Bucha after Russian forces withdrew, including 12 children.

On the evening of August 24 the same year, a traditional Ukrainian Motonka Doll, made by children rescued from a refuge in Bucha, was the symbolic centrepiece of a gala fundraising event at Melbourne's Hyatt Hotel to coincide with Ukrainian Independence Day.

Stefan Romaniw, the co-chair of the Australian Federation of Ukrainian Organisations and Vice President of the Ukrainian World Congress, took to the stage to solemnly present the doll to Melbourne financial adviser Chris Garnaut.

Romaniw described it as "a small but incredible token of appreciation from the Ukrainian Community" for the work Garnaut and his Fawkner Property Group had done to support resettling displaced Ukrainians in Australia.

In 2022 the deeply private but influential Melbourne financial adviser led the call for corporate Australia to raise $2 million dollars for the Ukraine Crisis Appeal Resettlement Fund after his Fawkner Group tipped $100,000 into the fund in mid-May that year.

The Fund provides professional support for the resettlement of displaced Ukrainians, including mental health and work-entry programs, and life skill programs such as swimming, first aid and driving lessons.

"The idea of the August function was one to raise money and two, to ensure we didn't have Ukraine fatigue in the media," Garnaut says.

"You get this new level of energy when you have a purpose."

The theme of the night was the Ancient Greek word "Philotimo", an amalgam of the virtues of honour, integrity, duty, pride, dignity and courage. Garnaut says they accord with his own "life beliefs".

Ironically when the Fawkner Property Team launched the "We Stand United for Ukraine" appeal in May 2022 together with Rotary Australia and the Australian Federation of Ukrainian Organisations, Garnaut had never met a Ukrainian person in his life.

"Now I think they are one of the nicest races of people I have ever had the pleasure to meet," he says.

The Melbourne businessman, a father of two, had watched enough gruesome television images of
children caught up in the conflict to want to take action.

"I found them totally disturbing, to the point where I could not watch them and then I couldn't read about them. So, I thought, "Well, I better just work out what I can do'," he says.

Also, in 2022 Garnaut was discussing the Ukraine war with the manager of Fawkner's The Square Mirrabooka shopping centre in Perth when she mentioned the number of displaced Ukrainians who had resettled in the shopping centre's catchment area.

"I suggested we have a sausage sizzle welcome ceremony to welcome them to Australia. Because these are primarily mothers and kids," Garnaut says.

Thousands turned out to the event, staged in conjunction with the Ukraine Association of WA and the City of Stirling.

Garnaut stresses his Ukraine crusade has been a personal one, although Fawkner Property unit holders were advised of the initiative in an investor communication in mid-September 2022.

"We have never asked the unit holders for money and never spent their money," he says.

He says it has also tapped into his long-held Catholic beliefs.

"I have a huge distaste for communism, and the oppression of communism. You can call Russia whatever you like. But it is a communist, Soviet state and its conduct is reflective of a communist, Soviet state. Most communists are dictators and bullies," he says.

"While this started out as a philosophy, now it has turned into a love."

## COMPANY VALUES

It is now 36 years since Garnaut – the cousin of famed Australian economist and academic Ross Garnaut – formed Garnaut Private Wealth, which provides financial advice to high net worth and ultra high net worth individuals with over $4.4 billion in assets.

The Melbourne-based firm has more than 650 clients mainly based in South Eastern Australia.

"We will continue to grow organically; we will never buy another company. For us, it is about cultural fit. The average Garnaut interview process, before you become a client, is five interviews," he says proudly.

One of the keys to its success has been its focus on investments, both liquid and illiquid, that don't show high amounts of price volatility.

"There is a really high care factor and a thoroughness to what we do. We want to provide clients with the "sleep at night" factor," Garnaut says.

"The Garnaut Absolute return theme is about active management and capital preservation, so we look for downside protection, low correlation and alpha generation."

Fawkner, which is a separate business, has more than $1.7bn in funds under management and sees itself as a deep value, essential services manager. It now has over 130 roadside retail, convenience retail and childcare assets.

"Fawkner will continue to grow as long as it sees value in the market. It is a fund manager, not a Funds Under Management (FUM) gatherer. That is really important," Garnaut says of the firm, which is separately managed by a team led by Owen Lennie.

Notably Fawkner owns more than 10 shopping centres including The Square Mirrabooka in WA, Traralgon Centre Plaza in Victoria and the Mount Pleasant, Earlville Shopping Town and Stockland Cairns centres in Queensland.

While the deals were driven by the opportunity to purchase assets at considerable discounts to their pre-pandemic valuations, there was also a personal motivation for Garnaut as the firm's chief investment manager.

The 62-year-old now wants to make every day count, five years since winning the biggest personal battle of his life. He was diagnosed with throat cancer in July 2016. One of his specialists, who is also a good friend, told him he would die by Christmas that year. The doctor even delivered the grim diagnosis to Garnaut's family.

But the man himself, who has never smoked a cigarette in his life, would have nothing of it. He started researching his condition and realised his probability of survival was quite high.

He started preparing for laser treatment, which commenced in August 2016.

"It takes two or three weeks to actually build your body kit and the body kit for throat cancer is horrible.  But it saves your life. It saves you having radiotherapy all over your face and your body," he says.

Every Tuesday, for 7 weeks, he had laser treatment and chemotherapy.

"I went in real match fit and lost 18kg. But I lost no hair, zero. The only hair I lost was off the back of my neck when the treatment burnt through my throat, through my head and burnt the back of my hair off. I gave up drinking and just had a can of Guinness every Friday. But I lost my taste completely so I couldn't taste the Guinness anyway," he says.

"I was exceptionally lucky because my son is involved in Garnaut, and I had such brilliant staff that were so capable that both businesses didn't miss a beat."

Patrick Garnaut, known as "Patch", is a Garnaut director. Garnaut's other son, Elliot, is a famed celebrity fashion stylist.

Their father now continues to get the all clear on his cancer diagnosis. Asked how the experience has changed him, the practicing Catholic says he has become "more Christian".

"I pray more often, I go to church more often," he says.

He even started taking his now 87-year-old mother, Angela, to her local Anglican Church in the Bayside suburb of Elwood. He says she loves it, despite being a Catholic.

His mother was widowed at the age of only 36 – with nine children in tow – when her husband passed away suddenly. Arnaut was only 12 when he lost his father. He says his cancer fight has also made him conscious of his own mortality.

"When you are punching along in life and you're doing okay, you think that you are immortal because you've had so many wins. The only time you think that you are not immortal is when you have a few losses. Then along comes a fucking good old life-threatening disease, and you have a real ripping fucking smell of the rosewood in the fucking coffin. All of a sudden, you are mortal," he says, displaying his trademark penchant for the odd swear-word.

Not once, he says, did he fear death. In fact, despite the initial dire diagnosis, he never thought he was going to die. But the experience has given him a new lease on life in business.

"I think it was this sort of 'Fuck this, I've had two years off in a holding pattern and there's no way I am a holding pattern sort of guy. I'm going to go in and absolutely swing this fucking hard'," he says of Fawkner's recent rapid expansion.

"God willing, the timing was perfect. Because when I was ready to go, the opportunities happened to be there for a deep value property manager. And we executed the opportunities."

# MAX GRUNDMANN

*Max Grundmann might be a larger than life character and responsible for co-founding one of the most iconic Australian homewares brands that is now a household name, but he has always jealously guarded his privacy. In 2021 an old journalistic colleague of mine talked him into finally telling his story to record the historic moment when he took full ownership of the Maxwell & Williams brand from his co-founder. In true Max style we did the interview over lunch and several bottles of fine French red wine at one of his favourite Italian restaurants, Cecconis, at the top end of Melbourne's Flinders Lane. Max was his passionate, colourful self. When the article was published, Max rang me to say how many people from his past had reached out to congratulate him for finally telling his amazing story. He was quite stunned. We have since been to several AFL matches together to watch his beloved Collingwood Football Club. He supports the Magpies in the same way he has always approached life. with hard work, pride and passion. He is truly one of a kind.*

In 1996, Max Grundmann was doodling on a paper tablecloth in an Italian trattoria in the Tuscan capital of Florence when an idea came to him that would change his life.

Inspired by sharing several bottles of fine Chianti wine with his fiance Kath to toast their Italian sojourn, he jotted down a name for a unique porcelain range of homewares being sold by his family's Melbourne-based importing business, HAG Imports.

It was a combination of his full first name and that of his business partner, William – better known as Bill – Ryan. That afternoon the brand name Maxwell & Williams was born.

This fateful piece of paper now sits framed on the front counter of the HAG offices in the Melbourne industrial hub of Brooklyn at the foot of the West Gate Bridge.

Today Maxwell & Williams (M&W) products are distributed widely around Australia in Myer department stores and other speciality retail shops, and in more than 60 countries worldwide, including Canada for the past two decades.

In June 2021 the 96-year-old Bill Ryan retired and Max – also a lifetime Collingwood supporter and a former owner of the North Melbourne Giants basketball team – took full ownership of the M&W business.

With HAG's global selling footprint, Max has ambitions to make it a $1bn enterprise which could even one day be listed on the Australian Securities Exchange. His two sons to his ex-wife, Michael and Daniel, both work in the business.

"There is only one thing that is absolutely perfect in this world. That is mediocrity. The reign of mediocrity is extraordinary. So you don't have to be that good to be exceptional. That is the reality," he says.

"When Bill and I became partners, we agreed our success was pretty much guaranteed. Not because we were that good, but because the competition was that bad."

The amicable negotiations for their separation took 18 months, assisted by another intriguing piece of M&W written history.

"We actually had a document which was prepared by the lawyers in 1978 about a separation. But we never signed it," Max says with a wide smile.

Bill joined HAG in 1978, combining his expertise in finance with Max's prowess in buying and selling.

"He stuck to his knitting and I stuck to mine and we trusted each other. We had what I call experience sessions rather than recrimination sessions when things went wrong. Experience is what you get when you didn't get what you wanted," Max says.

"Our relationship has always been cordial and friendly. But there was such a big difference in age and perspective. And he was very frugal; I am not. His frugality came from his life experience and my philosophy has always been that you only get one life."

## STARTING FROM NOTHING

Max's parents. Holocaust survivors Heinrich (Harry) and Anna Grundmann, immigrated to Australia from the Greek port of Piraeus in mid-December 1952 aboard the migrant ship "Cyrenia", an old Greek vessel built in 1911.

The ship stopped initially in Fremantle in Western Australia before Harry and Anna travelled on to Melbourne.

After working as a salesman, Harry – with only $700 in the bank – started HAG, named from combining his and Anna's initials. The company began life in a small garage at their home in Clinton St in the bayside Melbourne suburb of Brighton East.

"I'm very, very proud of the fact my parents started something from nothing," says Max, who turned 75 in 2021.

He left Melbourne High School in 1964 and then studied economics, politics and law while working as an assistant waiter, lifeguard, hamburger-maker, porter, lift driver and door-to-door salesman.

He joined his father's business as a junior salesman in 1974, its fifth employee. His father was then head salesman and his mother handwrote HAG's invoices.

"Dad was a commercial thinker who got it. Mum had fabulous style and taste. Not that she had the money ever to express that, because the family were refugees. The most fundamental thing Dad taught me was you can't buy integrity so you better not give it away. So it is not possible for me to do things in the business that would destroy their integrity. That has always been a huge lesson for me," he says. In 1978, his father suffered a heart attack and stepped away from the business to recuperate. Max and Bill Ryan – who he called the company's "favourite customer" – became joint managing directors.

HAG came to acquire the exclusive Australian distribution rights to household names such as Casa Domani tableware and world-renowned Polish glassware Krosno.

As part of his political studies at university, Max studied philosophy. He says this taught him to think in a way that has made HAG completely different to its competitors.

"Most people come at things from the product side; I come from the strategy and philosophy part. My thinking is completely different," he says.

For example, he says while many in business see advertising, marketing and communications as a cost imposition on a business, Max sees it as a "super fund".

"Business is the organisation and management of specialisation. That's it. It is not about making a profit. When you tackle things from that perspective, it changes the way you think," he says.

"Specialisation achieves the benefit of improving productivity and capability. The idea that business is ever at someone's expense is an impossible idea. The strategy in our business is I am responsible for the benefit received by every stakeholder. Because everybody needs to receive the benefit they should."

He says the values of HAG are expressed "in the way we do things".

"No stakeholders will be cheated or disadvantaged from the factory to the consumer," he says.

"We need to make great product that is affordable, fashionable, functional and we do it because we care. We have a passion about it and we are not going to let anyone down. That is what we do."

On the wall of HAG's head office boardroom is a plaque with a famous quote from legendary Walmart founder Sam Walton.

"There is only one boss: the customer," it reads. "And he can fire everybody in the company from the chairman down simply by spending his money somewhere else."

John King was appointed Myer chief executive in June 2018, and on his fourth day in the job he visited Max at HAG's offices. It was a first for a Myer CEO and the idea of M&W setting up in-store shops in Myer was born.

In 2019, Max took that deal to a new level when HAG severed its ties with David Jones, which since 2014 has been owned by the listed South African retailer Woolworths Holdings.

That same year, before the onset of the pandemic, Max also had his first meeting with a Myer chairman, then Gary Hounsell.

M&W now runs 60 in-store outlets in Myer department stores.

In July 2021 HAG also took over the Australian distribution rights for Woll Cookware, a cast-aluminium brand that has been manufactured in Germany since 1979.

He says the opening order was worth almost €2m ($3.15m), a figure the brand had never achieved before in Australia.

## PLAYING BALL

Max still wears the championship ring of the now-defunct North Melbourne Giants as a reminder to "never to buy a basketball team".

He was a board member and then subsequently chairman of the club at a time when basketball was growing rapidly at both the grassroots and elite levels in Australia.

But despite winning the NBL championship in 1994 and being runners up the following year, Max and his fellow owners were unable to make the business viable.

"We tried everything to no avail. The financial losses were massive, the fallout was devastating and I will never forget the experience," he says.

But two experiences during that period stand out among the darkest of his life.

The first was on a Sunday morning in late 1995 ahead of an emergency meeting of the NBL board where they were set to cancel the Giants' NBL licence, which would have severe financial consequences for Max and his family.

Before he went to the meeting, he warned Kath that their beloved Mercedes was likely to soon replaced by a bicycle.

"Her answer was unequivocal and spontaneous," he recalls. "'Just make it a bicycle built for two,' she said. I'll never forget the beauty and power of that moment. That commitment to our love and relationship was just super. It was extraordinary and under the circumstances almost made the whole episode worthwhile."

The second experience came not long after, when Max had to finally advise the team's players at meeting at its Olympic Park headquarters that he could no longer single-handedly financially support them and was putting the club into administration.

At the time he was talking to a number of prospective buyers for the franchise and to keep a deal alive, he needed the players to stay with the Giants.

They included league legends and Olympians such as Mark Leader, Larry Sengstock, Pat Reidy, Ray Borner and Paul Rees.

"I told the players the devastating news and made it clear that we could not offer them contracts because we were in administration and the only way we could be sold was if they stayed," Max recalls saying.

Not one player left the room. For Max, it was a show of spirit and solidarity the likes of which he had never seen before.

"The feeling of disaster had been replaced by a feeling of exhilaration. Though the end was still nigh, hope existed and made all the difference. The rest is history: the club was merged but sadly still did not survive the difficult business of basketball at that time," he says.

Max recalled the story during a 2015 speech he made to the students of Melbourne High, 51 years after he graduated. The staff and students gave him a standing ovation.

He told them that the ups and downs of life and leadership were obvious and inevitable. They could be both uplifting and soul-destroying, he added, telling the students they had the choice to take up the mantle of leadership or to decline it.

"However, life without leadership means progress is impossible. Progress demands change and taking the lead means taking the risk. The question now is: are you up to it? Are you willing to take the risk?" he asked.

"Many say 'Life is what you make of it'. But I say 'All of life is what you make it'. So do you want to learn how to make that difference? You can learn to be a leader and the starting point is now! I implore you to dare to be what you can be."

# DAVID HAINS

I had often walked past the elaborate building known as Portland House at Number 8 Collins Street wondering what lay behind its grand solid-oak door.

In the early months of 2009, I was to find out.

I long knew of the legend of Melbourne businessman David Hains, but only dreamed of one day getting the chance to meet him.

The opportunity came via Ron Walker, the late Fairfax Media chairman and a long-time friend of Hains. Paradoxically Hains had called Walker to complain about the accuracy of his write up in the annual Rich List published by BRW magazine, owned by Fairfax.

Walker was sympathetic, but suggested Hains – in response – decide for once to tell his story in his own words. In conjunction with then AFR editor Glenn Burge, it was decided that my then esteemed AFR colleague Andrew Cornell and I were to pursue the story.

I'll never forget our first meeting with Hains at 8 Collins Street.

After we breathlessly ascending three flights of stairs (Hains later had a lift installed for his beloved long-time secretary Marlene), Andrew and I entered Hains wood-panelled office and sat on old leather arm chairs. When Hains entered the room, he shook our hands and sat in his own chair, his green, bakelite phone within easy reach.

He was polite and charming, but cautious. He warned us that he had not told his sons that he was even meeting with us – let alone doing an interview – and that the whole project could still implode once he did.

After a bunch of initial fascinating on the record interviews, that day duly came. I'll never forget the morning Hains walked into his office to greet us with looks that could kill.

*He had bad news – his "boys" had vetoed him talking publicly, the game was up. Inside I couldn't stop cursing, but Andrew and I kept our eye on the ball. By the close of the hour, we had politely convinced Hains that he had gone too far to turn back..*

*He left the room with the resolve to finish the project and duly did.*

*On the day the magazine piece was published, the AFR printed giant flyers for the story that were plastered outside newsagents up and down Collins Street. I remember Hains called me in shock to say he'd never seen his face so many times in front of him during his walk outside his office.*

*But no harm was done. Inside, I'm sure he was quietly chuffed. Below is the magazine piece, now updated to the past tense.*

*In the years that followed the story, Hains and I would catch up for a relaxed off the record lunch at least twice a year, sometimes with my friend and colleague at The Australian, Rich List editor John Stensholt.*

*The billionaire was especially interested in my book on James Packer, "The Price of Fortune", and always asked after James.*

*Hains had his own table at the back of Cecconi's restaurant – known as the billionaire table, given it was also the favourite of his friends Lindsay Fox and Solomon Lew – where we would always meet. In his final years, as he became hard of hearing and more frail, he preferred to order in sushi in his office. He passed away at the end of January 2023.*

*To the end he was engaging, polite and always interested in what I was doing. He truly was one of the finest gentleman of Australian business. I miss him.*

Ask the average bod who David Hains is and, if a view is proffered at all, they might hazard 'business-man' or 'someone to do with horses'.

Ask the average punter at the TAB, and the answer might be a little more precise, if less accurate: he's the trainer. A few, no doubt, would be more accurate, knowing Hains as the owner of Kingston Park, home of some of Australia's most famous thoroughbreds – some of which indeed were trained by David Hayes, the legendary trainer.

Hence the confusion.

Yet, even in Collins Street, where Hains worked for almost 50 years in the same office and at the same desk, few recognised the slim, fit and unassuming man with an old-school air as the founder of one of Australia's most successful investment houses, the Portland House Group.

Hains prefered it that way. A fixture in the billionaire category on the *BRW Rich List*, he was no Howard Hughes. Nor did desire to be a public figure. Hains was fond of saying "keep your tongue in your cheek and your pen in your inkwell".

Never before had he agreed to a profile. "And this will be the last," he told Andrew and I firmly in 2009 after finally agreeing to talk to *The AFR Magazine.*

Yet Hains was always discreet rather than secretive; many more people would have seen and spoken to him, in Collins Street, at the races or on the Mornington Peninsula, than would realise it.

He was always unfailingly courteous. When the old Bakelite rotary phone in his Portland House lounge rang, he answered it himself.

"I just don't see the point," Hains told us in his quiet, precise voice, when asked why he didn't have a higher public profile.

With a private company and one of Australia's biggest fortunes, he choose as he pleased. What he pleased to do was work, following much the same pattern of deep, hands-on involvement in Portland House, constantly questioning the business model, starting up new ones.

"I have enjoyed every day of my working life – some-times more or less – and for that reason feel that I have never really worked a day of my life," he said.

"On top of that, I have been privileged to do what I enjoy doing and have been paid for it, as well." Indeed, I always came away from any encounter with Hains realising how totally engaged he was with the investment world.

His sharp questioning of received wisdom, whether about leverage or counter party risk or commodity prices, defined his investment philosophy and that of Portland House.

This was a man who had meetings with directors of the world's biggest banks; who put someone with a good idea in touch with some legendary investors and business figures around the world. The late former Fairfax Media chairman Ron Walker shared a mentor with Hains: former Melbourne retailer and prime ministerial economics adviser, the late Sir Frank Richardson.

Walker lived two doors down from Hains in Toorak.

"He has this ability to stay risk-averse and he's a deep thinker about his investments," Walker told us.

"He has always operated below the radar and hasn't sought publicity. I compare David and Lloyd Williams in the same way, in that they are both very good poker players."

Hains denied he was any good at cards at all.

"I can't even remember the previous hand," he said.

Williams, a regular golf partner of Hains for 40 years, told us the billionaire was a man of the "highest integrity".

"He's very well read; he's got a great understanding of issues. [Hains told us he was a four-newspapers-a-day man.] David's the type of person who wants to know and he knows what he doesn't know. You are fortunate to know somebody like David Hains."

## PASSIONS AT HEART

An engineer by profession, Hains started work at 15 and by 18 had moved into management, set up his own business at 20 and grew by buying, restructuring and selling businesses before stepping away from operations to become an investor.

It is a remarkable story, too: having managed companies through a succession of economic downturns in the '50s and '60s, he found the trauma of redundancies and the desperation necessary for corporate survival just too taxing.

He turned down several restructuring plays because he "simply could not face the idea of mass retrenchments, invariably part of a restructuring program".

So, in the late '60s, he decided to play golf.

Not just take it up as a hobby but play seriously, convincing the great Norman von Nida to coach him. Hains took nearly seven years off to play golf, returning to business only when he began to appreciate that he was starting to worry about things that "really weren't very important". Although very serious about his business, the one thing to which Hains was long committed was his two weekly golf games at Huntingdale and at the National on the Peninsula, in all weathers and with the same partners for decades.

They were high stakes games: the losers bought breakfast.

Retired Melbourne real estate agent Don Carmichael, who was a good friend for more than 40 years, said Hains was "a very good competitor on and off the course – he's a very interesting golf partner, yet he only very rarely talks about business at the club".

Carmichael also got to play many a round with Hains and von Nida.

"Even to this day, [on the course] we will say, 'Norm would have said do this!'," he jokes.

Von Nida also introduced Hains to horse breeding. The golfing legend and Hains became very close friends and Hains credited von Nida with more than just taking his game to low single figures during the years they toured the world.

"Norm's attitude to class and quality in sport gave me a clear picture of what class really meant," Hains explained.

"Top horses, for example, really do have class. If a horse does not have class it is no good hoping it will win classic races. Class enables participants to overcome problems and still win."

One suspects, though, even when playing golf or when Kingston Park was at its peak as a stud in the '70s and '80s, Hains still thought about business.

"My experience with golf and horses led me to evaluate people and business in the same way," he said.

"A business has to have class to be really successful. Customers patronise a particular firm because it provides something that others do not – or at least equally as well as others but with better service."

While Hains came through engineering, manufacturing, retailing, oil and resources in his business career, it was essential concepts, such as class, that informed his thinking.

He was fascinated by the inner workings of business, by how markets work, by individuals. And he was fundamental in his approach.

Despite his manufacturing businesses having been very early adopters of computer technology, and Portland House having massive computing power manned by physicists and mathematicians, he never had a personal computer.

His favoured accompaniment when driving was talking books – loaded on to a digital player by one of his sons.

In agreeing to speak with *The AFR Magazine* about his business history and the foundations of Portland House, Hains was adamant he would not speak about the group's businesses beyond very general outlines.

Moreover, he added with a mix of pride and wistfulness, that while he may have been chairman of Portland House, his sons run the business.

"I now take orders from them," he joked.

## NEXT GENERATION

The three Hains sons joined the business in 1987, Stephen from Citibank, Richard from a City of London broker and Michael straight from university.

Daughter Cathy also joined the firm in 1987 and ran the bloodstock business.

The youngest Paul, a commerce graduate, joined for a few years but later moved into psychology. Cathy has her own farm and is a serious commercial horse breeder. She literally took the reins as Hains himself wound back breeding at Kingston Park.

Even though three sons run the business, Portland House is not a family office but concentrates on group commercial activities.

The company runs as a hedge fund in the true sense, carefully managing risk and taking positions in diverse asset and debt classes.

"Family business is not easy as there are inbuilt family issues which have to be dealt with by both parents and children that are not always simple to balance," Hains said.

"I really enjoy working with my children, and the influence they have had on shaping and running Portland House Group has been instrumental to its development over the past 20 years."

Portland House is now one of Australia's largest private investment funds, employing around 100 people worldwide with offices in London and New York.

"We invest across the world equity and bond markets and run a sophisticated treasury operation handling more than 20,000 transactions a year," said David's son, Stephen.

The business has a bespoke technology platform, FMO, which is now available to outside investors. Stephen said that over its 50 years in business, Portland House had always had a strong inter-national focus.

"Back in the '80s, the local investment scene was very Australian security-focused and there were few portfolio management tools available for a fund with an emphasis on international shares and bonds," he said.

"We began developing some basic information technology capable of handling the complexity of multiple time zones, multiple currencies and multiple strategies. The arrival of the internet gave us the opportunity to link analysts worldwide and develop our systems significantly further."

David Hains was always hesitant to define the business and, indeed, given its history of global investments – covering asset and debt classes, including direct and indirect investments – most descriptions are accurate only in the breach.

But the business philosophy was perhaps best summed up by Hains now former technology specialist and chief operating officer, Gary Weatherley, who set up FMO with the Portland House culture built in.

"We are common-sense people and our system provides a common-sense way of asking common-sense questions about the world," he said.

## EARLY YEARS

Hains was born in Melbourne's inner north at Fairfield in 1930.

His father, who worked for the State Electricity Commission, was wounded at the Gallipoli landing in 1915 and died at 55 when David was 17. Hains said his father was mathematically sharp – and a brilliant card player.

Since childhood, Hains wanted to be an engineer. His father built him a work shed when he was 10.

"I can remember the final scenes from a film about a Birmingham steel mill I saw in my teens, in which the brother, who had finally won back control of the family mill, walked back through these scrolled iron gates to take control," he said.

"I suppose I dreamt of being in charge of a large industrial complex, even at this stage."

Hains would achieve that ambition in 1976 when, after long experience in manufacturing and retailing, he bought the large engineering firm Malcolm Moore.

He had started manufacturing part-time more than 30 years earlier – ornamental brass candlesticks, which he said quickly taught him the importance of gross margins – and then built his own company with an original-design washing machine and clothes dryer, branded the Hydromat, at 20.

In the early '90s, he even had his Birmingham moment when, after extraordinarily difficult negotiations with intransigent management, receivers and hard-nosed union officials, he and his partners took the failed Wheeling-Pittsburgh steel company in the US out of bankruptcy as a turnaround play.

"The entry to the main plant had a wrought-iron canopy over the gate, exactly the same style as the one I could remember from the film," he said.

"By then, however, I had learned how difficult the manufacturing industry could be and, while I was prepared to play a part in restructuring the company, I had no wish to run it."

This low profile disguises a career richly entwined with corporate Victoria.

He remembered moving his whitegoods factory to Footscray around 1952, near the Smorgon meatworks.

"The patriarch of the family drove along Somerville Road each morning and, if he saw me, he would pull up and talk for a few minutes," Hains said.

"It was Norman Smorgon – a very pleasant man who quite often gave me useful advice on how businesses should be run."

It's a quintessential Hains anecdote, capturing his humility – and connections – and one imagines there's probably quite a few people who have had the benefit of advice from Hains himself who may not have quite realised what they were getting because of the informality of the exchange. When he sold out of his first major business, Oriole Industries, Hains said one of the foremen said he was a decent bloke but a slave-driver while, "an English spray painter once told me all bosses were bastards but that I was a decent sort of bastard".

He admitted he was schooled in management in a very tough industrial environment. He subsequently mellowed.

In 1959, Hains and his wife Helen decided to buy a farm on the Mornington Peninsula, settling on Kingston Park, a cattle property with good rainfall in rolling hills.

"During the extremely difficult times of the early 1960s, I am sure the farm helped to keep me balanced and I would go there nearly every weekend with Helen and the children," he said. Kingston Park, of course, on the suggestion of von Nida, also became one of Australia's most successful thoroughbred studs, with a succession of winners, including Lowan Star, Rose of Kingston and the triple Cox Plate winner Kingston Town.

Some paddocks are right on the road and Hains cheerfully recounted how, in Kingston Town's heyday, visitors would be constantly knocking on the door to see the champ.

But the thoroughbred was notoriously antisocial and highly strung.

"We had another stallion, a spitting image, and we had him in the front paddock," Hains chuckled. "People would stop and look and you could hear them say how you could just tell he was a champion. But that one couldn't run down a well."

With 34 Group 1 wins, Melbourne, Sydney and Brisbane Cups, four Guineas, three Cox Plates, four Derbies, six Oaks and a Blue Diamond,

Hains was happy to hand over the breeding to his daughter.

In 1963 Hains was also looking for office premises and he bought, for what he thought a 'full price', one of the 19th-century buildings at the Paris end of Collins Street that he had long admired.

But the name of his company, the Portland House Group, comes not from its headquarters but from the name of the Portland Motel in country Victoria that he owned at the time.

He said the critical lesson from his long, varied business career was to expect the unexpected. "There are not many benefits of being 60 years in business but one of them is to have seen many major downturns over the years," he said.

"And you realise that any business caught short during the down cycle did not survive to reap the benefits of the recovery which inevitably will follow. The current cycle was probably always going to happen at some time, except that nobody could have expected it to be as severe or anticipated the speed of the onset."

He was never immune to the restlessness investors invariably have to do something or to "believe that this time is different. But, unfortunately, the reality is every bubble bursts. The experience of many downturns and recoveries has greatly influenced our relatively conservative culture [at Portland House]."

The myriad booms and busts he saw in six decades in business all had unique features, but even more similarities, he said.

"Every boom has a predominant theme – in the early 1950s, it was retail and hire purchase; the late 1960s, mining shares like Poseidon; the late 1980s, debt-driven conglomerates like Bond Corp and Quintex; the early 1990s, property; the late 1990s, dot-com companies; in the 2000s, it was a stock market boom with highly leveraged property and 'financial engineering' companies like Centro, MFS, Allco, Opes Prime. Any business which expands rapidly during a boom using high leverage can be vulnerable when the bubble bursts."

Lloyd Williams recalled a pleasant afternoon in the second half of 2007 when he and Hains had just played a round at Williams's exclusive Capital Golf Course at Heatherton, regularly used by Crown Casino's high rollers, and were chatting over a warm pot of tea in the clubhouse.

Williams said he started littering the table with major company balance sheets from Reuters.

They weren't happy.

"We both took the view back then that the major investment banks of the world, among others, were substantially over geared. We both thought this was a real worry," Williams recalled.

Hains was extremely reluctant to proffer business advice but, when pressed, repeated an early mentor's line that the difference between a bankrupt bum and a wealthy merchant was "about two and half per cent".

He emphasised there were too many factors to lay down fixed rules but that history revealed some key insights.

Here are two examples: In a young business, taking significant risks is not only justified but a prerequisite of success – while luck in timing can be a major factor.

But many a mature business has succumbed by adopting an excessive continuous expansion strategy financed by debt and fatally "betting the farm".

A growth rate of say 20 per cent a year compound means one in five people at year end are new. New to the organisation, new to the culture.

At the end of the next year, it is two in five relatively new, some learning from last year's intake. "Executives and staff need time to assimilate the culture and business model," Hains said.

"One can never overestimate the importance of a sound culture in business."

## MAN OF THE PEOPLE

In the '60s and '70s, Hains also toyed with politics, both federal and local government and was instrumental, behind the scenes, in John Gorton's manoeuvring to reclaim the prime ministership from Billy McMahon, even negotiating the release of some internal party polling supportive of Gorton to Rupert Murdoch.

But having lost a close-fought local government campaign, he decided politics was not for him. "The ensuing publicity [from both episodes], which was completely unexpected for me, dissuaded me from further political involvement," he said.

Hains's story is truly remarkable for having touched so many major people and events though so little known itself.

He was on several public bodies such as the Gobbo Commission, and he and his wife lived for 45 years in the Toorak house formerly owned by Rupert' Murdoch's parents.

His close friends long included Mark Leibler and broking eminence Sir Lawrence Muir.

Potter Partners executive and close Kerry Packer confidant, Muir first met Hains in 1950 when he was a "fresh-faced 19-year-old engineering graduate" and he subsequently worked with this "quiet achiever". "Despite his wealth, he is a modest, generous and charming man," Muir said. "He is very comfortable with working with his family and his family is very important to him."

Muir once approached Hains on behalf of the Baker Medical Research Institute, of which Muir is patron.

"We wanted an association with the racing industry, and David gave us some great advice and actually offered to pick out one of his best yearlings for us," he said.

"He is now trialling several and, when one is good enough, it will race for the Institute with its prizemoney donated to the Institute."

Hains had brief dealings with failed '80s entrepreneur Russell Goward and knew junk bond king Michael Milken.

Now former Australian Competition and Consumer Commission chairman Graeme Samuel acted as Portland House's legal adviser during several takeovers, including Malcolm Moore.

Yet Hains remained at heart a practical, counties-style but certainly never flashy man.

He was long able to fly first class – indeed he bought his first Bentley at 30, "a bit over the top", but he had the money and wanted something safe that could carry five kids and a Labrador.

He also owned a "very modest" boat on the French Riviera and a London house in Mayfair.

For many years he owned a Mercedes with variable suspension, allowing it to be bounced around the grounds at Kingston Park.

But he baulked at the price of an Hermes handbag when he popped into the Collins Street boutique to buy a present for his wife.

His driver, Chris, was hired because Hains wanted someone who was handy; whether that was maintenance on the house and garden or running confidential errands. (Chris always had time for other tasks as Hains always drove himself to work and to the Peninsula, and his wide brief included looking after Portland House.

"The boss likes you to be able to have a go at pretty much everything," said the multi-skilled Chris.

Hains always paid for lunch with cash (he tipped well but not lavishly) and the modest Kingston Park weatherboard farmhouse could well be mistaken for the gatehouse by someone who knew the stud only by reputation.

Indeed, were it not for the walls of pictures of Group 1-winning thoroughbreds that adorned the lounge room and framed family snaps in the living room rich in faces well known to corporate

Australia – often in exotic locations – the owners wouldn't even appear especially wealthy.

Air-conditioning was only installed in the late noughties.

"It is only a weekender, after all. It's comfortable," Hains said. A down-to-earth escape for a down-to-earth billionaire.

# MATT HAYMES

On the morning of June 23 2021, for the second time in less than two years, the flags above the Ballarat Town Hall flew at half-mast.

On the first occasion they marked a genuine national tragedy, the shock passing – on 9 September 2019 – of Australian football great and one of the Victorian regional city's favourite sons, Danny Frawley.

The second commemorated the death of one of Ballarat's greatest-ever businessmen, Haymes Paint patriarch David Haymes.

The 77-year-old long-serving CEO of the sole remaining large, Australian-owned paint company – its last big, local rival Dulux was purchased by the Japanese three years ago – had been on dialysis for his failing kidneys for years and had heart surgery after suffering Ciguatera Fish Poisoning seven years earlier.

"That was the beginning of the end. It buggered his whole system," says his eldest son Matt Haymes now.

"His frustration was that his body failed him, but his mind was still fantastic till the end. He still chaired the board even from a hospital bed. But it was very quick when he went, which was a Godsend."

David Haymes was surrounded by his family at home and unable to speak when he passed away on June 15 last year, not long after a fall during a visit to the bathroom from which he never recovered.

Rod Walton – now Haymes Paint CEO and the son-in-law of David Haymes who started dating David's daughter Belinda when they were only 16 years old – chokes back tears as he describes the legacy of his long-time mentor, teacher and father figure.

"He was an amazing person. He was the most visionary person you'd come across. He had a vision with an ability to inspire and communicate. Yet he would plan every detail. There are not many people in life you come across that can do both," he says slowly.

"But he could."

Between 1974 and 2008, when he stepped down from day-to-day operations to become chairman, David Haymes realigned and reinvigorated the business started by his father Henry in 1935, elevating the Haymes brand on a national level.

In 2016 local Ballarat historian Phil Roberts published a book about the business called "Haymes: Paint Flowing Through The Veins" and David Haymes' fingerprints are all over the company's constitution formulated more than a decade ago.

His son says its two core tenants are his father's trademarks.

"One is 'Blood is thicker than paint'," Matt says with a wide smile. "The other is 'Don't f... it up!'."

## IN THE VEINS

The business is currently in its third generation of family ownership under the guidance of Matt, Tim and Belinda Haymes and entering a new chapter of its history as it continues to expand nationally.

In 2022 Haymes Paint opened its new $10 million flagship Ballarat store, the largest ever investment at a single site in the company's history.

"The whole idea was 'Lets try something here and roll it out to the network.' To change the game. Retail paint in this country is dominated by corporate hardware. 80 per cent of sales go through that channel," Matt Haymes says.

"We wanted to bring people back into the family business environment where a lot of people say if it's as good quality, if not better ; if the process is good, if not better ; and if the service and the experience is as good if not better ; why wouldn't you support Australian made and local?"

20 years ago, Haymes Paint decided not to sell products through large corporate-owned hardware chains.

Instead, the paint maker stocks its products largely for trade buyers in independent hardware stores and specialist paint retailers, as well its own Haymes Paint shops.

Its national footprint has grown to over 350 stores, including 250 independent hardware and paint specialist stores, delivering the group annual turnover of more than $200 million.

Haymes Paint currently makes more than 12 million litres of paint in Ballarat each year, giving it just under 9 per cent market share in the Australian paint industry.

It is targeting 15 per cent share by 2035 when the business turns 100 by investing $40m over five years across various areas of its business, including its flagship store, manufacturing, research and development and its head office.

## FUTURE PROOFING

"Doubling the production means a big investment in plant and equipment and investment in environmentally sustainable practices," Rod Walton says.

"Achieving 20 per cent year on year growth predominantly through our trade channels is very doable. Once people use our products, they want to support us, given we are the only Australian-made and owned paint company left."

Haymes Paint has also launched an e-commerce site, initially servicing customers in metropolitan Melbourne, with a view to extending it nationally.

So far the firm has resisted the temptation to take big steps offshore. In Japan it has a strong local partner that represents the brand in that market, but the Haymes family decided over a decade ago to concentrate growing market share in Australia.

Yet its roots came from abroad. After starting the business, Henry Haymes moved to the United Kingdom in the second half of the 1930's to learn how to make paint.

He then returned to Ballarat to build the firm before suddenly passing away in 1950 when his son David – an only, adopted child – was just seven years old. David's mother Mavis was left with a 25 per cent shareholding in the business.

"Dad wasn't in line to go into the Haymes Paint business because he was adopted," Matt recalls.

Instead after leaving Ballarat College, David went into shoe-making with Paddles Shoes and Clarkes Shoes subsidiary Hush Puppies where he met a local shoe retailer named Alan Faull, who was impressed by his work ethic and had contacts on the Haymes board.

Soon David was employed by Haymes and it wasn't long before he was third in charge of the Haymes paint warehouse in Ballarat.

"Dad then worked his tail off over the next seven years, making his way to be the managing director in 1974 before he had turned 30," Matt says.

"In the mid 1980s, he and mum had a very generous bank manager. Again, with Alan Faull's guidance, they were able to borrow a lot of money and acquire the business."

The deal, struck in 1988, meant full ownership returned to the Haymes family fold after years of smaller investors having shares in the company.

In David's obituary published in 2021, Phil Roberts wrote of him being "big" on marketing and with mantras like "we never take short-cuts on quality" and that all customer enquiries should receive an "immediate response".

He became a household name through television advertisements depicting 'paint flowing through his veins'.

Roberts also noted David looked after his staff very well believing they should "share the rewards, the hurts, and the challenges."

David provided many generous sponsorships across the Ballarat community and in 2015 signed a deal with the Melbourne Football Club for the Haymes Paint logo to be printed on game-day footballs.

Between 2005 and 2009, David was also the third National Chairman of Family Business Australia, the peak body for the millions of family-owned businesses across the nation.

He held his wife Jenny and the family dear.

"Every night Dad would be home to enjoy dinner with the kids. He also would say that for the major decisions in the business, mum was always part of that," Matt says.

"They were fiscally responsible because dad didn't like debt. That was a really positive thing. So they invested heavily back into the business continually."

Their partnership in life and business meant David's passing has hit his now 78 year old widow hard.

"Since Dad passed away it has been tough on her. Her health has been up and down. She has been grieving terribly like every widow does," Matt says.

"But she is a resilient person. To be honest, we would be stuffed without her. She is the glue that holds us together."

Matt Haymes says one of the greatest teachings of his father was the importance of humility.

"Treat everyone equal – we were so lucky to have such an unprejudiced, unbiased upbringing. He had a genuine interest in people. It didn't matter who it was, he loved them," he says.

"The second one was 'Everyone makes mistakes. It is how you handle it. Learn from it, own it and don't do it again'.

Rod Walton says the outpouring of support for the family from the Ballarat community on David's passing showed the impact he had on people.

"There were people who nursed him in hospital who he only met a few times who were taken by the interest he showed in them. The fact the city decided by public demand to lower the flag above the town hall to half mast after he died, they have done that for very few people," he says.

"David's famous saying was 'Whatever unfortunate things happen to others, it could be me so there for the grace of God go I.' From a business point of view, he always used to say in board meetings. 'What is the worse thing that can happen if we do this?' Then we would tell him and he would reply 'So if that is the worst thing and we can live with it, let's go for it!'."

## SUCCESSION PLANS

In the final months of his life, David Haymes was conscious of his own mortality. Being an only child, he was a great collector. His passions were model trains from around the world – he even built a model Ballarat train station and track for them to run on – and stamps.

Well before he died, David ensured a succession plan for the business was put in place to provide an orderly transition to the next generation.

The main focus is to protect the business so it continues for generations," Matt says of the plan.

The family constitution also ensures the fourth generation of the family must work outside the business for a period before they can join Haymes Paint.

"The kids go away and develop their own identity. For a minimum of 5 years they must do something else. Through the family constitution there is also a way to introduce them to and educate them about the business," Rod says.

"The kids are urged to do what they are passionate about. To be the best people they can be."

Rod Walton and Matt, Tim and Belinda Haymes are now looking ahead to the 100th anniversary of the business in 2035 and beyond.

They – like their late patriarch – will never forget the families that have helped make Haymes a Ballarat and Australian icon.

"It's hard to not have the emotional side because you're talking about people that babysat us as kids that still work in this business and work with us," Matt says.

"There's multiple people that have done 50 or more years with Haymes, that started as kids and retired and their kids work with us as well now."

Today more than 300 families are involved directly with the Haymes business across the country.

"As a family business ourselves and dealing with other independently owned family businesses through paint stores or independent hardware, we feel an obligation to ensure their security, their sustainability and to help them thrive," Rod says.

"We're responsible for those people."

# MAX HAZELTON

*It was a typically cool, crisp Autumn morning in 2021 when I jetted into Orange to meet one of the legends of Australian aviation. Given I've always had a fascination with planes and covered the airline round at The Australian Financial Review for a number of years, meeting an industry pioneer like Max Hazelton was extra special. This rare interview was organised by Rex's then PR boss Michael Venus, who I had first met when he was doing the same role at Middle Eastern carrier Etihad Airways. Max had always held a special affection for Rex Airlines, given his important role in its heritage. We had our chat over a delicious morning tea at Max's Orange home with his beloved wife Laurel by his side. After a fascinating discussion, Max drove me to the airport in his decades-old Holden Statesman – that was still in immaculate condition – to give me a tour of the local aviation museum where his memories took pride of place. His deeply stooped spine did not distract from his enthusiasm in reliving tales of his legendary past. I now feel deeply privileged to have been the last journalist to interview him.*

Of all the aircraft Max Hazelton has flown on over his 95 years, the Regional Express flight from Orange to Sydney on the afternoon of February 28, 2021 was extra special.

At his side was his only son Graham, better known by his nickname Toby, who often calls his dad "boss".

The next morning, as the clock at Sydney Airport ticked over to 8.25am, they stood together at the arrival gate to greet Rex's inaugural 737 jet service from Melbourne. The carrier was formed two decades ago from the merger of Kendall Airlines and the regional carrier Max Hazelton and his brother Jim started in 1953 called Hazelton Airlines.

"It was very hard not to have wet eyes because it was such a big day. They were looking after me extremely well with a wheelchair. It was an amazing day," Max tells me, his now permanently bloodshot eyes again turning misty for a moment behind his spectacles.

The jet was flown by captains John Veitch and Brett Brown, both ex-Hazelton pilots who took voluntary redundancies from Virgin Australia last year.

"They came home again," Max says with a beaming smile. "(Rex deputy chairman and former federal transport minister) John Sharp has been a magnificent person promoting things."

After decades of competing head-on with Qantas on regional routes, Max is excited by what is known internally at Rex as "Project Mother", its move onto Australia's busiest air route using jets previously leased by the collapsed and now private equity-resurrected Virgin.

Rex is also flying jets from Melbourne to Adelaide and from Melbourne and Sydney to Coolangatta.

The airline's deputy chairman John Sharp describes Max as the nation's "greatest living aviator and an absolute pioneer in regional and agricultural aviation".

"Because of his ingenuity, the regulator had to keep changing the laws to accommodate new things Max came up with," he says.

"One of the great legacies of Max and Laurel is they created a family business culture which still runs thick through our business today and is the reason we have survived and a reason we are competitive not just in the regional space, but now the domestic space."

Sharp is speaking of Hazelton's wife of 64 years, who was missing from his side that February morning in Sydney after she couldn't make the trip from Orange.

For decades she kept the Hazelton business wheels turning while her husband took to the skies, organising catering, pilot rosters and looking after the books.

Today she is sitting alongside him in their cosy home not far from the Orange city centre after Max, who now has a deep stoop when he stands, invited her to join our interview.

Above the dining table atop a cabinet are a decorated array of model Rex and Hazelton planes. On the adjacent wall hangs a stunning painting of one of Hazelton's first Saab aircraft taking flight.

On the table is a signed copy of the book on Max's life by author Denis Gregory titled "The Hazelton Story", launched in 2014 by famed entrepreneur Dick Smith.

"I think I got caught. It was a busy life, I can assure you. Aviation is a very interesting, challenging life," Laurel says.

"We had well over 200 employees and they were fantastic employees."

## PLANE PIONEER

In 1953 Max started his charter airline service in a paddock at Toogong near Orange, after borrowing money from his mother to buy an old aeroplane.

He famously survived being lost for six days after walking 100km through thick bush when his plane crashed in bad weather returning from Sydney to Toogong, sparking what was then Australia's biggest single rescue effort.

In 1959 he moved his operation to nearby Cudal where he and his pilots hand-built a runway and terminal and Hazelton Airlines soon became renowned for its crop-dusting and then night aerial cropping, aerial firefighting, flood relief and rescue work.

It gradually expanded to be a major passenger airline feeding country areas employing 270 staff, carrying 400,000 passengers a year to 23 country ports.

Max still drives his immaculately maintained white Holden ute around the streets of Orange, occasionally falling foul of the law.

"A policemen stopped me six months ago driving from downtown to home. He asked to see my licence. I said it was in my wallet, which I had lost the day before, and that I was going to the motor registry to get another copy of it. He went back to his car, got on the radio and came back to me and said I was OK to drive. But a few weeks later a letter came with a $150 fine," he says.

"I rang the local member and he told me to write a letter so I wrote to Transport NSW and told them what I thought of them. And they dropped the fine."

Also in his garage is a 20-year-old luxury Holden Statesmen, which has only travelled 50,000km, including a single trip across the Nullarbor Plain to Perth.

Max once famously locked horns with Bob Hawke and the ACTU by defying a union ban to fly live merino sheep out of Australia. He also recalls flying Kerry Packer on several occasions from Sydney to his Ellerston polo property near Scone.

"If you had any magazines on board, he would say 'What have you got this bloody rubbish for?' He wasn't very talkative, but his wife was. His kids were small then," Max says.

While he hasn't flown in an aircraft for many years, he has fond memories of his time in the air, especially running Hazelton's commuter operations.

"The flying was great. It was always a challenge. No two days were the same. From a very young age, I was very keen to fly," he says.

But what he doesn't miss is battling bigger rivals.

"Everywhere we went, like Armidale and Tamworth, it was working quite well but then Qantas came in, cut the fares considerably, and basically killed us. Because we couldn't operate because we were paying higher fees each month on the SAABs. We couldn't cut prices to match them," he says.

"They were fair old buggers doing that. Anywhere we went, they would cut the fares. That is the battle we had. Taking on the big boys like that is a very difficult situation."

He still believes the 1994 decision to list Hazelton Airlines on the Australian Stock Exchange was wrong. A year later he stepped down as CEO of the airline after a boardroom fight for control of the company.

In 2001 the Hazelton family sold its Hazelton Airlines stake to Ansett after the then haemorrhaging domestic carrier won a takeover battle with Qantas. In September that year, Ansett collapsed and Hazelton and Kendall Airlines were also put into administration.

While he was no longer involved with Hazelton, Max was devastated.

"It was a silly mistake to go public and the whole thing was out of control. The float was the undoing of the whole show. Laurel and I were in America and someone from Ansett rang me at midnight US time and said they were going to make a bid for Hazelton. I said 'You can do that if you want to' because I was fed up with the board," he says.

"I thought Ansett would be the best thing for us the way things were going. Ansett were good to us over the years. Then Ansett went under. We were horribly disappointed then because the whole thing had gone. We thought there would be no future for it at all. Then the Singaporeans came in and it lived another day."

The executive chairman of Rex, Singaporean businessman Lim Kim Hai, bought majority control of Rex with his business partner Lee Thian Soo after it was launched from the merger of Hazelton and Kendall in August 2002. Interests associated with Lim now own 65 per cent of Rex.

While the Hazelton family has parted ways with Rex, Max and Laurel still have $10,000 worth of shares and attend each annual meeting as ambassadors of the airline.

The Hazelton name lives on in aviation through Toby Hazelton, who now runs his father's agricultural flying operation, Hazelton Agricultural Services.

"It made it easier for me clientele-wise because the name was there. But then I had to live up to the name. It has been a great thing for me," Toby says of taking over the business three decades ago.

His daughter Georgia is now also flying, while his youngest son Jock is studying for his pilot's licence while he completes year 12.

"It is a great thing for the family. I didn't have to encourage it (flying) with my kids – it is in their veins I think," he says.

Other members of the wider Hazelton family also fly for Rex, Qantas, Cathay Pacific and pilot private jets for wealthy clients in America.

Max will always consider his greatest contribution to aviation was to help country people travel further, faster than ever before. His legend will live on in Rex's motto plastered on the livery of its new jet fleet: "Our heart is in the country".

"In the early days we were using very small planes. It meant a hell of a lot to those people to spend the day in Sydney and be able to get home at night. That was the aim," he says.

"The aeroplanes coming up to the country towns, it has certainly helped them get bigger to support them."

My chat with Max in late April 2021 proved to be his final media interview. He passed away just under two years later on April 9, 2023 – Easter Sunday – at the age of 95.

Appropriately his memorial service was held in a hangar at Orange Airport beside a four-seater Auster Aglet – one of the first planes he flew – with a 34-seat turboprop Saab 340 sitting on the tarmac outside.

John Sharp told the hundreds gathered at the service that Max didn't simply follow the road ahead throughout his amazing life.

"He made his own path," Sharp declared.

"That's what pioneers do."

# TOM JACOB

Guenter Jacob worked like a man possessed.

Every evening, his clothes were soaked with sweat from hours swinging a hammer for the suspension parts manufacturer he started in his backyard in Melbourne suburbia in 1958 called Jacob Spring Works.

Jacob was known in business as the man with the cigar, given he smoked at least 20 of them a day. His firm, later known as JSW Parts, became Melbourne's largest producer of springs for trucks before he passed away in 1985 from a heart attack at the age of 67.

"When he died, his doctor said, 'You know, I believe that human beings have a vital force, a survival force. When they are confronted by death experiences, and particularly what he went through in his life - regardless of the cigars - that is finite," his son Tom now says.

Guenter had been running the family's metal business in Germany in the 1930s when it was taken over by the Nazis and he and the rest of the family were shipped to the Auschwitz death camp. His metal-working skills saved his life but not those of his loved ones.

"When you experience something like what he saw, it is not fathomable. He used to say he saw death every day, from 1942 until 1945. You can't think about what that means to a person," Tom says noting his father never shyed away from speaking of the horrors he endured.

After the war ended, Guenter emigrated to Melbourne. Tom was born in 1955, five years after his sister Barbara.

"So I grew up in a house where there was always a storehouse of tinned food, big pots of flour and big pots of sugar for an emergency. Because my father was always prepared for the worst. He slept with an iron bar under his bed."

Tom was 30 when his father passed away, and instantly became managing director and half owner of the family business. Barbara inherited the other half.

Over the decades it has evolved to be manufacturer and supplier of suspension parts around the world and today is known as Ironman4×4, providing accessories to meet all the demands of off-road-users in 167 countries.

It is the second-largest four-wheel drive accessories company in Australia, an untold story of Australian ingenuity and hard work in a family business that now turns over $200 million annually from its headquarters among the industrial sprawl of Dandenong South in Melbourne's South-East.

But Tom will never forget the day he lost his dad and the emotions he felt in the months and years after.

"The things that people don't understand about running a family business is how lonely it is. It is an extremely lonely experience. Solitary. You are surrounded by many but you are really on your own and you've got no one to fall back on but yourself. Some people can deal with this and achieve, some people can't. In my case, I didn't get a choice. We'd just travelled to Japan. I'd kissed him goodbye at Tullamarine Airport. He went home and died in his bed that night. It always struck me how lonely it was without him," he says, before a painful pause. Then, for a moment, he breaks down in tears.

Tom's eldest son Samuel, who has joined us for today's interview and works in the family business as an executive director, hands his father a napkin to wipe his eyes. After composing himself, Tom continues.

"I had the legacy of stepping into the work that my father had started," he whispers. His mother Mimi, who he describes as a "rock" and a "lioness" for the family, died in 2003.

"I've had a very beautiful, wonderful life. Great parents, great childhood, great opportunities. I've never had to be tested like my father was and I don't want to be. But there is no question that the experience of our family affects who we are."

He turns to his son and, once again choking back tears, asks him a question: "What did you ask me in Germany once? We were sitting by a river. You were very emotional."

Samuel looks me firmly in the eye and without flinching, replies to his father's question: "I asked him that day, 'How will I ever be able to fill your shoes Dad? Dad replied, 'You don't have to fill my shoes. You just have to fill your own'."

## REAL IRONMAN

In 1988, JSW Parts launched the Ironman 4×4 brand of springs and suspension parts and a decade later changed its name to match the brand moniker.

Tom Jacob, who is 68 this year, says the name was initially modelled on the quintessentially Australian beach ironman, who excels at running on land and swimming at sea and is adaptable to all conditions.

"But later on, I actually discovered what Ironman really meant to me. It was really my father. He was our Ironman," he says proudly.

"He survived the hell of Nazi concentration camps to be born second time, as he would say, in Australia. So he's the real Ironman."

The suspension kit products Guenter Jacob designed decades ago are still being sold around the world today and family now donates 10 per cent of those sale proceeds to secular and Jewish charities.

In 2014 Tom Jacob was recognised with an OAM for his charitable contributions to the King David School, Mount Scopus Memorial College, and Yeshivah and Beth Rivkah Colleges and other general community institutions.

"I think we live in a time where we need to have heroes. My father is a hero because he survived and he built us into a family, which is now into its third generation in this business. That really matters to us," he says.

For a time Tom Jacob turned his hand to journalism, working for The Age for six years after scoring a cadetship as a 17-year-old in 1972. But with his father's health failing, he and his sister joined the family business.

Their big break came in 2005 when Ironman secured a contract to supply the US military with vehicle accessories for the war in Afghanistan.

Today the firm's four wheel drive accessories are supplied to vehicles used by the United Nations, the World Food Program and the World Health Organization, as well as the defence, mining and agricultural sectors.

As Tom Jacob puts it, Ironman mantra is simple: "Follow the vehicles and find the opportunity."

Its secret sauce has always been engineering and its ability to design solutions for a global market.

The firm now has six distribution warehouses across Australia and has operations in Africa, Middle East and Asia. It also has 150 retail stores and is planning hundreds more.

On the board is businessman Steven Fisher, a former chairman of appliance maker Breville and current chairman of The Reject Shop.

"I had a call from my GM in Thailand to say that the emissary of the King of Bhutan wants us to prepare two vehicles for him. These people search out the brands or products that they want around the world and brand Australia means something," Tom Jacob says passionately.

"Australian businesses can look to people who believe that Australia can punch above its weight across the world. We so often undersell the ingenuity and the capability that Australians have always had. I think we need to believe that dreams can become reality."

## US OPPORTUNITY

Ironman's next big growth opportunity is the American market, which it entered in 2020.

So far the business there is up to 90 per cent online. But five retail bricks and mortar stores have been established and hundreds more are planned.

"The business in America literally took off from day one because the internet had already exposed our products to the world. The Ironman brand was already well developed and people have always looked back to Australia for the way we used vehicles, particularly in overlanding. Australian brands do well in America because they are absolutely relevant," Tom Jacob says.

The US expansion has been spearheaded by the now 29 year old Samuel Jacob, Tom's son to his second wife. Samuel planned to live in America in 2020 before the COVID pandemic forced him back to Australia.

Tom says he had no expectation his son would enter the business, even though deep down Samuel dreamed of doing nothing else.

"As a young boy growing up, you just want to be like your dad. You want to follow him. I remember playing at his desk and sending off pretend faxes and talking on the phone back when we were in Moorabbin. I've had the most incredible role model and mentor to look up to in my dad," Samuel says, recalling he was only 7 when he sold his first 50 load plus springs to Ballarat Toyota.

An image from that day hangs proudly on his father's office wall.

"I came to the end of my plumbing apprenticeship and dad offered me the choice of whether I wanted to join. He had one condition which was if I did join the business, I needed to travel. I needed to learn a bit about the world, which I did. So, coming into the business, there was a lot for me to learn practically. But it always felt very natural. It always felt like a second home."

Tom and Barbara Jacob each have two children and Samuel is the only one in the business. Barbara's son Daniel once was but is no longer.

Her daughter Rebecca is a cheesemaker and Tom's daughter Maggie is a singer in Ireland.

Barbara is now retired but Tom Jacob quips that his big sister is still "in charge of me".

"She is little and has an indomitable spirit. I think that is the spirit of my mother," he says proudly.

The group has always reinvested its profits in growth and had no debt. Tom claims the firm has achieved a compound average growth rate of 20% for the last 22 years, funded all internally.

But now he says the time has come to look for an external investor in America.

"We are very fortunate that we don't need it for the capital. But what we really want and seek is a large group that already has a retail footprint," he says, stressing a public float is not currently on the agenda.

He has no great wish to currently crystallise the family's wealth. Rather he wants to continue to grow, honouring his father's amazing legacy.

"We've still got a long way to go to build this business into a store footprint that could see us add 1000 stores across the world," he says.

He also loves working, especially with his son by his side.

"We walk this journey together and are very close. I'm really happy continuing doing what we are doing and building this future together. There is no obligation to build a legacy. There is work to be done. Being a true entrepreneur is not just about being resilient, it is actually about having a vision and then finding and putting together the right team to be able to execute that vision."

"My father would never, ever have dreamed of what we have achieved so far. I will probably never dream of what Samuel will one day achieve."

# JOHNNY AND MARKUS KAHLBETZER

It was supposed to be Markus Kahlbetzer's gap year in Australia, a world away from the bustling streets encircling his ritzy apartment in the Argentinian capital, Buenos Aires. Born in America, Markus had moved between the US and Argentina throughout his childhood before the Great Argentine economic depression took hold in 1998. His first visit to Australia a year later at the age of 18, where he met his now wife Sally, changed his life.

The trip would also forever alter the destiny of the billion dollar fortune built by his famous father John, a German immigrant who came to Australia in 1954 and built his Twynam Agricultural Group into one of the nation's most famed rural landholders.

In 1982, the year after Markus was born, John Kahlbetzer created his Argentine agricultural operation known as LIAG. In the decade that followed, he quietly hoped that his youngest son would one day take over that business and that his older son, Johnny – who joined Twynam in 1991 – might run the family's Australian operations. But his youngest son had other ideas.

"It was a depressing time in Argentina for many people," he recalls.

"Not necessarily for me. But I didn't have a support network that I might have counted on. Dad wasn't there and my mum hadn't moved there. So I was 18 in Argentina, and I met the girlfriend here in Australia. I'm like, 'Well, it's pretty shit being over there.' So I just kind of spat the dummy and said, 'I'm coming to Australia.' Dad thought it was more of a temporary thing, but it became a permanent thing."

Markus completed an agricultural economics degree at the University of Sydney, took Australian residency, got married, and then for five years worked in a management role at Twynam developing new projects. But he still had itchy feet.

"I'd watched Johnny sitting behind Dad for much of his young professional career. I thought, if I stay here behind Johnny, I'm going to be 60 by the time I can make decisions for my own destiny," he says.

In 2009 John Kahlbetzer supported his youngest son's creation of BridgeLane Capital, a venture capital firm seeded with cash and ownership of the 80,000ha of cropping and livestock country in Argentina he always hoped his son would one day run. Johnny, 16 years his brother's senior, was handed responsibility for Twynam.

Now in their first-ever interview together in Twynam's Darlinghurst offices in inner-city Sydney, the sons reveal that their now 91-year old father has ceded all economic interest in his empire to the next generation, completing the process Markus started nearly a quarter of a century ago.

For the final four years of his life, John Kahlbetzer had no operational involvement in Twynam. "The baton has certainly been passed," Johnny says. His brother concurs, adding that he has always admired and respected his father for supporting his wishes for independence.

"I've always appreciated that we were all able to sit around and discuss things and kind of set it out early. Dad was very conscious and able to do something, because it happened years ago, rather than now," Markus says. John Kahlbetzer passed away on October 27 2023 at the age of 92.

## TEXTBOOK SUCCESSION

Indeed the Kahlbetzers has been a textbook succession and over the past decade the sons have been reshaping the family empire in their own image.

A decade and a half ago Twynam boasted 22 broadacre cropping, livestock and citrus holdings and owned the Colly Farms cotton business, making it one of the nation's largest agricultural producers.

"We pioneered a lot of things in Australian agriculture and are glad we did it," Johnny says. "We created the biggest cotton growing area in Australia. In Argentina, we took irrigated cotton to the northeast of the country."

But after the global financial crisis, the Australian land portfolio was progressively sold down, aided by the Rudd government's $3.1 billion water buyback program, which in 2009 saw the controversial purchase of 240 million litres of water from Twynam for a record $300m.

Now only two smaller farms – Wingello Park and Johnniefelds, together spread across 1400ha near Marulan, south of Sydney – remain.

There Johnny has a family "weekender" and oversees breeding Angus cattle and polo ponies in a regenerative manner, preserving traditions that have been part of Kahlbetzer family history. He says in addition to the Twynam properties becoming dryland with the water buyback, there was another rationale to the asset sales.

"We just realised that we'd all had enough of dealing with drought," he says. "So I guess one of the negatives of having such a diverse portfolio of properties is you're always having a drought. Once we made that decision that we weren't going to be a really big company, we decided we should sell and Dad supported that."

Johnny moved to Monaco to focus on a venture known as Twynam Agriculture Africa to grow cotton and food crops in Sudan, but the project was eventually abandoned.

From the almost 100 per cent focused agricultural business built by their father, over the past decade the sons have diversified Twynam and BridgeLane into property development and venture capital projects.

Twynam is now backing a range of businesses involved in green technologies, sustainable farming and renewables.These include converting waste cotton fabrics into new fibres for clothes, recycling organic waste through insects, recycling $CO_2$ into chemicals and fuels, and supporting the production of alternative protein sources.

It also funds the World Wildlife Foundation's program to eliminate plastic in Australia and is working on ocean clean-ups across the globe.

"From my environmental side, we cannot create a sustainable world while we keep chasing more and more and more," Johnny says.

"That's not to say you should not replace something for something new but we are all accumulating a whole lot of junk, stuff we don't need and basically don't use." He notes that he inherited his environmental passions from his father.

"Dad has always been environmentally focused. If someone suggested cutting down a tree, in most cases he would prefer to keep it and work around it."

He hopes that in five years time Twynam will have moved out of most of its property development projects and be involved with a number of very successful decarbonisation companies and strategies.

"Hopefully, we will also have been able to make a big impact on the plastic pollution situation around the world," he says.

In his brother's world, since its inception BridgeLane has invested in companies typically in the online/mobile technology, sustainable food and agricultural robotics sectors. It now backs an eclectic range of businesses, including a hydroponic enterprise called Sprout Stack, which grows salad greens in transportable shipping container-sized farms in Sydney and Brisbane.

BridgeLane has also been a key investor in venture capital firm Tank Stream Ventures, along with Airtasker's Tim Fung, Jonathan Lui and former Renault Formula One engineer Rui Rodrigues, who managed the investments.

In 2022 the firm was rebranded as BridgeLane Ventures and raised $50m for a fund to invest in environmentally-conscious companies focused on sustainability.

"Tim and Jonathan were the first employees at [telecommunications and energy account company] Amaysim," Markus says.

"That was my first foray into venture investing and where we met. We've gone on to invest in other great startups, like [workforce training firm] Go1, which now is a unicorn and we invested much earlier than a lot of the VCs, which are much bigger than us today."

BridgeLane also inherited John Kahlbetzer's cropping and livestock country in Argentina, which were sold in September 2022 for US$201m to to the family of Gerardo Bartolome, the founder of global soybean powerhouse GDM Seeds

## FAMILY TIES

The Kahlbetzer scions have had their debates over time.

Johnny long believed his brother had a responsibility to return to Buenos Aires to oversee the Argentine agricultural business. But Markus was always clear that he would never again live in the country of his schooling.

Team development is something Johnny says he has admired watching his younger brother build BridgeLane. "That whole how you team up businesses I think is the biggest area of learning from him for me, and seeing the errors that I've made on that over decades," he says. Asked what he has taught his younger brother, Johnny replies with a wry smile: "How to manage dad! He's not an easy man.

"Where I do think it was harder for me than Markus is while Dad's always been difficult, he was a lot worse when he was younger. He has mellowed. Dad and I have had times when we haven't spoken to each other for a year or so. We have certainly had difficult times. But we are good now. I probably spend more time talking to him than Markus does."

Both brothers acknowledge they remain conscious of their father's mortality.

"In 2020, we thought it was very close," Markus says, noting that when the day does come they have peace of mind that at least succession in the business has been sorted, a testament to his father's foresight.

"If he's having a bad month or you think 'Oh no, this is it for Dad' or whatever, it's not like, 'Oh, my God, we've got to call in these lawyers or accountants and start from scratch'."

Johnny is more sanguine about the prospect of life without his father. "Having lost one parent, I guess it is maybe more front and centre for me, given Markus's mother [who still lives in America] is still alive," he says.

Johnny is referring to the passing of his mother, Virginia Kahlbetzer, who died in 2013 after a battle with lung cancer.

He reveals he and his family returned to Sydney from Monaco to spend eight months looking after her before she died and that they remained close to the end.

He will never forget being at a ski resort in Europe when he received a phone call from his mother. He was there with his wife Donna, once married to former world motorcycle champion Wayne Gardner.

"It was Christmas Day or New Year's Day. Donna had broken her leg skiing and I had a neck problem and that day, my cortisone injection had stopped working. We were lying in bed next to each other, really pissed off with life," he recalls.

"Mum rings up, we thought to say Happy Christmas or New Year, whatever it was. I say 'How are you? She goes "I'm fucked. I have just been diagnosed with cancer."'"

Virginia was given three months to live. She lived for five more, passing away in August 2013.

"My cousin was there when she died. I had gone to Double Bay to pick up something and when I came back she was gone," Johnny says softly.

Two years later Johnny made headlines when he sued the Garvan Institute of Medical Research – to which his mother donated regularly for

12 years before her death – after she left it the residuary of her estate.

He argued in the NSW Supreme Court that the will his mother made on June 25, 2013, less than two months before her death, was invalid because she "lacked testamentary capacity".

An earlier will made in 1990 made him a residual beneficiary, meaning he would receive everything not given to specific beneficiaries. He was shocked to see the new will days before she died.

"That was a media beat up. The deal that mum and I had made was she was going to leave me the money and I was going to give the money to the Garvan," Johnny says.

Which is why, as part of settling the case, he says he agreed to donate $11m to the institute as a memorial to his mother, with the request it be used to research a cure for lung cancer.

"The Garvan actually got more money out of the settlement than what Mum was going to give them," he says.

## STAYING PRIVATE

Both Kahlbetzer sons are deeply conscious of the legacy created by their father and have always respected his penchant for privacy.

"And with our experience of being in Argentina, anybody with wealth does not want to be seen. You just want to hide, because you become a target for violence," Markus says.

He acknowledges his father achieved great things, without the backing of his German family or anyone else. But he also believes he inherited his father's entrepreneurial spirit to build something of his own.

"I don't want to just have something that's been passed down to me. So I think about what is going to be my lasting legacy that I can pass on to my kids, other than maybe a bunch of assets? What am I going to do today to make a multiplier on that and really make a lasting legacy of my own," he says.

He hopes his sons and daughter will want to carry on the Kahlbetzer name in BridgeLane, but is conscious of his father's mantra supporting independence.

"Dad always said 'I don't care what you do as long as you do it well, or you love doing it.' I'd love all three of my kids to be involved in what I do and because our businesses are not operating ones, they are more accommodating to that," he says.

"But I love cycling and my nine year old does too, so maybe he runs a bike shop one day and maybe my daughter goes into the venture capital side."

Johnny, who still lives in a Vaucluse mansion once owned by his father, says the experience of splitting the Kahlbetzer empire has made him think deeply about the future for his two sons.

The eldest, who looks set to join the army when he leaves school, has shown an interest in farming. The younger hasn't.

"In five years, maybe my kids will be at university or maybe in the business and looking at what passion they have. We will see if any of the things we are involved in, they want to be involved in. Or we will be supporting them to do something which excites them," Johnny says.

He says he never does an analysis of his own or the family's worth. Never has and never will.

"The reality is an extra $10m or $100m, whatever, is not going to change any of our lives. It's a matter of whether you have enjoyment with what you do and you're happy with what you're doing."

"Very few people are happy with what they've got. I am very strongly of the view that the money does not make you happy. I think the burden is the expectation by society or parts of society that you should always be driven to make your wealth more. And quite often I give that the big finger!"

# JASON KIMBERLEY

The Springvale Botanical Cemetery, the largest memorial park in Victoria on the leafy outskirts of Melbourne, is the final resting place for a who's who of the city's famed and fortunate.

Among its graves are those of former governor-general Sir Zelman Cowan, VFL football legend Jack Dyer and TV star Bert Newton.

One far less known is that of a seven-year-old boy, born to a family that is part of Australian retail royalty.

Craig Kimberley, his wife Connie and her sister Chrissie changed the face of Australian fashion forever when they opened the first Just Jeans store on Melbourne's Chapel St in December 1970.

It became the largest specialty jeans retailer in the southern hemisphere and by the time they sold the business 30 years later it was worth more than $100m. But until now an untold part of the Just Jeans story is Marcus Kimberley, the boy Connie gave birth to in 1968.

"Marcus was born with brain damage. There is conjecture as to actually how. Was the cord around his neck? Was there some congenital issue? That was never adequately solved," says his older brother, Jason.

"He had calipers, he had a crash helmet, he would often fall over when he was walking and he had very little language. We had a program where 120 of mum and dad's friends would rotate through the house to help.

"They would educate and exercise him, moving him so his muscles wouldn't waste away because he was so skinny. It was a real hive of activity in our house and that was very much centred around Marcus."

Marcus died in 1975. His older brother was just eight years old.

For years he had looked out for Marcus, stood up to those who sniggered at the strange things on his legs, the weird helmet on his head and the way he walked.

To Jason, Marcus was the dear brother who he so wished could have been spared the trials he faced in his short life.

"I was very protective of him. I'd see a kid mocking him or saying something on the other side of the street and would cross the road and challenge them," he says proudly, as a tear trickles down his right cheek.

"I've always been really keen on the underdog and making sure that those least able to look after themselves get well supported."

Until the Kimberley family sold its interest in what became known as Just Group in 2001, Jason helped manage the company.

But during those years and in the decade after the sale, he also had 10 different careers in fashion, photography, warehousing, stockbroking, wholesale, building, fruit picking, cattle herding, roof repairs, and was for a time even as a restaurateur.

In 2008 he found his calling in life – a passion shaped by his experiences with his younger brother. It was to educate school-aged children about an environmentally sustainable future.

Kimberley initially launched the project, then known as Cool Melbourne, into 10 primary and secondary schools.

Since then his organisation, now known as Cool.org – formerly Cool Australia – has provided more than 175,000 educators with free educational content and activities to students and teachers, from kindergarten to year 10.

"I think my experience with Marcus is one of the main reasons why I'm doing what I'm doing in education. It is about the democratisation of quality education so the have nots can get as big a go as the haves," the now 56 year old says.

"My experience with my brother has really informed a lot of who I am. I really understand you are who you are because of where you were when and all the things that influence you at different stages of your life.

"You just absorb them and you become who you are because of those life experiences and those friendships and relationships. So I've always been for the underdog."

## THE MAKING OF MR COOL

In July 2023 Kimberley relaunched his business with the name Cool.org. He'd been after the domain name for years.

"I always thought that would be a great international brand," he says.

It had been owned since 1992 by a lecturer in anthropological documentary filmmaking at the University of Southern California named Dr Jennifer Cool.

Over the years she had been offered six-figure sums for the name, but was never a seller.

Kimberley sought her out and emailed her for many years before eventually convincing her to part with it for the cool sum of $US20,000. But after an administrative mishap, he had to wait some time before the sale date finally arrived.

He was having breakfast with his father in early February 2020 at the Chateau Marmont hotel on Sunset Boulevard in West Hollywood, just days after they had fulfilled a lifelong dream to attend the Super Bowl – which that year was staged at the Hard Rock Stadium in Miami Gardens, Florida,

"I remember the moment the message came through on my phone that she had sold. I just burst into tears in this restaurant," he says. "The waiter came up and said 'Sir, is everything okay?'. It was a special day."

Cool is raising $2.6m to support its new subscription product called Cool+, an unlimited access pass to premium teaching content.

"We've raised $1.5m and we've got another $1.1m to get to the $2.6m that we are after," Kimberley says.

"Another important part of it is the professional learning for teachers. What they don't get taught in university. How to manage your classroom, how to deal with difficult kids, all those critical skills. So that's what we've got a huge focus on in this new business."

Twenty per cent of the new subscription company is being sold to external investors in the raising. Kimberley and his co-founder, Jan Owen, are retaining 40 per cent.

The Australian Education Union, which has 200,000 members, has recently agreed to purchase all of its first-year teachers a one-year subscription to Cool+. International growth is next on the horizon.

"We've looked at where we are going to be in five years. Our valuation post our cap raising will be $12.3m and if we hit our targets we will be looking at a valuation of around $112m," Kimberley says.

"That also includes overseas expansion. We think it's got absolute, massive potential with our connections overseas, using our existing networks in Australia."

## ADVENTURE HUNTER

The launch of Cool Australia back in 2005 was inspired by Kimberley's maiden trip to Antarctica when he hauled sleds across the snow and ice with Peter Hillary, son of famous English mountaineer Sir Edmund. They have been good friends for a decade.

"Antarctica is a place that changes you. It is this pristine wilderness and it can go from that to something horrific in a matter of minutes," Kimberley says.

He has also travelled extensively throughout Australia and the world, including trekking Denali – the highest mountain peak in North America – and a month-long kayaking odyssey on Prince William Sound, both in Alaska.

More recently, Kimberley has trekked to Mt Everest base camp, traversed the Kokoda Track, and been dogsledding with his father in the Yukon Territories in Canada.

He learned from two near-death experiences in 1992 when he sought to conquer South America's highest peak, Mt Aconcagua, with another good friend, James Carnegie, the son of legendary businessman Sir Rod.

"There was a point where I was completely numb from the knees down and I couldn't feel anything. I had this feeling of a metaphorical door closing in my mind, and I could feel it shutting behind me," he recalls.

"I could see this sunny point ahead, which I thought was maybe half an hour away. It turned out it was about an hour and a half away. I thought if I can get to that sun, I'm fine.

"Eventually I got into the sun and I was alive. I didn't know if I was going to lose my feet and toes. But I thought, 'I've come this far, let's keep going'."

After reaching the peak and returning to their camp, the pair seconded an army helicopter that flew them off the mountain in a matter of minutes.

They then hitched a lift to Mendoza and jumped on the next flight to Buenos Aires.

"We thought we were geniuses until we hit a storm. The plane dived, quickly and steeply. Everyone was screaming and crying, James and I held hands as we plunged to a certain death. We eventually levelled off, landed erratically and kissed the ground on disembarking."

He attributes his thrillseeking nature to his long-held belief, perhaps shaped by the experience with his brother, that life is short.

"If I can jam as many lifetimes into my lifetime as possible, that for me is the adventure," Kimberley says.

"I love experiencing challenging scenarios. I love finding out what I've got in me and how I can help others with me, how we can all be better and stronger together, working as a team and being organised.

I also just love the pristine beauty of being in nature. It is silent, clean and so far removed from our day to day lives."

## SAYING GOODBYE TO JUST JEANS

Kimberley says he long lived with his father's expectation that he would work at Just Jeans.

"I loved it. From the age of six I'd go with Dad on the school holidays to muck around in the warehouse. I just loved being around what was happening and stuff like the orders, the marketing, the ads. It was always a really dynamic place," he says.

But eventually reality dawned on his father.

"Twenty years ago Dad said 'It wasn't until you were 30 that I realised you weren't me'," Kimberley says.

He left and rejoined the business four times, including working for Country Road for three years, before quitting for good – with his father's blessing.

He stresses none of the family's proceeds from the Just Group sale went to the next generation.

"I'm not saying I've missed out. I just didn't get a financial windfall in any way," he says.

"But I never had a sense of ownership or entitlement to the business. Mum and Dad are very generous people and I've obviously enjoyed some nice times with them on with trips and stuff. They've also supported me in a couple of businesses to a smallish extent."

His greatest shared passion with his father is the Sydney Swans Football Club, of which Craig was president from 1975-77. For a period Just Jeans bankrolled the club. Craig was also an AFL Commissioner from 1997-99.

Jason was so nervous during the 2005 Grand Final that he vomited in the carpark at half time. The Swans won their first AFL Premiership that day.

He also hosted a picnic on the hallowed SCG turf last year when he was one of thousands of spectators who invaded the field after Swans champion Lance "Buddy" Franklin booted his 1000th AFL goal.

"We'd grabbed a bottle of champagne and filled our pockets with beers and got a box of pies. We put a blanket in front of the Ladies' stand. Dane Rampe was the Swans captain, who I was quite friendly with.

"I said to him 'Ramps come over here, have a champagne, a beer or a pie. He said I can't have a champers but I wouldn't mind the pie. He quickly devoured one before the ground was eventually cleared and the game resumed."

## FATHER FIGURE

Kimberley says he has long admired his father for his "endless passion and enthusiasm for everything".

"He's going harder at 82 than anyone I know. He is off the charts," he says, before adding that he believes he has taught his father "that there's more grey in the world than he imagined".

"He's quite black and white in his thinking and I think I've introduced him to other ways of looking at things and considering other opinions. I've made him less stronger in his ideologies and more accepting of other ways of seeing and doing things," he says.

Kimberley also saw his parents in their darkest days imaginable.

"It was pretty terrible," he says of the seven years his brother was alive.

"But his life wasn't a brilliant life for Marcus. It was difficult and challenging and it took up a lot of their time. It was quite emotional seeing this person before you who was really a large toddler. It was a very tough existence for him."

He will never forget the day they buried Marcus. His parents go to the grave each year on his birthday and the anniversary of his death.

But Kimberley didn't go there for 30 years after his brother's passing.

"I have done a bit of work with psychologists – like half a dozen sessions – and not going to the grave was something that was discussed," he says.

"But I felt I didn't need to go. I don't know if I was avoiding anything. Nothing was pulling me to that site to go and visit him."

The turning point was the shock passing of his best friend, 23-year-old Michael Fox – the son of trucking magnate Lindsay Fox – who tragically took his own life in January 1991.

Kimberley still visits his best mate's grave at the St Kilda Cemetery every couple of months.

Now he also goes to the resting place of his late brother at least once a year.

"As I have got older and have my own kids, I now look back and think 'f-k, no parent should have to bury a child'," he says – the family's pain still clear in his eyes.

"But we all learned a lot from Marcus and the experience of having him in our lives."

# PAUL LITTLE AND JANE HANSEN

*Paul Little was in his final year at the helm of Toll Holdings when I first sat down to interview him at the logistics giant's somewhat non-descript headquarters at 380 St Kilda Road. Little was in a combative mood and proceeded to give a parting spray to some of the stockbroking analysts covering the company he had run for the previous 26 years. From that day on Little and I had a cordial relationship. He would always take or return my phone calls and help me when he could. I knew his wife Jane Hansen in name only, so when I approached him in late 2018 to do his first ever joint interview with Jane, I wasn't confident they would do it. History now shows they agreed and their first public chat together was published in The Australian's Richest 250 magazine the following March. The discussion was fascinating to hear the dynamic between them, their mutual respect and admiration for each other's abilities. They are truly one of Melbourne's top power couples.*

Jane Hansen had never seen her husband in such a state. Paul Little, one of the warriors of corporate Australia who turned the Toll Holdings logistics company from an 18-truck operation in Melbourne worth $1.5 million into a $4 billion global powerhouse, was under siege.

It was late 2013. A few months earlier, Little had taken over the chairmanship of his beloved Essendon Australian Football League club at the very height of the club's devastating supplements scandal.

The almost two-decade marriage of Little and Hansen – they married in 1994, three years after Little's first wife tragically passed away after a battle with cancer – was facing its toughest test.

"I have been with Paul for 24 years and seen him take on some big deals, like [taking over Chris Corrigan's] Patrick and some contentious M&A deals," Hansen says. "I have never seen anything like the stress he had with Essendon.

"None of the institutions knew what they were doing. It was such uncharted territory that everyone was feeling their way."

Hansen remembers one adversary dressing up as a cleaner so he could confront Little in his office.

On another occasion, Little was photographed filling up the petrol tank of his wife's car, whose registration plate carries her initials, "JH". The media seized upon the picture to claim that it showed the chairman's blind allegiance to Essendon's controversial coach, James Hird.

Hansen was deeply worried.

"Yes, most definitely I was," she says. "I just tried to maintain a sense of balance and be more distant from the emotion of it all, to step back and think about it rationally ... I do have the utmost respect for the way Paul handled it. He did do the best by the club."

Little describes Hansen as being "totally supportive" throughout the whole affair. "She didn't question the reasons for doing things unless she violently disagreed with me, which she did on a couple of occasions," he says. "I would like to have left it out of the home but when the press are camped on your front nature strip it is hard to do that.

"When it became personal, it affected my family, not just me. That was something we felt was below the belt. During that time, I couldn't walk anywhere without someone giving me their point of view. That was OK at first, but after a while it became torturous."

History now records that Little stepped down as Essendon chairman on December 14, 2015, shortly before the final guilty verdict was returned against Essendon in the supplements investigation. He knows he could not have survived the affair without Hansen by his side.

A month earlier they had launched the Hansen Little Foundation, a large-scale, active philanthropic enterprise that has since given significant donations to the State Library of Victoria and the University of Melbourne. The aim of the Foundation is to leave a legacy of significant and positive change.

Hansen, who spent more than 25 years in stockbroking, finance and investment banking, says they went into philanthropy together because they are both self-made, and have similar values and a shared interest in wanting to make the world a better place.

In January 2023 Hansen became the 23rd Chancellor of the University of Melbourne, after first being appointed to the Council in January 2016.

"I like watching the way Paul's mind works," she replies when asked what she has learnt from her husband. "He likes to pull problems apart. He has an analytical, flexible mind."

Little says he loves his wife's "rigour – how she doesn't avoid an issue. She brings a direct route to solving problems. Her willingness to confront things and deal with things is incredibly valuable."

Which means they lock horns from time to time, but never in public. And the issue is always resolved, even if – as Hansen puts it – they "agree to disagree".

"You get excited, upset, you argue, you thrash it out," Little says. "We are both quite robust and we can work through issues.

"If it wasn't for the fact I have so much respect for Jane, you might become less secure about what you are doing. But there is great underlying trust and belief between us."

## LIFE AFTER TOLL

Little will never forget the nervous feeling in the heady days of the mid-1980s when he started Toll.

"Looking back in hindsight, Toll was probably one of the things that you would not want to do because you had no history that you could point to, you were dealing with the multinationals, big and difficult companies to commercially compete with. So the early days were really tough," he recalls.

"The big company customers would say 'Come back and see us in a year or two'. I'll never forget the day we actually picked up a BHP account, and the leverage we were able to get from that was amazing."

The experience built Little into a street fighter, who famously took on Chris Corrigan in a bare-knuckle battle for control of the nation's waterfront in 2006. He retired as chief executive of Toll four years later.

But it also gave him a passion for the entrepreneurial spirit, especially given the number of small logistics businesses Little went on to buy during Toll's expansion phase.

That now lives in his private Little Group, which retains interests in real estate, aviation and transport, including the $100m VIP Jet terminal at Melbourne's Tullamarine Airport.

When he took me on a tour of the jet facility in early 2022 Little claimed it set the standard for private jet facilities anywhere in the world.

The Jet Base has capacity for 200 aircraft turns a month, full kitchen and function facilities, a fully accessible hotel-level suite available for guests, and a suite for pilots and space for a flight crew.

"The object of the facility is to get people to house their planes there, because by doing that there are a range of other services that we can provide for them," he told me during the tour.

"So we certainly accommodate people who just want to fly in and fly out, but the other category of people is those looking for a home to hanger their aircraft."

"To help that process, all the crews have their own office facilities overlooking a lot of the aircraft. That has elevated the importance we place on the crews, not just the owners of the aircraft or passengers on the aircraft. The crews are also very important."

Little said he believed that booming demand in the private jet market would take the Jet Base, which turns over $15 million per annum, to another level.

"Our long-range aircraft can go to Los Angeles in 12-13 hours nonstop," he said. "That's pretty compelling. And one stop to London.

"Being joined at the hip with Melbourne Airport, we also get to take advantage of the curfew environment, the cost of fuel, and the safety aspects of flying in and out of Melbourne Airport, which is much better than some of our competitors. So I think the facility is obviously world class, but we are also attached to a world-class airport that really values what we can do to help them and assist them."

Before the onset of Covid, the Jet Base was also starting to offer wealthy customers on commercial airlines a quick airport arrival and exit, away from the public eye.

"If someone wants to fly in a chopper, go directly to the plane, bypass the terminal check-in and security and meet an existing commercial flight, we can do that for them," Little said.

"We just love the concept and our customers love it."

"We had a couple of the very high-profile tennis players using it pre Covid and they loved it. They brought their families through. If you want total confidentiality, there is a big car park underneath the Jet Base building; you can come in a private car or a chopper and be gone. No one would even know you were there."

Little has also owned his own Gulfstream G650 for more than five years, the first business jet able to fly non-stop to Sydney and Melbourne from Los Angeles, Today it still looks as good as the day he took delivery of the $85 million private plane.

It remains his pride and joy.

## PROPERTY PASSIONS

In late 2018 Little Group sold the goodwill associated with future projects for its Little Projects business – a commercial and residential property developer – to directors Leighton Pyke and Paris Lechte, but has since continued to invest in the group's developments.

Little says he wanted to reduce the amount of long-term investment of Little Group in the construction industry. The lead time to conceive and deliver a project is usually around five years.

"I felt for some time that not only was I making decisions about where I was going to invest, but of course where was I going to be in five years' time," he said.

The pivot out of construction also allowed the group to focus on other development passions, such as working on a $10m refurbishment of the historic 133-year-old Grand Hotel at Portarlington on Victoria's Bellarine Peninsula.

Little Group's property management arm is known as Kolmeo, a business which helps property managers, landlords and tenants streamline workflows, automate tasks and communicate.

Kolmeo allows property managers to track requests, book inspections and manage portfolios in real time and remotely for a variety of tasks, including maintenance, rent reviews and payments.

"Our real estate business is probably one of the largest in the country for managing properties on behalf of landlords. In the old days, it might have been called a rent roll. There's a lot more that goes into it today than was originally the case. But the technology that drives that, from both a landlord' and tenant's point of view, is archaic. It's essentially manual and has been paperwork-intensive, and simply is very difficult to manage efficiently," he said.

"Kolmeo is a digital platform that covers everything from your PC or your phone or whichever way you want to do it."

One day Little hopes it can be publicly listed.

While he has now retired from public company roles and sold his interest in Toll Holdings in a multi billion-dollar takeover by Japan Post, Little remains chairman of Skalata Ventures, which started life as a Melbourne University Accelerator program developed as a mechanism to back young and bright entrepreneurial graduates.

More recently it has morphed into being a stand-alone, for-profit company with a high-powered board led by Little and relationships across the Victorian university sector.

Simply put, Skalata vets, invest in, and mentors business talent coming out of top universities and works collaboratively with them to support early-stage companies.

"I love relating to the companies. You see their enthusiasm, their lack of respect for the need for a contact with the banks and a contact with the accountants and everything else, which is kind of nice," he said.

"Really they are trying to focus on what it is they do and to be the best at what they can do."

# RON MANNERS

*Julio's Italian restaurant is a West Perth institution. In 1998, in my third year of service in the Perth bureau of The Australian Financial Review, my then boss Mark Dixon invited me there to dine with one of the doyens of the WA mining industry, Ron Manners. Also joining us that day was Ron's delightful daughter, Sarah, who I had known through her various PR roles in the small community that is corporate Perth. Ron was sharp as a tack, engaging and shared some hilarious stories of his life. I never saw him again until by chance I ran into him nearly a quarter of a century later at a Perth event run by the top boutique fund manager Cooper Investors. We got talking over the dinner that night and Ron shared a few more amazing stories.*

*Ron has always jealously guarded his privacy, so I wasn't expecting him to agree when a year later I asked him to do an interview documenting his incredible life. But he was only too happy to chat so we met at his non-descript Subiaco office on a sunny lunchtime in late June 2023. The office was completely empty, this being a Monday in the post COVID world when all his staff worked from home. But Ron, of course, was still there at his desk. Surrounded by busts of world-famous economists and walls adorned with memorabilia, we had a wonderful discussion at the make-shift board table in the office before walking around the corner for a quick and entertaining alcohol-free lunch at one of his favourite local Thai restaurants.*

*Ron is truly one of the absolute characters of corporate Australia. They don't make them like him anymore.*

Ron Manners' life changed forever one pitch-black evening on the highway between Kalgoorlie and Esperance in regional Western Australia when he was just 17 years old.

"I was driving with my parents when I saw the headlights of a truck approaching. Suddenly its lights went out and we didn't have any idea that they had overhanging machinery on the back of the truck. It tore the side of our car out and my arm went with it," he recalls.

"Dad drove me straight to a hospital in Kalgoorlie. I had about nine broken bones and my right arm was a mess. I remember being sedated and sitting in a wheelchair when the doctor pointed to the top of my arm and said to his colleague: 'We are going to take his arm off from here.'"

But his father was having none of it. He firmly insisted upon flying his son to Perth the next morning for a second opinion. Nine operations later, Manners junior's arm remarkably remained intact. But it would be locked at the elbow in perpetuity.

A budding musician in his youth, he had loved playing the piano and the old clarinet he pinched from his grandfather's coffin before his burial.

Sadly he never played the former again. But after the accident his father ensured the latter passion could continue when he paid 40 pounds to the local music shop in Kalgoorlie to design a special clarinet so his son's fingers could still reach the keys.

"I played every Wednesday night in a jazz ensemble for 20 years, until the gold boom happened.

Every couple of years something goes wrong with my arm and I've got to get it fixed. But every time I do my shoelaces up – you need two hands for that – I whisper to myself quietly, 'Thanks Dad'," Manners says with a wide smile.

"I also think because of that experience I now question everything. Things are never quite what they look."

In 2023 his Mannwest Group celebrated its 128th anniversary. Its predecessor, WG Manners & Co, was established in 1895 when his grandfather WG Manners – the son of a Ballarat prospector – set up a mining engineering business to design and build mining plants in Kalgoorlie.

Born with mining in his blood, Manners junior started out as an electrical engineer training at the Kalgoorlie School of Mines, and took over the family business from his father in 1955.

Now known as a legend of the local industry – he is Emeritus Chairman of the Australian Mining Hall of Fame – over the decades he floated a number of Australian-listed nickel, iron ore and gold mining companies.

But his greatest claim to fame was starting and building Croesus Mining, the firm named after the ancient King of Lydia (now Western Turkey) noted for his great wealth and the fact he was the first ruler ever to mint gold coins.

At one point Croesus was Australia's third-largest gold producer and during Manners' two decades as chairman it established 26 mines and produced 1.275 million ounces of gold.

Sadly in mid 2006 Croesus slipped into the hands of administrators due to disappearing orebodies and a nasty hedge book, nine months after Manners' retirement. Famed WA prospector Mark Creasy was then its largest individual shareholder.

Manners says Mannwest Group has always been an enthusiastic participant in the introduction of new technologies during the booms and busts of commodity prices.

He proudly describes mining as "the greatest creative industry in the world."

But in an era of massive global corporations and an Australian resource sector increasingly foreign owned, the now 87 year old says the industry will never return to its halcyon days.

"Back then we were doing stuff for the first time so we would help each other. There was a free exchange of information because we were all trying to do things better. It was an amazing spirit of camaraderie," he laments.

"That was an era that probably won't come back because everything is now corporatised. The average CEO wouldn't dare do that today."

## ROLE MODELS

Manners describes his late father – known as C.B Manners – as a great role model. They were very close.

After the Australian credit squeeze induced by the Menzies government in the early 1960's, he and his father started a farming operation at Esperance before the latter suffered a fatal heart attack while chasing cattle on the property in 1966. He was only 72.

"I was in Kalgoorlie that day running the family business and I still believe that if I was there helping dad on the farm, I might have saved him," he says solemnly.

"That would have been important because he would have seen the nickel boom. My grandfather ran the family business for 30 years and enjoyed the gold boom at the turn of the century. Dad ran it for 30 years when there was zero happening. In the month dad died they declared Kambalda as a commercial mining project and bang, off it went."

Manners' mother was ten years younger than her husband and started life as a schoolteacher.

But being in a mining town, she decided to visit the Kalgoorlie School of Mines to enrol in studying geology.

There she was told the language in the classroom would be too strong for a woman.

"So, she told them 'What if I don't listen!'," her son recalls with a proud smile.

"She never worked as a geologist but got the qualification. When I did geology many years later I used her notes, they were so detailed. They were really helpful."

The inspiration of his mother led to Manners becoming an industry pioneer in employing female geologists.

"They asked questions, they were unrelenting in showing up their male colleagues, and they lifted the whole industry as a result," he declares.

Manners' exploration work during his career was also assisted by his chance involvement at just 15 years of age in the now infamous outback crash of a De Havilland DH104 Dove aircraft owned by McRoberts Miller Airlines – the predecessor of Ansett WA – on October 16, 1951.

There were no survivors when the plane plummeted into the scrub at Kurrawang Lake near Kalgoorlie.

"We were out in the bush one afternoon and heard this almighty thump in the distance. When we got to the site, bodies were everywhere and there was vertebrae all over the place. I remember putting a few in my pocket as evidence of what I had seen, just because I thought the kids at school would never believe me," he recalls.

"I also managed to knock off the set of pilot maps that were printed on pieces of fabric. I then used those very detailed aeronautical maps throughout my exploration days. They had details that other maps didn't."

In 1997, after a ceremony that Manners attended marking the 50th anniversary of the crash, he was contacted by the daughter of the pilot.

"She came to my office in West Perth and I presented her with the maps because I wasn't exploring anymore," he says.

While he now lives in Perth, Manners says he was lucky to grow up and live in the "exciting" community that was Kalgoorlie during the second half of the 20th century.

Gold will always be his favourite metal. Last year he used a one kilogram gold bar he'd hoarded for four decades to pay for a fancy new Lexus.

"I've always had a fascination for gold. It is still the only mineral you can follow on from the discovery process of prospecting and exploration, to finding a mine, opening a pit, building a mill, processing the gold and pouring gold bars. You are in charge of all the processes and you can then market the gold yourself. There's no other mineral like it," he says with glee.

"There is also something when you pour your first bar. Women talk about the feeling when they hold their child for the first time. But that is nothing compared to holding your first bar!"

Remembering legends

His name was Arvi Parbo, a former chairman of Western Mining Corporation, BHP, Alcoa and at one point arguably the most powerful corporate executive in the country.

To this day Manners believes Parbo stands above the rest as the person he has most admired over the decades in the local resource sector, despite him hailing from Estonia.

He first met Parbo when he was 17 and they stayed in touch for decades afterwards.

"His first job was at Bullfinch near Southern Cross, out in the middle of nowhere. He was made the underground mine manger there because they couldn't find staff. We met up when I went there to give him some advice about new miners cap lamps that were better than the ones they were using," Manners says.

"He had a very heavy European accent and I remember driving back to Kalgoorlie in my Holden ute thinking 'The poor bugger will never make it because nobody will be able to understand him!. Yet he went on to become, without doubt, the most significant figure in corporate Australia in the second half of last century."

Manners also developed a friendship with WA mining magnate Lang Hancock, which now endures with the latter's famous daughter Gina.

"I was one of the few people that argued with Lang. He wanted someone to bounce ideas off and he had a habit of getting information from the source. He wouldn't accept anything second hand," he says.

"I think Lang's style is something Gina has inherited.. If she wants information about something, she goes straight to the source. So people in authority can expect to get a call from her."

Rinehart still has a celebration each year to mark her late father's birthday. Manners is always on the guest list.

"Despite her wealth, she hasn't changed at all. It is amazing. I think she's handling it well. There is a total responsibility to be in that position. Half the world is hoping you trip over."

As a long-time proponent of the free market economic model, Manners set up the Mannkal Economic Education Foundation in 1997, a think-tank that has sponsored over 2500 students to study opportunities in both Australia and overseas. It is now his great passion.

He says Mannkal has given Mannwest a new-found purpose. to permanently rebel against bad economics and bad education, however well-meaning, popular and respected.

As one of the elder statesmen of Australia's liberty movement and the author of 5 books, he still believes that individualism and personal responsibility are powerful drivers of change.

He has also long admired people displaying "heroic humility".

"The phrase best describes many of my role models and I admire this 'style' as it helps avoid the trap of 'self-burial'," he says.

From the age of just 16, one of his greatest mentors was famed American economist Leonard E Read, the founder of the Foundation for Economic Education – the first modern libertarian think tank in the United States.

Manners is now on the board of the Mont Pelerin Society that Read started with another top US economist Milton Friedman. A photo of Read hangs proudly on the wall of Mannkal's Perth office.

"He used to offer these little one-liners in letters he would write to me," he says.

"He once told me the best thing you can do is bring an idea to the threshold of someone's consciousness, and then back off. If that idea stays in their mind, it is theirs and it will be theirs for life. You will never persuade anyone by belting them over the head."

Despite turning 88 in January 2023, Manners continues to turn up to the Mannkal office most days. With his right elbow still locked. He wouldn't dream of doing anything else.

"I learn so much from the young people in the office because they have a different way of learning, a different attention span. My generation procrastinate, we are always looking for more information. The youngsters don't want that. They just want a quick grab so they can go and make their own mistakes and quickly. I love it!" he says.

"The mates that I've spent a lot of time with over the years often say to me, 'Why can't you just be normal like the rest of us and play golf or buy a yacht.' I tell them, 'Mannkal is my yacht.. I have more fun everyday than any of them that have yachts."

# ROBERT AND TOM MILLNER

Robert Millner was one of more than 40,000 people who ventured to Omaha, Nebraska, on the first weekend in May 2023 for what American business magnate Warren Buffett calls "Woodstock for capitalists".

The annual shareholder sojourn for Buffett's Berkshire Hathaway group, where one of the world's most revered investors and his vice-chair, Charlie Munger, this year explained how to avoid mistakes in life and business, has been a fixture on Millner's calendar for many years.

"Tom (Millner)  and I first started going over to Omaha before COVID-19 hit. We would be away for five to six days together," says Millner of his son, who could not make the trip in 2023. "We've done it together seven times now. To listen to those great men has been absolutely unbelievable. One regret we have is that we didn't start going 20 or 30 years earlier."

Robert Millner is only the fourth Millner family member to run Australian investment conglomerate Washington H Soul Pattinson (WHSP) throughout more than 100 years. It is the nation's second-oldest listed firm. Better known as "Soul Patts", the company is widely regarded as the closest investment vehicle Australia has to Berkshire Hathaway.Following Buffett's style of high-conviction investing has seen Soul Patts take large positions in disparate industries including coal, building materials, telecommunications, pharmaceuticals, retail, agriculture, property equity and listed investment companies.

"We are very honoured to be spoken about in the same breath as Buffett and we are a very similar type of business, even if his scale is a lot larger. We are long-term investors," says Robert Millner.

Tom adds that, like Berkshire Hathaway, Soul Patts is a closed-end investment company. "It is not like a fund where there are redemptions during a downturn," he says. "So you can genuinely wait, be patient and, as Buffett would say, be greedy when others are fearful. Sometimes, we've sat on $1 billion worth of cash."

Soul Patts has never borrowed money or missed a dividend payment, even during WWII when Robert's uncle Jim Millner was a prisoner of war in Singapore.

Robert notes that one key difference between the firm he chairs and Berkshire Hathaway is the daily diet of the chair. "I don't have a cheeseburger, a Coke and an ice-cream every day for lunch," he says, in reference to the 92-year-old Buffett's penchant for junk food.

A deeper difference between the two firms is the family business culture at Soul Patts. Robert is the great-grandson of Lewy Pattinson. The business as it is known today resulted from a merger of Pattinson & co and Washington H Soul. This venture grew through the Great Depression and two world wars into the multibillion-dollar public conglomerate that is Soul Patts today.

Over the decades, Soul Patts has been run only by Lewy's eldest son, William Frederick Pattinson, William's nephew, Jim Millner and, most recently, by Robert. He has been on the board since 1984, chair since 1998 and was joined by his son Tom as a director in 2011. Over the past three years, the company has gradually refreshed its board and management.

## CROSS-INVESTMENT

Soul Patts also owns 44 per cent of listed building materials group Brickworks, which has a 26 per cent stake in Soul Patts. This cross-shareholding structure has been criticised over the years, most notably by funds management giant Perpetual, which launched a Federal Court action in 2017 claiming the cross-investment structure had the effect of depressing share value and was therefore "oppressive" and costly to minority shareholders. Justice Jayne Jagot held that the maintenance of the cross-shareholding was neither oppressive nor unfair in all of the circumstances, dismissing Perpetual's claim with costs.

But Brickworks and Soul Patts, whose boards are also closely intertwined, claim the structure has long helped smooth the economic cycle and deterred hostile takeovers. Celebrating its 120th year in 2023, Robert says the secret sauce of Soul Patts is simply personnel.

"We have been very fortunate that we have had very good people," he says. "The people before me have always been conservative and well- mannered. Every morning, when I'm in the office, I walk around to the senior staff. There aren't many chairs who would do that. We're common people and we look after and support our employees. It has always been a good place to come to work.

The Millners like to be low-key. They have never owned a boat or a plane, and fly economy domestically. They have also carried on the family tradition of supporting the Royal Flying Doctor Service and donate to the Salvation Army.

Tom says another secret of the company's success has been its governance culture. "Being an investment house, the relationship of the chair and the board with management is really vital. You want the bad news in an investment company to travel even faster than the good news. So if you have got a good relationship with the management team and something doesn't go to plan, you can address it quickly."

## RISE OF COMPLIANCE

Some have argued that the ASX Corporate Governance Principles and Recommendations are overly prescriptive in Australia, leading to more pressure on boards for compliance and less scope for focus on strategy and growth.

Robert describes the rise of compliance regulations in recent years as "disturbing".

"We are in an era where 11 per cent of people's super money is being taken from them to grow their future, yet the average person with a self- managed super fund cannot understand a listed company annual report," he says, holding up a Soul Patts annual report from 1971, which is just 13 pages long. He then holds up a 190-page 2002 version. "There is nothing wrong with it, per se, but sometimes you just get bogged down in a board meeting talking about this other stuff."

Tom believes over-regulation is now a broader problem for Australia, with the consequence that the next generation of business leaders won't want to join public company boards.

"There is a lot of risk, you won't get rich by taking a director's fee, and you're better off being an executive or a CEO," he says. "So the age of the people who sit on boards is deteriorating, unfortunately. Going forward, if that trend continues, we might run into a sad state of affairs when it is very difficult to find good-quality board members.

Robert's advice for those who do choose to serve on boards is to "be honest with yourself" and when starting out, to "sit there and listen — read your board papers, use your common sense and don't say something stupid".

But once through the initial phase of joining a board, Tom says it is important to actively participate in the discussion. "You've been asked to join that board for a reason — because you bring a different background, a track record and benefits to the company. So you need to produce that at board level."

## SEPARATION OF POWERS

Robert has always lived by one golden rule as a chair and non-executive director: directors are not there to manage the company. He puts the mantra into practice at Soul Patts. The investment house has strategic shareholdings in a number of companies where it has board seats. Robert occupies several of them.

"That's a very important point," he says. "I've come across a few ex-managing directors who never liked the board asking too many questions. But when they become a director, they will throw darts at the present management. An important lesson for directors is that you're not running the company.

With the push to zero emissions, Soul Patt's investment in carbon-heavy assets — notably through its investment in coal miner New Hope — is becoming a focus for stakeholders. But the Millners see no issues resolving the tension between profits and corporate responsibility, and taking account of ESG issues.

Robert claims New Hope has long been regarded as being at the forefront of rehabilitating coal mines "as we go" and says that it has always been a good neighbour and integral to the prosperity of the nearby town of Muswellbrook in the NSW Hunter Valley.

"If an investment opportunity doesn't stack up from the environmental side, it shouldn't be investment-grade," says Tom. "If it leaves a bad social impact, that shouldn't be investment-grade. ESG has become quite a trendy term and at the forefront of a lot of people's supposed investment checklist. But deep down, we've invested in various businesses that have looked at those aspects over generations."

## FAMILY DYNAMIC

Tom Millner has long had a passion for funds management and equities. He wrote the prospectus for the BKI Investment Company, which he went on to run. Since listing in 2003 with $173m, BKI has now paid out over $1b in dividends and franking credits to its shareholders. Today, he is a full-time executive at Contact Asset Management.

"It wasn't forced on us as the next generation," he says. "That's the beauty of how the family has been so successful. I have liked funds management and enjoyed it."

Robert began working for his uncle at the family business after a stint as a stockbroker, straight after school. He says he has never expected his son to follow in his footsteps. "You can't force people to try to do anything.

They now talk at least once or twice a day and say there is no line between their business and personal lives, which blur into one, sometimes to the frustration of Robert's wife of 48 years, Janine.

"I'm very fortunate to be married to a lady who's very, very patient," he says. "I'm away a lot, so she doesn't get to see much of me at times. She is a wonderful mother.

Tom has been married to his wife for nearly 20 years and they have twins. "With the rock and grounding she provides, life is so much easier," he says, adding that the greatest learning from his father has been "downright common sense". "If you don't know enough about something, try to find it out, and if it's still above you, don't invest in it... you're probably better off putting your money elsewhere," he says. "The other big thing is alignment. When you're managing people's portfolios or wealth, you must be on the same page as them.

The Millner family tops up its shareholding in Soul Patts every six months. "Don't tell shareholders what they should do if you don't do it yourself," says Tom. "Put your money where your mouth is."

Soul Patts is now in uncharted waters as it transitions to the fifth generation of Millner family involvement. Formal succession planning on the public company board remains a work in progress.

Robert notes there are no public companies left in Australia with a history quite like the firm he has now chaired for a quarter of a century. But his son is confident that, like Berkshire Hathaway, its ability to make long-term bets will stand it in good stead, with or without a Millner at the helm.

From the next generation coming through, the guys we've got in our team have that ability," says Tom.

"Knowing it's closed-end and we don't have to fund all these outflows in a bear market, we can actually fund the next long-term investment. That's where the continuation of our outperformance will come from. People that have already done it before will do it again. We can because we have a really good team and we look long-term. That's been the secret of our success over generations and it is still very ripe today."

# GRAHAM AND KERRIE MUNRO

Kerrie Munro's most important motto for life is a very simple one.

"Never ever give up," declares the matriarch of the deeply private Munro Group, the largest privately owned player in the $3 billion Australian footwear market with more than 290 stores nationwide and a turnover of more than $300 million.

Her three adult sons are now entrenched in the business her 84-year-old husband Graham started more than half a century ago.

The previously untold road-to-riches story for the 60-year-old and her family is an inspiring one of a mother who brought her husband and her children back from the brink.

Almost two decades ago Graham Munro went broke.

The business he started in 1950 making shoes on the shop floor of Melbourne's Myer Emporium and which 12 years later launched Australia's first footwear brand specifically designed for teenage girls grew strongly through the 1970s and 80s.

But Munro stayed in shoe manufacturing too long and paid the ultimate price.

"We should have been getting out but we didn't. We were stupid," he told me alongside his wife and sons in the boardroom of the group's Collingwood headquarters in inner-city Melbourne in early 2018.

All he could save was the family's fibro holiday shack at Cannons Creek on Melbourne's Western Port Bay, which was also mortgaged to the hilt.

The Munros lived there for a year, struggling to put food on the table. They shared a single shower cubicle and regularly got up in the dark and arrived home at midnight.

Graham Munro learnt plenty from the experience, but one thing stands out from the pack.

"To never forget it," he says bluntly.

"And I instilled into the boys it can happen and make damn sure it doesn't."

His wife is far more effusive, as are his sons.

"It taught me you don't trust banks. The banks have treated manufacturers very tough. I have always taught these boys to never let them have control of you," Kerrie Munro says, gesturing across the table to her three sons.

"We have worked really hard but we haven't taken any fancy holidays. We haven't taken any money out of the business. One thing I learnt is you can't be cash-poor. It is very hard to run a business if you are undercapitalised."

The CEO of the company, now 41-year-old Jay Munro – who used to drive container ships at sea before joining the family business – recalls "going to the supermarket and having to put all the food back because we couldn't pay for it".

"It was something I will never forget," he says.

"I never got angry. We saw how much mum worked and we always respected it. Mum used to work 7 days ... Mum is the hardest-working person I have ever seen. She is loyal to all of us and the rest of her family. Mum really has been the driving force behind the business for the past 20 years."

His younger brother 39-year-old Lee Munro says there was one positive that came out of the experience: that the family got to spend time together, which has held them in good stead in subsequent years.

"I understand and appreciate the hard times and I am probably the most conservative in business because of that," he says.

"I remember having a great time on the drive to and from Cannons

Creek. We each had four minutes in the shower cubicle each morning. But it was fun. We bonded together. It was a fun way to grow up."

## ON THE FRONT FOOT

As Paul Keating's "recession we had to have" took hold in the early 1990s and her husband worked through his bankruptcy, Kerrie Munro looked to earn an income by starting her own agency business selling shoe brands.

She paid her first visit to China and found products that were not available in the Australian market.

In 2001 she launched the Django and Juliette footwear brands, named after her twin nephew and niece that were born the same year.

She opened a shopfront in inner-city Clifton Hill and used the outside footpath as a warehouse.

Her sons, who had once played games of Cowboys and Indians around the stock in their father's shoe warehouse, often stayed home from school to help unload the shipping container straight off the docks from China. Or they were hauled out of bed during the middle of night to do it.

But Kerrie Munro says the business luckily had the right products at the right time and doubled in size every year. It was always profitable and all of her sons subsequently joined the business.

"Our success has been our products have always been wanted in the marketplace. We run a unique business in China where we have a number of small factories. We didn't have the money early on to deal with big people – we couldn't take that risk. It has made us a very disciplined business," she says.

Munro Group made seven acquisitions in 10 years, in the process picking up brands such as Midas, Mollini, Mountfords, Wanted, I Love Billy and Silent D.

In 2013 the group took control of the nation's leading online shoe store known as Styletread. Lee Munro became its CEO.

Lee Munro sees the US online retail juggernaut, which launched in Australia in late 2017, as a positive for Munro Group.

"We are keen to list our products on Amazon and work with them. We are seeing it as an opportunity. Whether that comes with a lot of challenges remains to be seen. They will generate a lot of hype and traffic to their site, and that was traffic we would not have had," he says.

"We have spoken to them. We are a registered seller on their marketplace and are working through the technology to make that happen."

His father, almost half a century his senior, says he is not frightened about Amazon, "because we have been heavily involved in that world for the past few years.

"If you had asked me that question before we did Styletread, I would be frightened to death."

His wife, who is now responsible for product development and still spends six months of the year in China liaising with the company's 25 suppliers, concurs.

"The online thing is inevitable so I am with them," she says, again pointing to her sons.

"Join it. All our wholesale customers are scared of it, they are worried about it. But these guys (her sons) have made the business grow through their ability. We (parents) don't have that so I am with them. They aren't doing too bad. But you've got to have your eyes open."

## TRANSFORMATIVE DEAL

In June 2017 the Munro family completed the biggest transaction in its history, the acquisition of Fusion Retail Brands, formerly known as Colorado Group, in an all-scrip deal after 15 months of negotiations with Godfrey's co-founder John Johnston's private company Couper Finance.

The deal added footwear brands such as Williams, Mathers, Diana Ferrari and Colorado to Munro's stable and gave Johnston a stake in Munro Group. He is also now a director of the company.

In 2018 Munro also decided to close or rebrand the retail stores of Diana Ferrari and wind up its clothing line.

Looking at raising external capital through an initial public offering has always remained an option.

"It is something we are keeping our eye on; it is something we foresee in our future. But we are focused on getting Fusion back to the powerhouse it should be in our industry," Jay Munro says.

"We are learning every day about it (a potential listing). It is something three years ago we would not have contemplated. But it is definitely something we are looking towards and we are trying to understand what it means. It is something we are thinking about."

And there is little doubt Kerrie and Graham Munro are looking for some reward from their decades of persistence and hard work. "I think that is a fair assumption," their son says with a smile, before his mother interjects with a euphoric "Yes!"

"Mum and Dad have worked hard for a long time and they deserve to take some risk off the table," he adds.

While his mother declares she would like to "step back a bit" and see more of her grandchildren, she says she will never be comfortable not working. And her sons will always live by another of her mottos.

"Never forget the past," Jay Munro answers when asked what is his mother's greatest teaching.

"Celebrate the good times but be humble about them."

# JENNIFER NASON

She is the global chair of investment banking at JP Morgan, based in New York City. She's been a key figure at one of the world's top investment banks for decades.

Yet Jennifer Nason still describes herself as a "novelty". And she hates the tag.

"Therein lies the problem. My experience shouldn't be scarce and novel," she says.

"I long for the day when I am just part of the pack that have graduated from Melbourne University, have had a career and, certainly in other people's eyes, am worth having a conversation about. Irrespective of my gender."

In March 2023 Nason was the keynote speaker the Melbourne University Foundation for Business and Economics annual dinner in Melbourne, where the theme was "women in business and economics", a topic she is deeply passionate about. But part of her wishes she did not have to be.

"I wish these labels didn't happen anymore. There is a part of me that it is always bothered by the label," she says.

She might be the most senior Australian woman on Wall Street, but the Melbournian's story is far more complex than the taglines suggest.

Nason went through a difficult divorce and brought up her four children on her own in America after earlier losing her parents within 18 months of each other, her father to a heart attack and her mother to ovarian cancer.

But the biggest hit came in 2011 when she lost her dear brother, David, after his battle with cancer. The former journalist with *The Australian* newspaper was just 57.

"It was terrible. It makes me emotional now just talking about it," she says slowly. David was seven years older than me, he was the black sheep of the family, he broke all the rules."

After being pulled out of high school, David forged a career in journalism and eventually became Darwin, Brisbane and later New York correspondent for The Australian.

There he reunited with his sister and they became close. He even interviewed her for a trade press article in 2006.

"It was a little weird. We were standing on the steps near the New York Stock Exchange. He had a photographer with him. We had such mutual pride in each other that day – here he was a journo in New York and here I was.

"He was a great journalist, he broke the mould. I still have that photo in a frame. Our parents, who had passed away before that, would have been so thrilled," she says.

All the Nason family were with David when he died in an Adelaide hospital.

"I spent a lot of time with him in that last year. I flew back to Adelaide many times. We were all there for the funeral which was a great celebration of his life," she says.

David's ashes were scattered on his favourite football field, Marrara Stadium in Darwin.

"My sister and I went to Darwin with some of his friends. He was a very good footballer and kicked most of his goals in one forward pocket at that ground. So we spread his ashes there."

Nason will always treasure the time they had together in his final years of her brother's life.

A framed caricature of David and one of his business cards now takes pride of place on the desk of her JP Morgan Office in Manhattan.

"We found each other later in life," she says. "I had tremendous respect for the course he had taken. I wish I had been more of a risk taker like he was and I think he wished he was a bit more like me. So we just found each other. Then he was gone."

## HOME LIFE

Nason describes her household growing up as one of "chaos".

Her father was an accountant and her mother worked five nights a week at Melbourne's Royal Children's Hospital.

Her parents didn't own a home until the last two years of their lives, so the family moved between rented homes frequently.

"The chaos in our family built character strengths. I have always been very good in disorganised, unstructured environments," Nason says.

Despite also being pulled out of school, another of her three elder brothers – Robert – eventually became CEO of Racing Victoria. The other, Stephen, became a well-travelled writer while her sister, Helen, is now a healthcare worker living in country Victoria.

Nason and her sister Helen were the only children her parents could afford to educate privately. She says they "killed themselves financially" to send them both to Firbank Grammar School in Brighton.

For her final year, the school trialled a year 12 economics course for girls. Nason and four other girls took it up.

"It was a game changer for me," she says.

"I grew up in a household where the dinner conversation was very political, economic and global. We were left of centre, working class, with strong family roots and always felt suspicious of the system. So when I actually studied economics, that dinner conversation gave me the applied aspect. Economics can feel very esoteric, conceptual, analytical and not very real life. But I came to it with a real life understanding of issues."

After graduating in 1983 Nason started her working career at the

Victorian Treasury. She moved to New York in 1987 with JP Morgan and eventually specialised in technology investment banking.

But her first decade abroad brought one of her biggest challenges, dealing with her sick father back home who eventually lost a long battle with heart disease.

"He died very suddenly. I had flown home to Melbourne on vacation with my young daughter and husband. We were due to go to Bendigo where my parents lived and he died of a heart attack the night before we went up there. So we never got to see him," she recalls.

Within months of her father's passing, her mother was diagnosed with ovarian cancer and died just 18 months later. She now quotes the many mottos of her parents frequently to her children.

"My mother gave me that steely determination to just get on with it. There is no way in life I could handle as much as she did and make it look effortless. So I am no nonsense, very efficient and have that perseverance gene which is the single most important factor in lasting as long as I have in this industry," Nason says.

"Then I got from my father a sense of worldliness and curiosity. He never left the country but he was an awesome armchair traveller. He was the push for me to go abroad and live overseas. So that curiosity and interest in every client I meet today comes from him."

Nason also went through a difficult divorce from her husband Alex Lipe, who she met at Melbourne University and who followed her to New York to become an investment banker with Morgan Stanley.

"It was a long and protracted divorce because points can be different on how things are divided. Then he got sick and he died shortly after we divorced at the age of just 56," she says solemnly.

"Marriages have their life cycle, it wasn't always easy and I was incredibly guarded about that. In fact maybe I felt some guilt about it and I found the process of coming to the decision to divorce harder to share with others than the decision itself. I am not angry or bitter. I wish it was otherwise. But I went through a thoughtful process and we made the right decision. I am always comfortable with the decisions I make. Divorce is one of those. I am not ashamed of it. It is just a fact, a part of my story."

She has been on her own ever since. "The most common question I get asked is whether I am single or not. I find that kind of funny – like who are you if you don't have a partner," she muses.

"I have a busy, full, interesting, entertaining life and it is not incomplete if I am on my own. I can go to a dinner or an event on my own and I am happy."

Her children – Caroline, Thomas, Eleanor and Sarah – are now all adults and have their own careers.

Nason says being a working mother has actually helped her navigate the rough and tumble of investment banking.

"I am very good at things like making decisions, allocating my time, taking calculated risks and having a full and varied life. I didn't have time to bullshit with people. I had to get on with the job. Investment bankers have an amazing capacity to fill the available time like I have never seen. I am not interested in doing that," she says.

Importantly, she has found a way to do the job differently, which she believes should be a lesson to those seeking more diversity in the industry.

"They want a rainbow of seats at the table yet they want us to do it all the same way. We have to find seats for those who have found a different way."

## MENTORS

Nason has spent the past two decades learning from one of the most decorated figures in Wall Street history, JP Morgan Chase chairman and CEO Jamie Dimon. She describes it as one of the great privileges of her life.

"The only thing he is interested in is what value you can bring to the table, whoever you are or wherever you come from," she says. "I don't think a lot of people would attach the word humility to him but people who work here do. He has very high ideals and the structure in this organisation is very flat."

It was Dimon who approved Nason taking her first external directorship in 2020 when she was approached to join the board of mining giant Rio Tinto, reconnecting her directly with her homeland.

She accepted the role because "the sheer breadth of issues Rio deals with are incredibly intellectually challenging and appealing. I would rather have a front-row seat to the China question and Rio is at forefront of that."

She says she wants to be an "insider" dealing with issues like decarbonisation and climate change, while Rio also gives her an experience far removed from the CBD glass towers of investment banking life.

"I think there is something very tangible and earthy about what Rio does versus what I do in my job everyday."

Nason joined the board just as Rio Tinto made the fateful decision to blow up two ancient rock shelters at Juukan Gorge in the Pilbara. The incident triggered an international controversy and the eventual resignation of the CEO and chair.

She believes it was useful for her to come to the boardroom discussion as an "outsider", although the Rio board was widely criticised for its response to the disaster.

"I had no history. I could be completely impartial and I think that was useful to the process. The board and company is now enormously focused on ensuring something like that doesn't happen again," she says.

Despite the trials in her life, Nason remains an optimist. She keeps a "mental top 10 highlight reel" every day to remind her of "what a great ride I am having."

But the challenges have also given her a steely resolve and a zero tolerance for unnecessary risk-taking, big egos or "bullshit" from her colleagues or clients.

"I work at a great company. I have really smart and great colleagues. But there is still an element of bravado and Masters of the Universe that I have no time for. I wish my male colleagues in the industry were more open minded about what it takes to be successful in this field," she says.

She's been criticised, called "an empty suit" and some have "scratched their heads" at how she wins deals and keeps clients.

"That has been damn hard. I have certainly questioned and doubted myself in those moments," she says.

"These days they are just curious about it. But they don't question if it is happening. I think the proof is now in the pudding."

# RACHAEL NEUMANN

Rachael Neumann and Jodie Auster took their first born on his first long-haul flight when he was just six weeks old in April 2011.

"We went to America to introduce Miles to my family," says Neumann, a management consultant-turned-venture capitalist who hails from Long Island, New York, but has lived in Melbourne since 2009.

"Most normal, sane parents would not have travelled with a six week old back to New York."

It is a trip now forever burned in her memory. It was the last time she hugged her younger brother, Jacob.

"That was the only time that my brother ever met Miles. I have this beautiful picture of him holding him. I feel really grateful that at least that happened," she says.

On September 28, 2021, Jacob Neumann was killed in a motorcycle accident in Arizona. He was only 21. The day before Jacob died, he Skyped with Miles and his sister for 40 minutes, exclaiming how much he "absolutely-freakin-lutely" adored his nephew.

"It was really something that was not even on my radar as a possibility," Neumann now says of his passing.

"It hits you losing a sibling. Then in this moment of early motherhood, you think about what it might be like to lose a child. I joke I've only been to therapy with my wife twice in our 15-year relationship.

"One was to deal with her lateness. The other one was to work through the fact that I didn't want to have a second child.

"I thought the more kids I had, the more risk of something happening to them. So I actually had to work through that. I'm glad I did, because I now have a beautiful daughter." Juliet was born in 2015.

Neumann and Auster were married in America in August 2013, two months after the US Supreme Court formerly recognised marriage equality.

"We went to City Hall in the morning to get married and to the courthouse in the afternoon to finalise my son's adoption. We just thought, 'Let's tick every box there is to tick'," Neumann says.

Nearly a decade on, Miles is almost a teenager, Juliet is eight and Neumann and Auster have carved their own paths in the Australian technology and corporate sectors.

Neumann is the co-founder of Flying Fox Ventures, a rapidly expanding early stage venture capital firm. She is also a former managing director of event management tech platform Eventbrite Australia and now on the Council of Trustees for the National Gallery of Victoria, fulfilling her long-held passion for art.

Auster is a strategic adviser to the global chief executive at ride-share giant Uber after previously running its food delivery subsidiary, Uber Eats, in the Asia Pacific.

In July she started a three-year term as a director of Australia Post and is on the board of listed investment company AMCIL.

Neumann also has another, less-known claim to fame: She is one of the best friends and an ex-school buddy of Academy Award-winning actor Natalie Portman.

In August 2023 they spent a month together while Portman was visiting Australia and New Zealand for the women's soccer World Cup. Neumann is also an investor in Los Angeles' Angel City Football Club – the US soccer team Portman founded in 2020.

"It is always the best to spend time with her. I've been papped by photographers at many things with her and I'm slightly offended I am not identified as her new love interest," Neumann quips with a smile.

She believes that dealing with the grief following her brother's passing was a profound turning point in her life. Initially, she threw herself into her work. But then she recalls standing in a coffee queue a few months after his death.

"I remember thinking, 'No one here knows that my brother just died and this pain that I'm feeling'. It made me realise that you literally have no idea what's going on in people's lives," she says.

"Everyone is fighting their own battles. So that was one kind of insight that I try and take through my life."

It has also shaped her work with thousands of start-ups around the globe, including as head of start-ups for Amazon Web Services in Australia and New Zealand, and now at Flying Fox.

The latter firm has already deployed $25m in funding into 50 companies and is raising at least $20m for a more traditional fixed-term fund that will make 30 to 40 investments in early stage start-ups.

One of its backers is Rachael's friend and mentor, Reserve Bank of Australia director Carol Schwartz and her husband Alan.

"I think living in this world of start-ups where anything can happen, where all of a sudden you get a pandemic or the sentiment around the industry changes overnight, you can't control those things," Neumann says.

"You just manage through it with as steady a hand as possible. So I think that's actually what my brother's death taught me is everyone is fighting a battle that's invisible to you and there is no rhyme or reason. You have control over very, very little."

## RISING FROM ADVERSITY

Neumann's father's parents were Holocaust survivors who escaped from Vienna and Berlin to settle in New York. German was never spoken in their home. They would never buy a German car and deliberately gave all of their children Anglo-sounding names.

Her mother was one of eight children born into a Lutheran Church-going family outside of Buffalo, New York, who had never met a Jewish person until she met Neumann's father, Peter.

After leaving school, Neumann completed an undergraduate degree at Stanford University and two Masters degrees from Columbia University.

Her stint at Stanford came after she scored a scholarship there to play soccer and lacrosse. She played goalkeeper in both sports. Her mental coach at Stanford was famed sports psychologist Dr Jerry Lynch.

"This was very early in the days of the mental game as being important as your physical. We did visualisation on 'How do I fail and how do I reset?'. My coach would have me mentally play the game 10 to 20 times more than I played it on the field," Neumann says.

"Those skills are things I bring forward in my life. I always ask 'What is the worst case scenario here?' Once you have identified it, play it over 100 times in your mind and you are ready to deal with it if it happens."

She still has two mental coaches – one in America and one in Australia.

Neumann believes her experience of elite sport has taught her to challenge what she calls the "hustle culture" of the modern world that she believes is detrimental to financial returns in business.

"Elite athletes always work recovery into their training. It is absolutely essential. Hustle culture ignores all the science and data around rest and recovery. It assumes the ends justify the means," she says.

"A start-up is always a marathon, not a sprint. So you need to do what is necessary for endurance."

Neumann has always believed that athletes make amazing business people because they know how to play in a team, pursue excellence, and to endure pain and setbacks. She now wants to find a way to get more athletes into business.

"One of the things I have noticed is how much sport has given me in my business life," she says.

"Many companies don't see this treasure trove of talent that sits within elite sports people. It is a market failure. I want to help fix that.

"I want companies to benefit from their skills. I'm actively working to make this happen at a larger scale than has been done before."

She stresses her interest in the Angel City soccer club is an investment in, not a donation to, Natalie Portman's cause, which is also backed by stars such as Jennifer Garner, Eva Longoria, Serena Williams, singer Becky G, Billie Jean King and Mia Hamm.

"On paper this is one of the best investments I have ever made. Put your capital to work to build the thing you want to see," she says.

"The timing of this was perfect because never before have we had a confluence of things around gender equity, sports and women sport."

She and Portman have been close friends since 8th grade.

"We were paired together when we were 12 at school. Our principal made us buddies. She is brilliant academically. She went to Harvard like me. We are both book worms and love learning," Neumann says.

"She is a great friend to bounce ideas off and gives me wise counsel.

"There is something so special about a friendship that is 40 years old. There is an unconditional love that will always be there. She has a handful of friends like me who were there well before her life in the spotlight began."

## LOVE CONQUERS ALL

Neumann met Jodie Auster, an Australian-born doctor, at a Boston Consulting Group recruiting dinner while both were earning their MBAs at Columbia Business School.

"We both have non-traditional backgrounds to business. We are not afraid to follow our intellectual curiosities to a career that is a non-traditional path," Neumann says.

"The defining word for both our careers is 'Yes!' We are not afraid if something doesn't necessarily work out."

But the trials they have endured in obtaining dual citizenship for Miles, who was born before marriage equality was legalised in America, have been truly testing.

Neumann is listed on Miles' birth certificate as his legal parent, which should automatically grant him US citizenship as it would to any other child born abroad to at least one American parent.

But they are still waiting.

"We have been in bureaucratic purgatory for about 12 years. It hasn't been resolved," Neumann says.

She also describes the adoption process she went through for Miles as "very demeaning".

"You are the first person to hold your child when he's born and you have raised that child. To then go through an adoption process where you have a social worker in your house, observing you and reporting like 'Miles seems to have a bonded relationship with Rachel.'

No sh.t. I'm his mother," she snaps.

"The whole thing was an exercise in bureaucratic box ticking and was highly offensive."

Neumann became an Australian citizen in 2021 to ensure they now have at least one citizenship in common for the family.

She now wonders whether they will even bother pushing for Miles' US citizenship.

The family's retreat from the world in these difficult moments – and to de-stress generally – has been a farm they purchased in 2017 in the Macedon Ranges outside Melbourne near a tiny town called Bullengarook.

The catalyst for the move came one morning when Neumann and her children were watching an ABC TV program titled Dirt Girl.

"When she signs off she says, 'Don't forget kids, get dirty'. I just had this visceral reaction that my children – who at the time were probably one and five – had nowhere to get dirty like I used to," Neumann says

"I know this is crazy, but at that moment I said 'I think I need land'."

The family now goes to the farm most weekends.

"To me, it represents an opportunity to think outside the box and literally go and be in land. It represents giving my kids the freedom that I had to explore and get hurt, be dirty, and be free," she says.

Neumann can never bring her brother back. But his memory has inspired her in the decade since his death to never waste a day.

"Losing a sibling is like losing a limb. It is such a terrible loss, especially when it is unexpected and when he was so young," she says.

"It is now 12 years since his passing. Over time, I've realised that life is short and unpredictable and it is about how you spend your time in the moment."

She still recalls thinking to herself in the week after his death "This isn't fair, why did this happen to me?"

"And then my inner voice quickly said, 'Well, who should happen to deserve this?'," she says.

"Life is all just a game of chance. S-t happens and you just have to figure out how to live through it."

# FIONA PAK-POY

It was the longest and hardest plane trip of Fiona Pak-Poy's life.

She had been in Southern California doing work experience for a global engineering company in the first week of January in 1988 when she got a call from her older sister Cathryn that she will never forget.

Her father, Patrick, had died suddenly while skiing in the Italian alps. He was only 54.

"He'd had a lovely day out skiing with mum and all his Italian friends and sat down for a lovely meal. Then he had a heart attack."

She immediately boarded a flight to her hometown of Adelaide, where her father's body was being flown.

"It was just the most horrible flight ever. I remember when I was checking in I asked for a window seat because I was so upset. I'd spent the day with my brother's friend's mother, this lovely lady who wanted to sort of cocoon me and wrap me up and took me to the airport," she says. "They wouldn't let me. So, I had to sit in the aisle just bawling my eyes out for 12 hours. Strangers were walking by and asking if I was fine. It was just so horrible. That feeling of being so helpless and just totally thinking 'This can't be happening, this is not true'."

Patrick Gerald Pak-Poy was one of Australia's most notable Chinese-born entrepreneurs.

His parents were born in Darwin after his grandparents emigrated from China in the late 1800s. The family evacuated to Adelaide during the Japanese bombings of the Second World War.

After leaving school Patrick moved to Sydney and became one of the earliest graduates of the Master of Engineering Science (Transportation and Traffic) from the University of New South Wales, where he also studied Town Planning.

In 1965 he returned to Adelaide to start what became a famed international consulting group called PG Pak-Poy & Associates.

It worked on iconic projects such as the construction of Adelaide's iconic Rundle Mall, the Adelaide casino built inside the city's historic railway station, and Canberra's iconic Hyatt Hotel.

He also served as an adviser to the Federal and State Governments on economic development, trade and tourism and worked for the World Bank.

Fiona, the youngest of his children, studied engineering at Adelaide University thinking she would eventually work in his business. But upon his shock passing, she was thrown head-first into it as the sole family representative. Her siblings were not involved.

She was forced to take a year away from her passion of playing hockey after making the Australian Under-21 team and just missing the senior squad for the Seoul Olympics. That year it became the first to win an Olympic gold medal.

"Dad was my mentor and a true optimist. His philosophy was always success breeds success. So that is something which I've always thought – that if work hard, you can achieve," she says.

They were skills that steeled her for a career as a management consultant with The Boston Consulting Group, then as a General Partner in a venture capital fund that invested in high tech startups. She also secured an MBA from Harvard Business School.

After serving on the boards of MYOB, Novotech and Insentia, she is now the chairman of listed payments group Tyro. It is her first public company chairmanship after she took over from David Thodey in March 2023.

For the previous nine months Tyro had been in takeover talks with private equity group Potentia Capital Management, which collapsed in spectacular fashion in May 2023.

Despite the failure of the talks, she is philosophical about the process and the outcome.

"Having worked with on both sides of deals, lots of transactions, . lots of IPOs, you can see and understand different motivations. When you are in negotiations, it is not really helpful to just put a wall up and say, 'Well, this is our view, take it or leave it' You really need to try to understand what the other party is thinking," Pak-Poy says.

"That doesn't mean it is easy. It was a really challenging process."

She reiterates that the board and management remain confident and excited about the company's outlook, especially after Tyro recently upgraded its earnings guidance and announced that it now offers 'tap to pay' on iPhones which can accept contactless payments.

Tyro is one of only a handful of public companies that have both a female chair and a majority of female directors and going forward, Pak-Poy says her focus will continue on being "exceptionally well organised" in her thinking and leadership style.

"You've got changing leadership teams, you've got growth aspirations, you've got market change, you've got an uncertain economy and then you've had a complex M&A situation. So there is a lot to get your head around," she says.

"You certainly need to be fair when considering all shareholders, which requires good people skills where you can really try to draw the best out of the board."

She says she has learned a lot from Thodey, a former chief executive of Telstra.

"One of my favourite quotes is that on a board, if everybody is thinking the same thing then no one is thinking, because you want people to voice their different opinions. But at some point, you need to draw the discussion to a close. David was good at that," she says.

"I would like to think that I have learned that skill. You have to pick your battles. But as long as people understand that their views are being heard, that is what is most important."

## ANNUS HORRIBILIS

1989 was the year from hell for Pak-Poy as she was single-handedly forced to keep her family's business going while still grieving over the loss of her hero.

"It was really our business yet I wasn't sitting up there in dad's office in the front. I had no title, no nothing and I was still incredibly emotional," she says of being given a "cupboard size" space at the back of the office to work in.

"It was just the most stressful year ever because I had to work with the lawyers, the accountants, the management and the board. I had to learn about balance sheets and profit and loss and try to understand whether what the accountants was telling me was true."

But she remembered her father's life lessons: What doesn't kill you makes you stronger; be fair, honest and always believe in yourself; and on big decisions, think carefully about the pros and cons.

Eventually the business was sold in a management buy-out a year later.

"What we didn't know at the time was that we had been approached by significant overseas companies, including (US engineering giant) Parsons Brinckerhoff. The family was not told, so were sideswiped by the management," she says.

The sale generated enough wealth to keep her mother Barbara and the family "comfortable", but by no means rich-listers.

It retains Patrick Pak-Poy's original family home in the Adelaide Hills, which he purchased from Reginald Murray "R.M." Williams, the famed Australian bushman and entrepreneur. The family still returns there for holidays.

Fifteen years later in 2015, Pak-Poy had just finished playing in a hockey semi-final in Sydney when she went for a routine mammogram. After being sent for a biopsy, she was told she had breast cancer.

"I was like, 'What? That can't be true. I thought I didn't have any risk factors as no one in my family ever had it. I was fit and healthy, I breastfed the kids, I had not lost weight. So why would I have it?"

But the diagnosis was definitive.

She immediately told her husband and together they prepared to deliver the devastating news to their three teenage children when they came home from school.

"It was literally a massive shock for them and we just sat together holding each other, talking, crying and hugging. It was actually a really beautiful afternoon in a very sad way because we were just so close as a family. I didn't know what to expect," she says.

"But I've always been a very positive person, partly due to my dad's perspective on life. So I thought, 'Well, I'll just tackle it with gusto, find out all the facts and get the best information I can. I studied all the research."

Pak-Poy then went through a traumatic period of treatment while one of her daughters was finishing the HSC. She was so sick she couldn't attend most of the final graduation events.

"I did come out of hospital one night after three operations in three weeks and went to the second graduation dinner. I had to keep people around me as bodyguards because I didn't want to say what had happened. But I got through it," she says.

She finished her radiation treatment on December 23, 2015, returned to Adelaide for Christmas and started training with her son to return to the hockey field. Remarkably she then played the 2016 season.

"It helps to be fit when you face adversity because I think the fitter you are before anything happens, the easier you can get through it. Then you need to have the mind strength and mindset to rebuild your fitness afterwards," she says.

"But worrying doesn't help. The more you are positive, the more it can impact your family because you don't want them worrying."

She still plays hockey and will forever miss the motivational notes her father used to slip into her training bag when she aspired to be an Olympian and got within touching distance of playing in a a gold medal winning team.

She has represented South Australia, New South Wales and Australia in under-age, Open and Masters hockey and is still involved in the sport as an administrator.

Last year she took time away from hockey to walk the 211-mile John Muir Trail, a world-famous trek in the Sierra Nevada mountain range of California, passing through Yosemite, Kings Canyon and Sequoia National Parks.

She was in the wilderness for 3 weeks, walking at elevations as high as 4000 metres above sea level.

"It was extremely challenging, but a lot of fun," she says.

She still regrets losing the family business three decades ago, but isn't sure the family would still have it even if her father was alive today.

"I think times have changed. Dad's mindset was to build a business and stay in. He had such a huge commitment to his employees," she says.

"But I think these days, particularly with my experience of going in and out of businesses, there would be more of a realisation that it is okay to sell if you get to the point where you can actually make some money. Yes I am sad that we didn't have the business longer because dad wasn't around. But ultimately I think that perhaps we would have moved on to something else anyway because he just had so many ideas."

She still misses him.

"I wish I could still get his feedback and advice because I relished it so much," she says.

"I think he'd be very excited by what I have done with my life so far. But also extremely proud."

# JIM PENMAN

David "Jim" Penman celebrated his 70th birthday in May 2022.

The man whose famous smiling bearded caricature – complete with hard-yakka hat – is splashed across the thousands of vans and trucks of his famed Jim's Group in Australia and in three countries abroad, told me in an interview ahead of the milestone that he could not believe how good his health was.

But it had not always been that way.

"I had a problem many years ago with fits, I would lose my memory and sometimes even collapse. It was very worrying. My mind would go blank. Originally, they thought it was something like transient global amnesia because I would forget everything that happened, briefly, in the last 24 hours," he told me.

He saw many doctors and specialists, but none were able to diagnose his condition.

"Then I started doing some reading myself. One thing I recognised is that cold water on the head can trigger these things. I used to and still have cold showers most mornings, but I used to put my head directly under the cold water in the middle of winter. As soon as I stopped doing that, it all stopped. So I went to see these really, really specialised people, but nobody ever asked about the triggers," he said.

Penman is a big proponent of the Medicare universal healthcare system in Australia but claimed his experience showed him it is, as he put it, "too superficial", leading doctors to conduct shorter and simpler consultations with bad outcomes for patients.

It is one of the reasons why he wants to take his Jim's Group, one of the largest franchise groups in Australia offering more than 55 different services operated by 4000 franchisees and attracting 35,000 customers every day, further into health.

Physiotherapy and optometry services were in his thinking, as was a Jim's Doctor service. Four years ago Jim's expanded into personal training, where trainers visit clients with mobile gyms.

After starting as the Jim's Mowing franchise in 1989, Jim's Group now offers services such as cleaning, removals, pool care, dog grooming, traffic control, computer services, pest control, painting and locksmiths. Laundry started last year and has 23 franchisees.

The group has also started a scratch and dent repair service for cars.

The Jim's Group empire is run from the Foothills Conference Centre – a former Swinburne University campus, a two-minute walk from the front door of Penman's home – nestled in bushland on a 9-hectare property at Mooroolbark, 31km east of Melbourne.

In March 2022 the property hosted Jim's annual family and trade day, the first for two years because of Covid, themed around Jim's Group's commitment to going green and incorporating more environmentally friendly technology and practices into its day-to-day operations.

International brands such as Milwaukee, Mikita, Dulux Construction Solutions, LDV, Renault, EGO, Ecoteq, MeanGreen and Pellenc offered incentives and discounts to help Jim's franchisees use green technology in their work. More than 2000 people attended.

But in our interview Penman revealed he had bigger ambitions for the business beyond its move into health and going green.

He wants to take Jim's into North America and Europe and has been seeking an external investor to sink $100m into the Jim's Group parent company to supercharge its growth. Jim's is already in New Zealand, the UK and Canada.

He had a similar dream a decade ago when he made an unsuccessful bid for $10m in funding for expansion, including a float on the ASX that never happened.

This time he believes the group's sophisticated franchise management softwear systems will make it more match-fit for external investment and international growth.

Jim's Group in Australia grew revenues by 10 per cent in 2021 to more than $500m despite the pandemic, when Penman was a vocal opponent of the Andrews government's lockdowns in Victoria.

Penman said the booming demand for home services meant that over 40 per cent of leads for services were being unmet because Jim's Group didn't have enough franchisees. By his count 90,000 leads remained outstanding in 2022.

So that year he launched a Registered Training Organisation based at Mooroolbark to provide a fresh pipeline of skilled workers for his franchisees.

"We have a big advantage over TAFEs in that the people teaching will be people in the field, running their own business. I think we can actually do extraordinary things," he said.

## COURTING CONTROVERSY

Penman's story was first fully documented four years ago in his biography by novelist Catherine Moolenschot, titled The Surprising Story of Jim Penman, Australia's Backyard Millionaire.

The warts-and-all book explained how Penman turned a few mowing rounds in Melbourne in the late 1980s into a nationwide corporate juggernaut.

But in it Penman spoke of his "profoundly flawed" life and Moolenschot wrote of his "temper and unorthodox communication style", and some of his business decisions that "put many off side" over the years.

These included his estranged sister Gill Moxham, whom he sacked from the business in 2011. She claimed four years ago that Penman's move had left her "poverty stricken" and while her brother feels sad about their falling out, he doesn't regret his decision.

"You can't keep someone on just because they are family if they're not doing the job because it demoralises every other staff member. You can't just give someone a job, they have to deserve it," he reiterated resolutely.

In 2010, Jim's Group's master franchisors – who effectively run the divisions or are responsible for regions within those divisions – also held a "referendum" demanding Penman stand down because of concerns with his leadership style, alleged breaches of contract, and steep fee hikes.

He eventually reached agreement on the fee and master franchise issues, but not before the dispute made national headlines.

Penman has been married four times and has 11 children. He has been with his fourth wife, Li, for nearly two decades and she is the mother of his four youngest kids.

When I asked if he wanted the children to succeed him in the business, Penman firstly declared his deep concern that any potential future corporate owner of the business could "destroy it" by ignoring long term thinking in the pursuit of short term profits.

"You could probably double or triple your short-term profit, if you really did it in a certain way, but it would destroy it and it would destroy the franchisees that are my people, my tribe. So, my biggest concern is that whoever takes over will just go for short term money. So, I'm hoping it will be possible for some of my children to take over," he said.

"My daughter, Jasmine, she's a wonderful young lady. I'm hoping that one day she might be somebody who could do it. The main reason for that is Jasmine is not just capable, she's also very ethical. She would not allow franchisees to be treated like that."

In addition to being estranged from his sister, Penman doesn't speak to three of his older children, which pains him greatly.

"That is their choice," he said.

"I've got a complicated history. When you get divorced, even though it wasn't really my choice to get divorced, it causes strains in various ways. Divorce is a terrible thing. I always thought I'd be married for life. So when it does happen it hurts kids."

Asked if there was a motto for life he has learned from the tough times, he replied instantly, with a wry smile: "Be really careful who you get married to."

## OTHER PASSIONS

Outside work, Penman's treasured pastime is scientific research, particularly studies on mental illness.

He has authored bio-history titles and co-authored numerous papers in journals, although his early writings were criticised for being too extreme and "wild" for serious scientific consideration.

"The research project I am working on now is actually really important," he said of the project dealing with mental illness, depression and anxiety to which he donates $1m each year, run with RMIT and The Florey Institute of Neuroscience and Mental Health.

"I'd like to really expand that. I hope as Jim's Group grows, that will happen. My will, such as it is, is basically going to donate Jim's Group to the Research Foundation. The children get a little bit of help with buying houses, but that's it. They are never going to live off the business. I don't believe in inherited wealth. It's bad for kids and bad for society."

Despite his wealth, Penman still drives an old Mitsubishi Outlander which hasn't been washed for months. He doesn't take overseas trips or own expensive clothes and prefers a meal at the local takeaway over fine dining.

He is now an evangelical Christian after being a militant agnostic until his conversion at 28.

His passion for religion has made him more conscious of his personal failings, but immensely proud of what he does do well.

"I'm very introverted and was extremely introverted when I was growing up. I don't read social clues very well. Everybody has their strengths and weaknesses, I have very considerable strengths. I'm intensely creative. Even at 69, my mind is full of new ideas all the time, some of which are actually quite good, most of which are complete crap, of course. I'm very idealistic, very passionate, I care deeply about the people I deal with – my franchisees and my family and people like that," he said.

"But there's other sides to me that are not so positive. I get impatient easily. I really have had to control my temper. I can easily say things that I regret and sometimes I just don't notice the way people are reacting to me.

"One of the most important virtues that anybody can have in business and in life is a degree of humility. If you look upon yourself as being a perfect person, then you're not going to take action against the things that are wrong with you. Whereas I am struggling to be a better person, to be a kinder person, to be more thoughtful. It's a lifelong struggle."

Penman still takes a cold shower most mornings, always after a vigorous session of 30 minutes of treadmill running, then rowing and weight training.

He said he would he never retire from the business he founded.

"I will die in harness, unless I go senile. Not a year goes by when my role doesn't change in any way and I love that," he said.

Australia's Backyard Millionaire might be viewed by some as a polarising character, by others as a hero. He detests the latter tag.

"I wouldn't like to be in a situation where people look up at me and say, 'Oh, that guy's so amazing. I couldn't possibly do anything like that'," he said.

"I'd rather they look at me and say, 'Well, you know, okay, he's achieved good things. He's got all these faults and failings and weaknesses. Now, if Jim can do that, surely I can do it'."

# ELIZABETH PROUST

It was to become an all too familiar experience for Elizabeth Proust.

Shortly after being appointed chief executive of the Melbourne City Council in 1990 – the first woman to hold the role – she was invited to attend a Christmas cocktail party at the NAB's stuffy Bourke Street headquarters.

"Bill Irvine was chairman. I went there because they were bankers to the city. Bill started the night by saying: 'Elizabeth and gentlemen.' This was in a big room. And at that point I realised the only other women were the waitresses. There have been many such times," she says.

At 37, Proust became the first woman to run a Victorian government department – the Attorney-General's – before going on to be secretary of the Department of Premier and Cabinet under Jeff Kennett.

When she quit halfway into a five-year contract to be the first big hire by the ANZ's new CEO, John McFarlane, in January 1998, she still stood out from the crowd.

"Of the top 60 staff in the bank, I was the second woman. So it was a very white Anglo-Saxon male company. A number of women, including Alison Watkins (who later became the chairman of Coca Cola Amatil and Graincorp) were hired while I was there."

Fast forward a quarter of a century and Proust went on to build a storied boardroom portfolio, which has made one of nation's most respected directors.

As well as serving on the boards of listed public companies Perpetual and Spotless, she has been the chairman of Nestle Australia and the Westpac-owned Bank of Melbourne, and a director at Insurance

Manufacturers of Australia, Sinclair Knight Merz and the Australia Council's Major Performing Arts Board.

In 2010, she was made an Officer of the Order of Australia for her service to public administration and business and as a mentor to women.

As one woman who has succeeded in breaking into the so-called directors' club, her advice to aspiring board members is simple – and she says the tricks are the same for men or women.

"I have lots of cups of tea and coffee with aspiring directors, both male and female. I say to them, especially if I think they lack the experience and the skills, that they need to have a track record that gives boards a compelling reason to hire them. It isn't enough for a thirty-something to say: 'Being on a board suits my lifestyle.' That is not what it is about. And it underplays the reputational, as well as financial, risks," she says,

"I also encourage them to work with a school council, charity or not-for-profit. Boards are increasingly looking for diverse skill sets. There are some great boards in the not-for-profit space and you get good experience at an early age. It is not just giving something to the community and learning something. It is networking."

Indeed, those who know her well say Proust is a consummate networker. She's also a rarity in having crossed the public-private divide in Australia.

"I found in ANZ some puzzlement about what I would have done all day in Premier and Cabinet," Proust recalls.

"There is still not enough movement between the public and private sectors and that does contribute to a lack of understanding and maybe suspicion. So the private sector can often be ham-fisted in dealing with government."

## TOE CUTTER

In her big public-service jobs, Proust earned a reputation as "queen of the toe-cutters".

In her tenure at the Melbourne City Council, she oversaw substantial change and cut staff from 3000 to fewer than 1000. And, according to insiders, when she joined ANZ as its global head of human resources she brought in an aggressive approach to restructuring the business and took on the unions.

However, it is difficult to imagine the impeccably polite Proust as a hatchet woman. Educated by Catholic nuns in NSW, she moved to Melbourne after her schooling to do youth work with the group Catholic Social Action.

There she met her husband, Brian. She is still a practising Catholic, although she says "it is hard to be one these days with all the scandals".

Proust is "outcome-oriented", says Jeff Kennett.

"With us, she was more an executor of ideas and programs than an originator of them. But she is a very practical lady. She has good strong values, she has a clear, analytical mind and – most importantly – she executes."

Proust says she always got on with Kennett.

Not once did he ask about her politics, though she was a member of the ALP until she joined the public service.

"We had disagreements on policy issues, but it was about affairs of state. We had a very cordial, professional relationship." So he never lost his temper? "No."

Her time at ANZ (she left at the end of 2005, after moving from HR to run metropolitan banking, then Esanda) is viewed positively.

McFarlane saw her as a strong administrator, but lacking the background for bigger roles. Proust admits that was always an obstacle. "I had never been a banker and even after eight years there I never described myself as one as I think banking is life-long learning."

She will not comment on whether McFarlane or ANZ chairman Charles Goode stayed too long, but expresses puzzlement at ANZ's involvement in the $700 million collapse of stockbroker Opes Prime.

ANZ was the company's banker when it failed in 2008. "I find Opes Prime inexplicable really, because it was a hands-on board. The credit and trading risk committee was a group of hands-on, senior executives. Knowing how things worked while I was there, I don't know how it happened."

At Perpetual and Spotless, Proust had to deal with private equity approaches for both companies – always a challenge for a director, not only for what is riding on the outcome, but for the time it takes up.

KKR's unsolicited offer for Perpetual in 2010 took several months to resolve.

"The board met almost every day through the KKR process, on the phone or face to face. So you need to make sure when you take on your board roles that there is enough time for the unexpected, whether it's private equity or something else," she says.

## THE DIRECTOR'S CLUB

In 2015 Proust took on the role of chairwoman of the Australian Institute of Company Directors, the peak body for the nation's directors, where she was never backward in coming forward with a view – especially when it came to advocating for the advancement of women on boards.

When Proust took up her role as AICD chairman, the peak director body's own statistics showed the ASX 200 only had 20.6 per cent female representation on its boards. That number had risen to 28.5 per cent by the end of August 2018.

In late 2018, when Proust finished her three year term, she granted me her only exit interview and did not hold back when I asked her whether she believed the treatment of former AMP chairman Catherine Brenner, which led to her leaving the company in 2017, was "sexist".

"I think it was," she declared.

"Male and female journalists talked about what she was wearing, did she spend enough time with her family. It was all said through a gender lens."

Brenner and AMP CEO Craig Meller resigned from the company after the Hayne royal commission revealed AMP had charged clients fees, despite providing no services.

The inquiry also revealed attempts by AMP to interfere with an independent report into the scandal being prepared for the corporate regulator.

In the interview Proust also expressed her fears that more talented business people would shun serving on listed company boards because of the increased risks of being a director, especially in the wake of the scrutiny and publicity of the Hayne royal commission.

Proust said it would be "bad for the country" if talented, properly qualified people avoided listed company directorships.

She was clear that she would not be one of them.

"I don't focus so much on the risks, but I am mindful of them. You do the due diligence before you join and then you are there for the good and the bad," she said

"The thing that's more in my mind is ensuring that there's enough time to focus on the strategy and growing the business. The danger is that you might spend so much time on compliance that what you are really there to do – to add value – can be pushed to one side."

Yet she claimed she had heard anecdotal reports of people stepping down from chief executive and other management roles in public companies – who would normally take up directorships – saying words to the effect: "There is too much risk – I am going to do something else."

"Memories are short, we may all forget what it was like to look at somebody on television in the witness box, being glad it is not us. But I think people will make a decision that the risk-reward trade-off is not there, especially if you are in financial services," she said.

"I know directors by community standards seem to be highly paid but if effectively you are being expected to be a full-time director of one financial institution, then compared to all the executives in the institution, you are not highly paid."

Proust also said demands for directors to hold shares in their companies and pay for them with after-tax dollars could also lead to a situation where only wealthy people would serve on boards.

"Do we only want people of means on our boards? I think that is absolutely a question we need to ask and answer," she said.

"The risks have only increased. People do have choices, they can be consultants, they can go into private equity, they can do other things. Who do you want on boards and what experience do you want them to have had? It is now not just direct shareholders that have an interest in this. Every Australian, with their superannuation in shares, has a very big stake in the success of these companies."

While the AICD has more than 43,000 members across ASX, private, government and not-for-profit boards, Proust said commentary flowing from the Hayne royal commission showed there was a misunderstanding in the community about the role of directors.

"I think there is a view that they are there to stop anything bad happening. The royal commission might have inadvertently given them that impression," she said.

"It doesn't matter if you are running a business of 10 people or 10,000 people, you can't give guarantees. You can give guarantees about having a culture that lets stuff-ups be known about very quickly and rectified and people compensated, if that needs to happen. Two million people in Australia call themselves directors. The sports club, the charity. So that means one in 12 of us is a director. But do people really understand what it means?"

# ELANA RUBIN

It was one of the most intense periods of Elana Rubin's corporate career – and also the most thrilling. As chair of BNPL (buy-now-pay-later) juggernaut Afterpay, founded by millennials Anthony Eisen and Nick Molnar, Rubin was at the centre of months of intense private negotiations in 2021, which ended in the $39b acquisition of the Australian trailblazer firm by US digital payments giant Square – now renamed Block – founded by former Twitter CEO Jack Dorsey. This all-stock deal was the largest merger in Australian corporate history. Block would subsequently take a substantial hit in the market.

Rubin had joined the Afterpay board in 2017, when it merged with Touchcorp, whose board she had been on since it listed in 2015. Touchcorp provided the technology platform for Afterpay. After Touchcorp's CEO died suddenly in November 2015, the board undertook a strategic review of the business and commenced discussions with Afterpay about merging the two companies. Rubin became chair in 2020. A year later, Square executives held their first discussions with Afterpay co- founder Nick Molnar in Hawaii for the deal that became known internally as "Project Pocket".

As the COVID-19 pandemic was in full swing globally, all the negotiations were done virtually. "We had an adviser based in the US, we had advisers in Sydney, one of our advisers was across the Tasman, our staff were working remotely and our directors were in all different locations," says Rubin. "We also had an adviser to the board separate to the transaction. So we had a wide range of players and were spread across the world."

She says the internal Afterpay team working on the deal were utterly forensic in tracking the issues, "documenting and listing literally everything". Rubin herself chaired a board subcommittee for the deal that met at least twice a week.

"That gave us a degree of confidence we had our arms around the transaction," she says. "We spent a lot of time not just around the financials, but around the strategic rationale, because we'd all been involved in things that looked sensible on paper, but the opportunities never really came through because there was a lack of clarity about the strategic alignment. Where the culture wasn't right, the purpose between the two groups was different."

Afterpay and Square are both disruptors, providing their customers with financial freedom and giving them alternatives to traditional banking products. What their merger deal was really about was bringing AfterPay's merchant relationships into Square's seller ecosystem and converting AfterPay's existing customer base into Square app users.

When it was eventually struck in August 2021, the deal valued Afterpay at 42 times its annual revenues and made it core to Square's payments ecosystem, which includes a consumer app used by 70 million Americans, and payments hardware and software used by more than one million US merchants.

Rubin never doubted it was the right strategic move for Afterpay. However, she still held her breath when the deal was publicly announced to the Australian Stock Exchange on the morning of 2 August, 2021.

"Afterpay was a company everybody had an opinion on," says Rubin. "So there is an element that while you believe the deal is the right thing and you have tested it thoroughly, you still just hope that when it sees the light of day, other people will share that and you can be confident about it. But there's always just that little bit of baited breath as you see people's reactions. What was interesting is once the transaction was announced and we went out and spoke to shareholders and merchant partners, they all got the strategic piece. That was really pleasing, in that having tested ourselves and really worked through the issues, when we were able to explain it and put it forward publicly, everybody said, 'Yep'."

## M&A FRENZY

The deal was the biggest of a total of US$256b in merger and acquisition transactions announced in Australia during 2021, far and away the highest annual value on record, amid an explosion of corporate activity after the abrupt lull brought by the pandemic.

The frenzy continued in 2022, as the spectre of interest rate rises failed to offset other powerful factors driving M&A activity, including board confidence and cash looking for a home.

Elana Rubin says having the right process for any M&A transaction is vitally important at the outset for its success. "That may differ by transaction, but having a very clear process and the right team is really important. Having the time available to explore the ideas, test the assumptions and work through all the issues is really important," she says, noting the Afterpay board met at least twice a week once the initial discussions started with Square. "Being clear, not only around the financial story, but the strategic rationale for the transaction, and being as confident as you can that you're able to deliver the opportunity of bringing together two organisations, are also really important."

Afterpay ensured it had a number of different points of contact and work streams with Square during the negotiations. "So it was very much a collective effort to reach the positions that we took," says Rubin. "Then it was a matter of having the best person or group to convey those during the negotiation."

Remarkably, for such a massive deal in financial terms, it didn't leak. Rubin made her position on the issue of confidentiality loud and clear to the company's advisers from the outset.

"In an industry that is rife with leaks, it was really important to us, our shareholders, our employees and our stakeholders that we managed the process," she says. "This meant that we could manage and work through the issues without leaks."

The timing of the decision to recommend the Square deal by the Afterpay board – and more recently, its shareholders – now looks to have been ideal. While initially seeing its share price surge after the Afterpay deal was announced, it has subsequently fallen heavily.

However, Rubin says the strategic rationale for the transaction remains. "I don't think we predicted what would happen in the rotation from risk to defensive assets," she says. "So I don't think we had that timing in our heads.

## CAREER PATHWAY

Rubin's parents were both immigrants from Eastern Europe. Her father worked on the wharves in Melbourne until the early 1970s, when he set up an accommodation business.

After completing a degree in industrial relations and labour economics at Melbourne University, Rubin joined the Australian Council of Trade Unions in 1985, where then secretary Bill Kelty AC persuaded her to do postgraduate studies in applied finance and investment instead of labour law. It opened a pathway in the early 1990s to the burgeoning superannuation sector, now worth more than $3 trillion.

In 1997, Rubin joined Australian Retirement Fund, a forerunner to AustralianSuper, as chief investment officer. There, while working in her executive role, she also took on her first chair role in 2001, when she became chair of WorkSafe Victoria – then known as WorkCover.

It would be the start of her non-executive career, which blossomed in subsequent years as she became chair of AustralianSuper then non-executive director of life insurer TAL and property company Mirvac. She also sat on the advisory board of Infrastructure Australia. More recently, she has become a director of telco giant Telstra and law firm Slater and Gordon.

During 2010–16, she sat on the board of SecondBite, a charitable organisation that works with a range of food suppliers to rescue surplus fresh produce from suppliers and redistribute it to local charities and NFPs around Australia. Interestingly, given her union background, the charity was chaired by former Liberal Party state president Ian Carson AM FAICD.

"If you believe in diversity of thought – that no-one has a monopoly on good ideas, that we all share an objective of building stronger communities and a community that is safe and inclusive and provides a sense of security for all its participants – then I think we get the best outcomes by working across different groups," says Rubin. "What Ian and [Ian's wife] Simone Carson did in creating SecondBite was just remarkable. It just goes to show that political labels often don't give any value to the good work that people do. I would say political labels can be a distraction."

## THE ROAD AHEAD

Rubin has always believed in the powerful role women can play in corporate and political processes and says the most recent federal election reinforced that women belong at every table where decisions are made.

"No political party should take women for granted again," says Rubin. "The increase in the number of women in parliament will change not only the political debate, but also the culture of parliament as a workplace."

In the post-COVID-19 world, she says the priority for her companies has been focusing on employee wellbeing. The changing way of work and the rise of the work-from-home phenomenon has increased workplace flexibility, especially for women, but Rubin stresses there is still a very positive incentive to bring people back to the office for some time each week. "We've seen over the past couple of years the importance of technology and being digitally connected," she says. "The whole discussion around digitalisation in organisations has been accelerated and the role of technology in digital platforms, how we use them and how they've developed in parallel. So there is now some forward thinking about the skills we will need for the future. How do we access those and help develop our staff to take advantage of those opportunities?"

Rubin sees ESG as at the centre of corporate strategy, driving shareholder value, rather than simply being part of a company's regulations and compliance obligations. "Minimising your environmental impact and environmental resources is a core part of what companies should be doing," she says. "We focus a lot on the environmental aspects, and rightly so, but there are some really important initiatives under the S and the G."

Rubin rejects any suggestions that women on boards might care about the environment any more or less than their male colleagues. "But women bring a different perspective, based on their experience, career path, lives and education," she says. "We bring a different perspective to board discussions. Without diversity, the risk is we have groupthink and all we do is reinforce each other's views based on past experience. Diversity is really important to enable some of the more contemporary issues to be fully debated."

Rubin says boardroom discussions have become more powerful with two or three women present in the room. Gender suddenly becomes irrelevant and women account for more than 35 per cent of directors on ASX 200 boards. "Women are not all the same. We actually have differences among ourselves and so the issues stop being female issues or gender issues and become broader business, commercial issues. It is also my experience that having a number of females around the board table has given a licence to some men to say things and act a little bit differently than they may have if it was just a male group. Because sometimes, for some men, this groupthink has meant that they have been stereotyped into a position – an economic rationalist, not interested in soft issues, whatever it may be. When there's a diversity of thought and people around the board table, everybody has got the licence to say what they think."

## WOMEN AT THE TOP

More women have risen in recent years to sitting at the head of some the nation's top boardroom tables. They include Catherine Livingstone at Commonwealth Bank of Australia, Catherine Brenner and Debra Hazelton at AMP, Kathryn Fagg at CSIRO, Anne Templeman-Jones at Blackmores, Ilana Atlas at Coca-Cola Amatil, Kathleen Conlon at Lynas, Diane Smith-Gander at Zip, and Elizabeth Bryan at IAG.

However, Rubin worries that too many women have stepped up to take the role during difficult times for their companies. "My view is: full credit to them for stepping up and having the courage and conviction to lead a board and an organisation to rectify the issues," she says. "But more often than not, it appears it's much harder to get a chair role when you're a female director of a company that's going swimmingly well."

She also believes that where a man fails in a chair role, it doesn't condemn his gender. The same cannot be guaranteed when a female is accused of failure. "We can have men who are perceived as not being very good in their roles, but it doesn't condemn the entire gender," says Rubin. "I've had comments made to me about speaking to a particular woman, because there were concerns about her performance and that it was going to be bad for all women. Wouldn't it be a tragedy for the nation if we, in a sense, scared women off from taking big roles? Women who are absolutely able to do it with capable, skilled experience? But the level of commentary is so gendered they are actually put off?"

Rubin has long been on the board of Teach for Australia, an organisation committed to achieving equity in education, highlighting her passion for learning. She believes directors must always be curious and willing to embrace environments of learning. "One of the great privileges and benefits about being a director is that if you are naturally curious and you have a love for reform and a desire that things are always better, you want to build a better world going forward," she says. "There is a sense of continuous learning and education, both formally and informally. What the AICD does is bring together a community of directors, and – particularly over the past few years – enable different voices to be heard and different views exchanged. That is part of the process of learning. You should never stop."

## LESSONS LEARNED

Rubin says she has learned something significant in all of her board roles. "It's not about getting on trophy boards. It is about finding organisations that have a purpose that speaks to me.

"When I think back on my different roles, I can find a purpose and talk to that purpose in all of my organisations. It may not be the purpose that speaks to everyone, but it's been the purpose that has spoken to me and that has given me an incredible sense of learning and satisfaction by being involved.

"I'd say to anyone starting out and looking at a non-executive director career, it's not a chessboard where you go from small to large. If you do that, you might actually miss some of the most inspiring and fulfilling roles. It's about finding those roles where you can make a difference and your organisation can make a difference."

Rubin has always split her directorships between the listed public, private and government sectors. She notes that her engagement with the latter has long highlighted her belief in the benefit of exchanging skills and information between the public and private sectors.

"There is a transparency and timeliness around listed boards," says Rubin.

"For some government boards, that immediacy is something they are not exposed to as much. It is incredibly stimulating. There's a complexity that is often underestimated by outsiders. But if you think about WorkSafe, the complexity in the stakeholder relationships and the multiple touchpoints, it's a very complex organisation. The private sector sometimes underestimates the complexity and how much the community depends on and engages with these government organisations. There's a very real accountability that those organisations feel every day."

# NIGEL SATTERLEY

*In the three years I worked for The Australian Financial Review in Perth from 1996-98, weekly coverage of the property sector was my primary focus. Yet I never met the legendary land developer Nigel Satterley. Fast forward nearly a quarter of a century, I was taking my seat in the VIP area at the Melbourne Cricket Ground to watch arch rivals Carlton and Collingwood do battle in August 2022 when I introduced myself to the man seated next to me. With impeccable politeness, he said his name was Nigel. As we got chatting, we soon discovered our shared passion for the West Coast Eagles Football club – the AFL team I have followed since March 1987 – and for all things West Australian. We caught up for dinner in Melbourne several months later when I suggested Nigel consider doing a rare, wide-ranging interview for my newspaper column. He agreed without hesitation. In the interview he was colourful, open and engaging. To this day he remains one of the best connected people in Perth. I now only wish I had met him decades earlier.*

Bernie "The Godfather" Prindiville was long known as the patriarch of Perth's Catholic business community.

Knowing he had only weeks to live in August 2005, Prindiville – also the former long-serving Western Australian Cricket Association president, who has a stand named after him at the famed WACA ground – invited Nigel Satterley to join him at his hospital bedside.

"I was asked by the Godfather to visit him in the month before he died. He was a great friend of mine. He used to call me godson. He asked me 'Godson, who is going to take over? But he already knew. He had one simple phrase to describe Kerry Stokes: 'He's a beauty. He's a beauty'," Satterley told me in May 2023.

"Kerry is now the Godfather of Perth. He took over from Bernie, who was the Pope's business representative around Perth. I have known Kerry since the 1960s. He is a very decent person. Despite his limited education and dyslexia, he is incredibly streetwise. He knows two days ahead if the dog catcher is coming. He is very good."

Stokes might be the godfather, but Satterley describes himself – tongue firmly planted in cheek – as simply "a helper".

"I go up the plank," he says with a wide smile over breakfast at the suave Gordon Street Garage cafe, a stone's throw from the head office of his Satterley Property Group, one of the country's biggest private residential land developers.

But he has long been more than just hired help in the Perth business elite.

He might have turned 70 years of age, but Satterley – along with Stokes, Fortescue boss Andrew Forrest, Wesfarmers chairman Michael Chaney, top barrister Malcolm McCusker and several others – remains one of Perth's most powerful and influential businesspeople.

You might even call it a business mafia. Its critics certainly do.

Satterley doesn't disagree with the tag, but quickly notes that Perth is no different to any other big city in Australia.

"Every city is controlled by a mafia. So, in Melbourne, Lindsay Fox is the head. Then there are 30 people around him. Sydney has the mafia, so does Brisbane. So, Perth is most probably about eight people that are seen as the mafia," he says, adding that they differ in one important respect from the traditional Italian criminal variety.

"They are all good people. The Premier has businesspeople he goes to for advice and they are all good people."

For decades Satterley has proudly played a powerful role behind the scenes in promoting Western Australia's interests in state and federal politics and beyond.

But the achievement he is most proud of came five years ago when he helped WA secure a fairer deal on the GST distribution after a year-long campaign.

"I'd known then Premier McGowan since he was councillor with the City of Rockingham – and he knew he could trust me. We formed a powerhouse coalition with Michael Chaney, Twiggy Forrest and John Poynton. We funded independent reports researched and compiled by Rick Newnham, who at the time was WA Chief Economist for the Chamber of Commerce and Industry. We all felt a strong obligation to do what we could for the WA community and to achieve a fair outcome," Satterley recalls.

"When we secured a meeting with then Prime Minister Malcolm Turnbull, he told us he wasn't an ATM machine. I told him that we weren't coming for that ATM machine. We didn't go in hard asking for 100¢ in the dollar, but rather what was fair and reasonable."

The GST Fix announced in 2018 by Turnbull introduced a GST floor of 70 cents in the dollar from 2022-23 for two years. The floor increased to 75 cents in 2024-25.

Satterley said Michael Chaney's ongoing influence on Mark McGowan regarding debt control when he was Premier was "terrific".

He also made no apologies for remaining close to the now former Premier, who he said consulted him regularly for advice on property industry issues. McGowan surprisingly resigned from the role in the last week of May, coincidentally only days after my interview with Satterley was published.

In 2022 it was revealed McGowan attended a Penfolds Grange wine tasting dinner at Satterley's Peppermint Grove mansion. At the time the Premier said there was nothing improper about the dinner, which was not a political fundraiser.

Satterley, who is a Liberal party member, has previously hosted events for WA Labor. He disputes suggestions McGowan has got too cosy with Perth's business "mafia".

"I think McGowan has been an outstanding Premier. He listens, consults and I think he's got very good steel. He is respected," the property developer says.

"So he can make a decision and it might not be what people agree with but he can respectfully say 'This is why I'm doing it'. I think he's got some very good trusted leaders he talks to. With low debt and a good economic outlook, this state is in good shape."

## EARLY YEARS

Satterley spent most of his childhood in the small WA pastoral township of Cunderdin before moving to Perth in his late teens. His first job at the age of 20 was WA Representative and distributor for Levi Jeans.

Later in his 20's he formed Statesman Homes, a real estate business which became one of the State's largest residential homebuilders.

By 1980, after selling Statesman Homes, Satterley had moved into broad-acre land development under the Satterley Property Group banner.

Today the group has more than 30 communities in progress across WA, Queensland and Victoria, annual project land sales turnover of around $850 million and 25,000 lots still to be developed over the next decade with an end value of approximately $8.5bn.

Satterley divides his time between his firm's Perth, Brisbane and Melbourne offices and says the secret sauce of his business is "doing what you say you are going to do".

"Integrity is important, as is transparency to earn the trust of our investment partners, the government and the banks. My motto is to be fair. What we do has to be fair for our stakeholders and government but the ultimate test is the consumer. Are you offering something consumers want and can afford," he says.

Interestingly he has never considered taking on a partner or a pursuing a public listing. For five decades Satterley's house banker has been ANZ.

"We can nurture the assets, so we don't have to be trying to drive the share price with substantial discounting. We have seen some of our competitors discounting by $30,000 a block. We also don't have to engage in creative accounting to bolster executive bonuses," he says.

The firm's independent chairman is former Hawaiian Group boss and West Coast Eagles football club president Russell Gibbs. Deputy chairman is Mark Hunter, the firm's former managing director who was previously the CEO of Stockland Communities.

Satterley is CEO. He reveals he is now looking for a new managing director "so the business can continue if something happens to me."

"I have always had the philosophy that nobody is irreplaceable." He has one son, Sam, who is not in the business.

On the outlook for the property market, Satterley expects the most recent – and potentially further – interest rate rises to trigger a further 5 per cent fall in residential prices in the growth areas of Melbourne, Sydney and Brisbane.

But he sees no price corrections in Perth because of ongoing strong demand and a shortage of supply.

"Perth has now got the cheapest established home price in growth areas of any capital city at a median $550,000. Our median land price remains cheaper than the other states. Then what has happened over the last month or so, the listings of dwellings has dropped to 5150, where experts say the balance of established dwellings for sale should be around 10,000. The time to sell an established dwelling now is 17 days, very low. So that is terrific," he says.

He says Perth's median rental price rose from $500 on January 1 to at least $550 by the end of March.

"The home builders here are just about getting through their backlog. So Perth is in a reasonable recovery. I think from September onwards, we are going to have a very much improved buoyant market. What we are seeing now is the shrewd investors – surprisingly, from Adelaide, Melbourne and Sydney – are looking at Perth to buy properties to rent knowing that the rental market is quite solid."

## FAMILY BATTLES

Anyone who shakes Satterley's right hand will immediately notice his right index finger is missing what in medical terminology is called its distal phalanx. Or in layman's terms, the top has been cut off.

"A virus ate through that 10 years ago. It ate through the bone," he volunteers when I ask about the deformity.

"They sent me everywhere to fix it but couldn't. I had two procedures – they even put in a plastic, surgical screw – but it didn't work. The third option was just to chop it off. You psyche yourself up for something like that and we did it. My only thing I can't now do properly is pull the collar down on my shirts."

In October 2015, Satterley's wife Denise was also diagnosed with breast cancer.

It was initially devastating, having seen her late mother battle crippling motor neurone disease.

"My wife religiously does all her medical tests. She went for her normal test and the first scans weren't that good. They got the imaging done and they could see straight away, stage one breast cancer. It was one of the biggest surprises because my wife is so fit for her age. We were stunned," her husband says.

Professor Christobel Saunders, internationally recognised as one of Australia's most prominent research-orientated cancer specialists, operated within days.

After daily radiotherapy sessions, which lasted a month, Professor Saunders has said there was a 90 per cent chance the cancer would not return.

"Denise got through that well and there are now no issues," Satterley says.

Football remains one of his greatest passions and big name politicians and business people are regular guests at the Satterley private box for AFL matches at Perth's Optus stadium.

In 1989 Satterley negotiated with then WA Premier Peter Dowding and Treasurer Joe Berinson to lend money to his beloved West Coast Eagles to keep the club afloat. In 1990 he also managed negotiations to convince Victorian Michael Malthouse to become coach of the team, who led the Eagles to 2 AFL Premierships and 3 Grand Finals.

"We needed to get someone who could help us win football matches. I think the coach drives membership," Satterley says.

"Malthouse, in my mind, made the biggest impression in the history of WA Football. It is my greatest achievement in football here. I still have a very close relationship with Michael and his wife. I was the one, I'm very happy to say on the record, who tried to convince him not to coach Carlton."

Malthouse's record in 2015 at the club known as "The Blues" was his worst in 30 years as an AFL coach and he was sacked by the board.

Satterley this year marks 50 years of supporting WA Telethon, Perth's annual charity fund raiser for sick children broadcast for 26 continuous hours by Channel Seven each October.

Kerry Stokes, the Seven West Media chairman who covers its costs every year, is widely known as "the father" of the event.

Over five decades Satterley Group has donated land for 41 Telethon

Homes valued at more than $18 million.

There are now 103 beneficiaries for the event, which is quintessentially Western Australian.

Satterley wouldn't dream of living anywhere else in the world.

"When the heads of banks come to WA and they go to the Pilbara, they say 'It's a massive thing'. Perth might still viewed by many as a big country town or just a mining town. Be we are lucky it is now also perceived as a medical town and an agricultural town," he says.

"We make up 10 per cent of the Australian population but provide 43 per cent of its exports. I think that is now getting us more respect."

# LES AND RONALDO SCHIRATO

Vittoria coffee king Les Schirato still has fond memories of his only son Rolando in the aisle of a supermarket when he was six years old.

"He'd been watching me fix supermarket shelves. Then I went to another store to buy something and I turned around and he'd got all the Vittoria coffee packs. But rather than fixing them up in the aisle, he'd laid them lengthways all the way along in front of the tomato sauce," Les Schirato told me in an interview in June 2022.

"You don't realise but the kids grow up watching you and being a part of it. I guess, subconsciously, because they're in it, they get to learn a lot about it very early in life."

Rolando was then 39 and the heir apparent to the $250m Vittoria Food & Beverage business, now the nation's largest coffee-bean company, which sells Vittoria coffee to supermarkets such as Woolworths, Coles, IGA and other independent outlets.

Its parent company, The Cantarella Group, also has the distribution rights in Australia to Jarlsberg cheese, King Oscar Sardines and Santa Vittoria water.

Les still comes into the group's Silverwater headquarters in western Sydney every day and remains chief executive, while his son is managing director.

At the ripe age of 70, the former has no plans to retire and believes the partnership with his son, his wife Luisa and only daughter Gabriella underpins the success of the family business.

In a joint interview, Les and Rolando revealed the secrets of their partnership, their work on succession planning and the lessons from a bitter dispute that led to Les and Luisa taking full control of the business six years ago.

## STRONG HERITAGE

Vittoria's history in Australia stretches back to 1947, when two Italian brothers, Orazio and Carmelo Cantarella, began importing Italian products such as mineral water, parmesan cheese and pasta.

In 1958, they started roasting 100 per cent Arabica beans for Italian cafes.

Les, the son of Italian immigrants – his father Rolando senior is still alive at the age of 90 – married into the Cantarella family and joined Cantarella Brothers in 1972.

One of his biggest achievements was taking the brand into supermarkets in the 1980s and transforming the company from a debt-riddled importer to a profitable mid-sized group. It has often been said that Vittoria's strong presence on supermarket shelves has set it apart from other family-owned coffee roasters that share a similar history.

Rolando Jr studied arts at university, majoring in anthropology, and joined the family business 25 years ago despite initially declaring he didn't want to work there.

"Not for any reason other than the fact that I wanted to do something different. But at uni I got ingrained in the really great Vittoria marketing team essentially pretty early on and was really enjoying the work that I was doing with the business," he says.

"I found the more time I spent there, the people in the business were huge. I also got exposure to things that I might not have gained for some years otherwise. Rooms were always made available for me to listen. That was a huge learning opportunity."

Rolando stepped up to be managing director in 2014 and now runs the business day to day while his father concentrates on larger, strategic issues.

The former says while they challenge each other a lot and don't agree on many things, they are aligned on the fundamentals of the business.

"We are alike in how we approach strategy, how we approach investments and the way we think about what the future of the business needs to look like," he says. "We have also had a really stable family life outside of the business. When the family structure isn't there, it is a recipe for disaster."

He says his greatest lessons from his father have been the power of determination and resilience, being able to wear the scars that come with longevity.

While many children of famous fathers wear their name as a burden, Rolando says being a Schirato has provided an ongoing sense of motivation.

"I don't know if I would have had that working in someone else's business. Twenty-five years on, it is something I am conscious of. I still feel I need to prove myself to the people around me and earn my stripes," he says.

Les says his son has taught him that while history is important, at the end of the day "you have to prove yourself every day and change with what's happening".

"It's in our blood and its personal. When you are a family business and its your name, it is all interlinked," Les says.

Their current polite disagreement is over staff working from home in a post-pandemic world. Les is adamant that after two years of the pandemic, cafes and restaurants want to see people.

He wants his people back in the office to help rebuild the culture.

"There are some people who have worked for us for the past two years who don't understand our culture," he says.

His son has a different philosophy and believes flexibility is now essential for a post-pandemic workforce. But for the moment Rolando has resolved to support his father's position.

"As you bring new people into the business, it is hard to feel part of the fabric and the culture when you are working from home," Rolando says. "So I agree that, long term, having a few days in the office is critical to the success of the business. A hybrid working scenario is where it will land. But for now, I see merit in everyone being together more. So he is winning that argument for now. Ask us again in six months."

When Covid-19 hit, Vittoria experienced a 60 per cent fall in sales to cafes and restaurants. Trade with hotels dropped by 80 per cent and key client Qantas stopped buying altogether.

But despite the setbacks, Les credits Rolando for still pushing to launch new products such as instant coffee, a new tea brand with Coles called Queen Victoria, and two boutique coffee brands.

Export markets in America, Southeast Asia and beyond also offer the greatest area of growth potential after, as Les puts it, they were "knocked for six" by Covid.

## BLOOD BATTLES

Les gained a controlling share of the Cantarella Brothers in 2002 after buying out his father-in-law, Orazio Cantarella, and four family members. He and Luisa bought out the latter's sibling, Clelia Cantarella – who owned 49 per cent – six years ago. That was after a nasty court battle in March 2011, when Les and Clelia went to war over a $20m subsidiary. It owned $20m worth of vacant factories and warehouses in four states, a $1.6m Princess motor yacht and kept at a berth on Sydney Harbour at Woolloomooloo reportedly costing $4000 a month.

The company was eventually wound up, releasing $14.6m to be shared between the families through the sale of the factories.

Two years earlier Clelia had sued her sister, Les and 11 other family members and companies over the money contained in two family trusts.

The case was reportedly settled, with the judge reportedly describing the case as "bitterly fought litigation over significant amounts of money".

Les describes the litigation as "incredibly difficult".

"It was a 10-year issue," he says. "In some ways, like all crises, there are silver linings. You learn things and avoid certain things happening in the future. It also meant Rolando blossomed. When I was tied up in litigation, it meant he grew and he was there to be a backstop." His wife has since made peace with her sister.

"Louisa's view is that she would not allow the business to damage family," he says. Asked if he has been as forgiving, he only replies: "We bought Clelia out and we moved on."

Louisa has been the glue that has kept the Schiratos together for decades, especially in the years when Les was travelling extensively, doing early starts and late finishes to turn around the business. Her son says she is a woman of few words. "She is not someone who throws her weight around. It is not her style. But when she does speak, it is taken very seriously. It carries a lot of weight. Her main objective is ensuring the business does not get in the way of family," Ronaldo says.

Luisa is one of the five members of the Schirato Family Council, which is chaired by Sydney lawyer John Churchill. The private company Cantarella Brothers Pty Ltd also has its own board with two external directors, including former Ernst & Young chairman Brian Long.

In recent years the Schirato family has also been taking advice on succession planning from former Harvard professor John Davis, who in 1989 founded the Cambridge Family Enterprise Group that specialises in assisting multigenerational families.

Les describes the succession as "a process, not an event".

"For too long it has been the young lion has to kill the old lion to take over the pride. Maybe it is like the American Indians. If you can get the young braves who are always fighting and have the energy appreciating there is some wisdom that comes with age, when it combines it can be powerful," he says. "What I'm hoping is whether people want to come into the business or do their own thing or have another business, the thing that is important is that we are lucky the business is big enough that we can separate responsibilities."

Les's only daughter Gabriella now runs Vittoria's people and culture division. He describes her as a "very competent, capable young woman" but more outspoken than her brother.

"She will point out everything wrong I am doing everyday. She is my life coach," Les quips. "They used to call me coach as a joke because I always used to coach them on things I didn't know. So now it's their turn. I'm getting exactly what I deserve."

Rolando says he has no expectation his two young children will one day follow in his footsteps to join the business and will never "consciously promote" the idea.

For the time being at least, their grandfather will remain the patriarch. Les admits he is "not 100 per cent ready" just yet to step back.

To the Schiratos, the Vittoria business will always be about much more than selling coffee.

"I grew up in Cabramatta. I certainly don't take for granted how lucky we are as a family to have the great opportunity that we do have," Les says. "Part of that is to understand that it is also our responsibility to do the right thing by others and to look after others."

# CAROL AND ALAN SCHWARTZ

*I have always admired and respected the billionaire Besen family. I will never forget the evening many years ago when Carol Schwartz introduced me to her legendary father Marc, as he anonymously shuffled his way into the annual dinner of the Business Council of Australia. He was impeccably polite and sharp as a tack. But as Carol has reminded me many times, she might be a Besen but she does not live in her father's shadow. She and her husband Alan, who I have also got to know over the years, have quietly carved out their own amazing family business focussed on investment and philanthropy. Their passion for Israel and the Jewish people has always been clear, and nowhere was that more apparent than one afternoon at the world-famous Yad Vashem Holocaust memorial when I stood and watched them at their most vulnerable. Their emotion – and mine – that day was palpable. Both deeply private people, I am still honoured that seven years later they would grant me their first interview together. It was worth the wait.*

It was a typically warm mid-spring afternoon in the ancient city of Jerusalem in April 2012 when Alan and Carol Schwartz stood together, hand in hand, in a corner of Yad Vashem. Surrounded by the delegates of an Australia-Israel Chamber of Commerce mission led by Carol and BHP director Carolyn Hewson, they watched in silence as their niece Delilah lit a candle below a headstone marking what is known as the Path of Remembrance and Reflection.

It was endowed at Yad Vashem seven years earlier by Alan Schwartz's father, Andor, and his mother, Baba, in memory of her father Gylua Keimovits, who perished in the horrors of Auschwitz.

Delilah then slowly recited one of the writings of her grandmother about the last day she saw her father on May 22, 1944, when Baba, her mother and sisters were tragically separated from him at the Nazi death camp in southern Poland.

As Delilah spoke, her voice wavered as tears began to trickle down her cheeks. Looking on, her uncle and aunt were crying, as were most members of the delegation.

"It completely defines me," Alan Schwartz told me seven years later before a poignant pause when I ask about the Path of Remembrance, dedicated to all Hungarian Jews who perished in the Holocaust.

Schwartz is sitting alongside his wife of 40 years in the boardroom of the offices of their Trawalla Group, perched five levels above Melbourne's chic Flinders Lane in a heritage-facade building they bought nearly a decade ago and renovated to include two new floors and a yoga studio.

Carol and Alan Schwartz had never done an interview together until May 2019 when they agreed to talk to me about their shared history, the importance of their Jewish heritage and detailed for the first time the inner workings of their $400 million family office.

Carol, a director of the Reserve Bank and a former director Stockland property group, is renowned as one of the most well-connected people in Australian business.

She has been a vehement public advocate for gender equity (she founded the Women's Leadership Institute Australia and has been a member for many years of Chief Executive Women, a networking group and forum for female leaders), regularly trolling business leaders and journalists on Twitter on the issue, which has irritated some in the business establishment.

Eyebrows were raised among her critics when she was appointed to the RBA board and when she became chairman of listed online furniture and homewares retailer Temple & Webster in 2016, which was one of the worst floats on the ASX that year.

She stepped down in October that year but remains a shareholder and the shares are now back above their issue price.

Less is known about her Israeli-born husband (even though he has his own website, as does Carol) who has created, acquired and sold a number of successful businesses, the most significant being a legal software and publishing group called Anstat, which was sold to SAI Global for $50m in 2005.

In addition to running Trawalla, Alan Schwartz is the former chairman of the nation's peak philanthropic group, Philanthropy Australia, and is known as one of Melbourne's most astute entrepreneurs, especially in the not-for-profit sector.

Just don't call them a power couple, a label Carol detests.

"Definitely not," she snaps when asked about the tag, describing her RBA board role "as an absolute privilege" before pointedly musing: "And what does the term 'power couple' even mean anyway?"

## SHARED HERITAGE

Alan Schwartz's parents emigrated to Melbourne from Israel in 1958 and struggled for years before his father, Andor, became a successful property developer. Together, they became titans of Melbourne's Jewish community.

Two of their three sons, Morry and Danny, have followed in their father's footsteps in property development. The former is also now a renowned publisher.

Baba died at the age of 89 in June 2017, only a week after she attended the wedding of one of Carol and Alan's daughters, Hannah, in Israel.

Carol says she learnt important lessons for life from her mother-in-law, especially in her latter years.

"I had a difficult relationship with her in our first 10-15 years. But once I had children and she fell in love with her grandchildren, it brought us closer together," she says.

"My relationship over the last five years of her life was absolutely fantastic. We were very close. I learnt a lot from her about an approach to life and always being incredibly optimistic and positive. But also she was fabulous at spending time alone, which I think is a real art. She would read, write, sing and be really content and happy. I thought that is something one has to cultivate in one's life – to not always be surrounded by people and busyness. We miss her every day."

Carol's grandparents, Fay and Sam Gandel, were also Jewish immigrants from war-torn Europe before they established a women's hosiery business known as Sussan on Melbourne's Collins Street in 1939.

They ran Sussan for more than a decade before it was acquired in the 1950s by Carol's parents Eva and Marc and her uncle John.

Eva and Marc Besen then further developed the Sussan chain and built Melbourne's Highpoint Shopping Centre (which Carol ran for many years), while Gandel went his own way and developed Melbourne's Chadstone shopping centre, becoming a billionaire in his own right.

Alan Schwartz says he has learnt plenty from his father-in-law, Marc.

"He has been successful at everything he has done but he is a genuinely loving person with a big heart," he says.

However, the final years of Marc Besen's life were the most trying as his wife was struck down by illness. Eva Besen passed away in 2021 at the age of 93. Marc was 99 when he died two years later on November 8, 2023.

## TRAWALLA IS BORN

It was the restructuring of Marc Besen's empire in 2003 that saw Carol's elder sister Naomi Milgrom buy her parents and siblings out of Sussan

Group, and the sale of Alan's Anstat Group two years later, that led to the birth of the Trawalla Group in 2007.

The group has three divisions: Trawalla Property (whose assets include The Tasman Hotel in Hobart and Rydges Hotel at Mount Panorama near Bathurst), the philanthropic Trawalla Foundation (a fund that invests in the arts, ideas and innovation that is chaired by Carol) and the Trawalla Capital Group.

It also owns a transport company called BagTrans, which has a fleet of small and medium-sized trucks.

"We have really spent the past 10 years working out how to be the kind of investors we are proud to be, which is active investors that create value," Alan says.

"What Carol and I have tried and I believe been successful in creating is a high-governance, high-entrepreneurial model for our group."

Trawalla has an independent board led by Computershare chairman Simon Jones. Also on the board are Seek chairman Graham Goldsmith and former Deloitte partner Kevin Slomoi.

While Carol is a director and Alan is both managing director and owner, he is what he terms an "employee CEO", fully accountable to his board.

He and Carol have separately established a family council on which they sit with their four children (who all live overseas), which each year presents to the Trawalla board a two-page mandate on the family's risk appetite, asset allocation preferences and return expectations.

The most aspirational return assumptions are expected from Trawalla Capital, which has three platforms: the Qualitas Property Partners real estate financier and investment manager, the Armitage Associates growth equity business and the funds management start-up known as Stonehorn Global Partners.

"One of our key strategies is to create and incubate asset managers,"

Alan says. "This is the part we are the most excited about because it gets the best returns and is the most active. It is very entrepreneurial because each one is a start-up. We are approaching it with great partners and a strong governance structure."

The activities of the now sharemarket listed Qualitas are arguably the best known in the Trawalla stable, having more than $2.5 billion worth of investments across a range of commercial, industrial and residential property assets.

Alan calls Armitage Trawalla's "growth equity platform", which directly invests in 10 to 15-year-old companies where Trawalla can see a simple path to doubling or trebling the size of them.

"They are solid and stable businesses. They are not necessarily hi-tech businesses but they are businesses that use technology," he says. "We take long-term positions. We are growth equity, not private equity. We have structured everything in Armitage to enable us not to be private equity."

Its investments include Iron Capital, an industrial asset financing business; Bluefit, an operator of aquatic leisure facilities and learn-to-swim schools; Sash, an animal veterinary hospital business; and Osteon, which makes dental implants.

But perhaps what is most interesting about Armitage, which is chaired by Graham Goldsmith, is the make-up of the boards of its investee companies. Former Incitec Pivot boss James Fazzino is the chair of Osteon, while former Bunnings CEO-turned CSR chairman John Gillam is the chair of Blue-Fit.

Trawalla has backed a trio of former Macquarie Investment Management stock pickers who have established the Stonehorn Asian public equities funds management business.

Trawalla's initial minority investment in the business, founded by Sam Le Cornu, Duke Lo and John Lam, is $US50m ($72.6m).

"We thought this was a terrific asset class to create an asset manager in because we felt that Australian investors were severely under-invested in Asia," Alan says.

"The Australian super funds are increasing their exposure to Asia. We don't believe they can internalise that – it is too hard. So we expect to get some capital out of the super funds, high-net-worth family offices, and the bulk of the capital will come from offshore."

The deputy chairman of the billionaire Myer Family's investment company, Peter Yates, says Alan and Carol Schwartz have made an "extraordinary contribution to Australia by solving social causes, building great businesses and at the same time nurturing a rich family life filled with love and many friends."

"Their thoughtful, down-to-earth and disciplined way is a role model that I have had the special privilege to observe, enjoy and learn from. I think the 'Schwartz way' could be a great Stanford business school case study," Yates says.

Yates is one of several friends who regularly join the Schwartzes on walking trips in different parts of the world. Alan and Carol also practise Vinyasa yoga together and regularly spend weekends at their coastal retreat near Point Addis on Victoria's Surf Coast.

They have always split their work and family life "very easily".

"The line is pretty seamless. Occasionally you might get worked up and agitated, but we are pretty good," Alan says.

They resolve their rare quarrels by simply "having it out". Neither is ever left in any doubt what the other is thinking.

"We work incredibly well together because we are very aware of what our roles are," Carol says.

A prime focus throughout their lives has been making time for their three daughters and son.

"We have always been home for our kids. We have had none of the children complain that we were not around," Alan says.

While all are members of their family council, Carol stresses there is no expectation they will follow their parents into the family business. "It is not important at all. They are all following their own paths. Who knows what is going to happen but there is no plan whatsoever for them to take over," she says.

# KERRY STOKES

*Kerry Stokes did me an amazing favour when he agreed in 2018 to be interviewed for my book on James Packer, The Price of Fortune. His revelations, especially of James's various engagements with Mariah Carey and her manager, are now part of corporate folklore. I had known Stokes for the previous two decades and over the years we'd always had a polite, cordial relationship. I'll never forget the day in 2001 when I had been scheduled to interview him in my role as media writer at The Australian Financial Review. It was September 11, and I called his PR boss first thing in the morning to confirm the interview had been cancelled. But, to my amazement, he told me: "The interview with the chairman is still on." When Stokes appeared at the door of the boardroom at the Seven Network's Pyrmont head office later that morning to greet me, he looked terrible. He told me he'd been up all night out out at Seven's master control room at Epping, helping direct the network's national coverage of the September 11 terrorist attacks. His chilling warning to me in the interview that day was simple. "The world as we know it has changed forever." How right he has proven to be. When he chose to retire as Seven Group chairman exactly two decades later we would talk again. This time it was on the phone from his West Perth office. He hasn't done another significant interview since.*

Kerry Stokes was at his adoptive father's side the moment pneumonia claimed his life in Royal Perth Hospital in November 1990.

As he said his final goodbye to the man who took him in as an orphan 50 years earlier, he reached into his pocket to find the worn rosary beads Matthew Stokes had carried all his life. The adopted son still has them today.

"They are a touchstone to my past," Stokes whispers in his trademark soft, raspy voice on the phone from the office of his family company in Kings Park Rd, West Perth, a plush mix of marble and wood and home to one of the nation's best art collections.

It is now legend that Stokes was born John Patrick Alford on September 13, 1940, and adopted out to Matt and Irene Stokes, an impoverished Catholic couple that for a time lived at Camp Pell, the postwar slum housing area in Melbourne. They renamed their son Kerry.

"I just am grateful they did. Even though it was a strange relationship, had it not been for that, I wouldn't be who I am today and I am grateful," he says.

Stokes struggled to control his emotions as he gave the eulogy at his adoptive father's funeral at the Holy Rosary Church in Nedlands. Some say it was the most upset they had ever seen him. Stokes agrees it was "up there" as one of the toughest days of his life.

"Matt was a hard-working, unskilled labourer who actually never got a great deal of enjoyment out of life. He just contributed. He did whatever he had to do for us to eat at night," he says.

"Before he died he was pretty chuffed back then at what had been achieved. He said to me he was most proud of the fact that he didn't try and influence me – he left a blank canvas. It has got some colours on it now."

Three weeks before celebrating his 81st birthday in 2021, Kerry Matthew Stokes decided one part of the canvas had been painted to perfection.

The entrepreneur, who arrived in Perth in 1960 and got his start fixing TV aerials to suburban rooftops before getting into real estate and later building a media and mining services empire, revealed he felt confident enough in the talents of his eldest son and his board to cease chairing the family's most important public company, Seven Group Holdings.

Ryan Stokes has been putting his stamp on Seven Group ever since taking over as CEO in July 2015, overseeing a refocus on its WesTrac mining services franchises in NSW and Western Australia and government infrastructure investment through its Coates Hire division, as well as gas development through its stake in Beach Energy.

Seven acquired a 70 per cent stake in building products giant Boral following a year-long campaign to wrest control, and Ryan took over as Boral chairman on top of his role as Seven Group chief executive and chairman of WesTrac and Coates.

Asked if the Boral deal had been the making of his son in the public eye, Stokes replies:

"With due respect, I think Ryan has been an excellent CEO since the time he was appointed. In a number of activities. He was responsible for selling our Caterpillar business in China in 2017. The reason we got the price for it is because, under his direction, the company improved its profitability," he says.

"I am proud of what Ryan has achieved. I remember seeing him off to the States when he went to Merrill Lynch (Ryan worked briefly in New York in the late 90s before joining the Stokes family's private company, Australian Capital Equity or ACE). He didn't want to come home from Merrills because I wasn't going to pay him enough. So I had to pay him a bit more to get him to return."

Given his US apprenticeship, it has been said that Ryan thinks like an investment banker. His father agrees, but with a caveat. "Yes, but with an eye to detail. He wouldn't accept the overviews like a merchant banker would; he would still want to understand the detail himself, which is most important."

He says his son's strategic thinking has been "demonstrated in what has been achieved" at Seven Group, also noting the turnarounds of Coates Hire and Seven's listed subsidiary Seven West Media – the owner of the Seven TV network and West Australian Newspapers.

With Boral, Seven had a less than 20 per cent stake in the embattled building group last September but gradually increased its holding via creep provisions in the Corporations Law, before accelerating its efforts in early 2021.

It was a classic Kerry Stokes play – to stalk its prey and agitate before securing the prize for less than a full price.

It is a modus operandi that has long angered his opponents. It once forced James Packer to part with some of his most prized assets in a panic to fight off a Stokes advance on his media company.

"We have used the model before," Stokes says with a chuckle. "This interpretation of it was in fact Ryan with his team and his selection of (corporate adviser) Barrenjoey and (its co-founder) Matthew Grounds. Ryan and I have known Matthew for years. I had a lot of confidence in Matthew. The strategy they put together was executed exactly as it was planned, to the cent.

"I didn't have a lot to do with the transaction. I overviewed it. The Seven directors had very strong input. The strategy they outlined was followed to the letter and it was successful."

## FATHER AND SON

Asked how Ryan is like him, Kerry Stokes initially brushes the question off as one for his son.

But pressed, he replies: "Like me he is detailed, persistent and very hard-working. I also want to make the point I have another son who I also love dearly who works in our private company. He is doing a great job there. He is very quiet because ACE is very quiet."

Bryant Stokes was born in 1977, a year after his brother, when their father was married to his second wife Denise. They were about to turn 11 and 12 when she left the marriage in 1988. She now lives in Queensland.

Their father says the now Sydney-based sons are close.

"Even more so since they have had children, which is very rewarding for me," he says.

Ryan has always been wary of talking publicly about his father. Once asked if there was a secret to the success of their relationship, he said they worked well together before adding: "Never lose sight of the fact that while you might be family, he is still the boss."

Ryan has always known his place in the empire, yet now remains the only Stokes on the board of the family's biggest public asset.

But when Kerry Stokes stepped down as chairman, Ryan also told me that there would be no decrease in the Stokes family's financial exposure to the success of Seven Group and that his father would remain involved, albeit in a different way.

He claimed his father's decision to exit the board was a sign of confidence in the calibre of the independent directors and management, and where the company and its diversified assets were positioned.

Kerry Stokes concurs.

"The Seven Group was in such a good position. The board had been so strong. And Ryan and his management team had performed so well that it was the right time. I did want to see the Boral transaction concluded. It has always been my intention to make sure I left before it was too late. You never know when it is too late until it is. I had no intention of staying past when I wasn't needed."

Stokes remains a strategic adviser to the Seven board and management for an annual fee of $475,000 to maintain what he terms "continuity of knowledge".

"My knowledge of history and the company is probably better

than anybody else's. And for them to have access to that is valuable," he says.

"They are paying me a good sum so I have to earn it. If I want to I will attend a board meeting. If I want to I will give advice to the board or to management. We will see how it goes."

It sounds like a Clayton's retirement.

Indeed, ask Stokes more about Boral, the $3.5bn pile of cash inside the company and the work-in-progress turnaround of its Australian business and you quickly appreciate his passion for the asset he first dealt with as a Perth property developer decades ago.

"The potential I see in their transformation is much greater than they are contemplating. It has an opportunity to gain market share, improve its efficiencies and to control and restructure its cost base," he says.

What Stokes won't miss about Seven is wading through its detailed board papers each month. His dyslexia was not diagnosed till he was in his 30s and it still troubles him, but he gets by.

"We are a company where our governance will meet any standard and to achieve that means you have to have an eye not just to statutory requirements but to a broader view of all of the associated issues. That is making it much more complex for boards today. I'm concerned if we make it any more complex we will struggle to find the right directors."

Stokes retains his chairmanships at Seven West Media and ACE, which owns a 57 per cent share in Seven Group.

ACE has property, pastoral and industrial activities, including bankrolling Australia's biggest new salt project in 20 years, BCI Minerals' $913m Mardie project in northern WA. It also owns several assets in China, which Stokes says it plans to retain despite ongoing geopolitical tensions.

"We have always had a very good relationship with China. Our investments have been very profitable. We have had no problems with the government there," he says. "I don't think China will close its borders to money or walk away from foreign investment."

His passion remains Seven West, which under the guidance of prodigal-son CEO James Warburton – who once defected to Channel 10 – now boasts its best balance sheet, cost base and growth outlook for many years.

Some analysts termed it a "Lazarus-like recovery" from 2019 when there were fears it could go broke. "Most analysts were not aware of what was happening inside the company. The year before last we set our plan which addressed all the obstacles. It involved an Olympics, the schedule, a whole host of things that would have seen us to debt reduction and solid earnings. We were not prepared for Covid … it caused a series of difficult events we weren't ready for," Stokes says.

"We were never, ever in the dire straits that the market seemed to believe. I was surprised anyone would ever think I would let a company that I was involved with not be in a position to meet its obligations. I can say over my entire my life we have never, ever missed an obligation."

In the past some who know him well have asserted Ryan Stokes would sell Seven's stake in Seven West if it wasn't for his father's passion for the assets.

"Ryan is more hard-nosed on those issues than I am, and that is a good thing. But if you asked him today, I think he would say he is seeing the value in the transformation of Seven. Now we see a pathway we are excited about," his father says.

He doesn't disagree that his son would have felt differently 18 months ago. "Probably, but that was because he was focused on other issues. He was running a large company and Seven West was just a small part of it," he says.

## UNFINISHED BUSINESS

In our wide-ranging interview in 2021, Stokes then said he was confident accused Victoria Cross recipient Ben Roberts-Smith would clear his name after being labelled an alleged war criminal.

Roberts-Smith had taken leave as boss of the Seven Network's Queensland operations as he pursued defamation proceedings against Nine newspapers over articles, which alleged he committed war crimes while on deployment in Afghanistan.

In 2023 he lost the defamation action and resigned his position at Seven, but subsequently appealed.

Stokes's private company Australian Capital Equity agreed to cover Roberts-Smith's legal costs in the initial defamation case and the former SAS soldier offered up his Victoria Cross and other war medals as collateral for the loan facility.

In April 2021 it was revealed $1.87m was loaned to Mr Roberts-Smith for his legal costs via a subsidiary of the Mr Stokes-chaired Seven West Media, owner of the Seven television network. The loan was repaid with funds from ACE.

"ACE stood behind it from the beginning," Stokes says.

"At the end of the day we had always agreed ACE would stand behind his legal fees. At the time Ben put up his medals as security, which he didn't have to do. It was always going to be by ACE. It got to a point where some charges were put through that had not been sent to us and ACE paid."

In the interview Stokes rejected criticism of his reappointment in June 2021 by the federal government as chair of the Australian War Memorial Council for another year, amid his public and private support for soldiers accused of war crimes in Afghanistan.

"I decided that if I could help them, I would. Because they should have the same access to the same opportunities of defence as anyone else. Since they are troopers and soldiers, they don't have a great deal of money. So, they need support and I am prepared to do that. It is not about me making a judgment whether they did right or wrong. The thing they deserve most is a fair go," he says.

Stokes personally guaranteed that a $500m redevelopment under way at the War Memorial would not run over budget. He described his reappointment to the council as "unfinished business".

"We have to get the final approval for the final drawings for the final construction. I am keen to see that achieved," he says.

"Never has it been more important to demonstrate that if you put on the uniform of our country, you shouldn't have to die to be recognised."

## THE HOME FRONT

In June 2021 Stokes welcomed his first grandson to carry the Stokes name, Rafferty Kerry Campbell Stokes, born to Ryan Stokes and his wife Claire. But the grandfather said carrying on the Stokes name was not important to him.

"I love all my grandchildren the same. I have yet to meet Rafferty because of Covid-19. I am looking forward to the day that I can," he says.

Stokes had significant surgery in late 2019 and in 2020, because of his extended recovery, he and his wife Christine were granted a government exemption to home quarantine in Perth upon their return from Colorado, where they own a hunting lodge in Vail.

"When you lead an active life and you do what I have done to my body, you are going to get times when you need repairs and maintenance," he says.

"I'm having those. But I'm still going diving and I intend to go skiing this year."

He said Christine Simpson-Stokes, his fourth wife and a former television newsreader, had dramatically changed his life.

"For 25 years to have someone who has been so consistent and so supportive, it's something I had never experienced before I met Christine. Her input is also appreciated and she is a very strong woman in her own right," he says.

The couple have been renovating their riverfront mansion in the Perth suburb of Dalkeith.

"Christine is heavily involved in building our new home, which is good because I don't want to be involved," Stokes says.

A member of the Australia Council for the Arts, she also has a key role in helping oversee the Kerry Stokes Collection, one of Australia's largest private art collections.

It features hundreds of paintings, manuscripts and artefacts, including works from medieval times as well as the Renaissance.

The couple have been looking for a new building in Perth to house the entire collection.

"The problem is we keep buying more art. What is more important, the home or the art? Every time we get that question something amazing comes up and we can't resist it. We will at some stage," Stokes says of relocating the collection under one roof.

"I am enjoying the collection a great deal. And enjoying having new parts added to it. Originally, I started collecting Australian art and I thought the important thing isn't just the art, it is the Australian story. So, I started getting involved in exploration and the founding of Australia. So as a result, the collection diverged into so many other areas as a result of that. That was 50 years ago."

Stokes told biographer Andrew Rule years ago that he will forever be a "restless" soul and he remains so, in so far as he remains curious and wants to be involved in business. He sees himself as "a chameleon", which reflected his ability to switch between being a businessman, philanthropist, art collector, esteemed photographer, skier and diver, amateur historian and most importantly, a father.

"In my past life I have been a chameleon in attitude," Stokes now says.

"Now it is more a maturing of what my lifetime ambitions are. I am not exactly going away, with Seven West, ACE and working with the war memorial. So I still have a full range of activities."

Fellow Perth billionaire Andrew Forrest once claimed Stokes felt a great responsibility to create a legacy, claiming it was "hardwired into his nature."

Stokes vehemently disagrees.

"My name appears on nothing at all other than a chair for telethon at Curtin University. That was generously done for me," he snaps.

"I have never been concerned that I get personal recognition. I am not building a legacy. I am hopefully building a foundation for other people to build on."

# SAM AND CHRISTINE TARASCIO AND SONS

*I had never met "Sam senior" Tarascio until 2020 when I was introduced to him by former Western Bulldogs AFL club chairman David Smorgon. David had very kindly convinced the Tarascio family patriarch to talk publicly for the first time about the family's successful succession transition with his sons Sam and David. When I arrived at the offices of Salta Properties for the interview, the Tarascio's were polite but wary. After a while they warmed to the task and we enjoyed a wonderful discussion. That day Sam senior spoke of his passion for producing Taralinga Estate olive oil from groves surrounding his holiday home on Victoria's Mornington Peninsula.*

*In 2022 he kindly invited me to visit the stunning property to meet his wife Christine and discuss their support for Chabad Youth, the largest Jewish youth organisation in the Southern Hemisphere, based in Melbourne.*

*After proudly giving me a tour of the olive crushing facilities, Sam sat down with Christine and I in the grand lounge room of the property where he revealed that David had survived a life-threatening episode a year earlier.*

*I have always admired the Tarascios. Theirs has been a textbook handover to the next generation, for which they should be congratulated.*

During the speech he gave before beloved friends and family at a surprise party to celebrate his 70th birthday in 2014, Salvatore Tarascio mused that he couldn't help feeling he was born under a Sicilian lucky star.

The billionaire, now better known in the property development industry as "Sam senior", arrived in Port Melbourne from Italy in 1949 as a five-year-old "outcast migrant child" with parents who had left behind their life in Sicily. They lived with two other families in a 12sq m house in the Melbourne suburb of Werribee.

The parents instilled in their son a work ethic and values that came to the fore when in 1972 they founded Salta Properties, now one of Australia's largest privately owned property developers.

A decade earlier he was recruited as a rising star goalkeeper by the Melbourne Jewish soccer team Hakoah while studying at Williamstown Technical School in the city's west.

There Sam was taken under the wing of legendary Jewish businessman Les Erdi, the founder of the Mercure Hotel group.

"At Hakoah, every person I met – including Les Erdie – had a business. You'd be playing a game and a supporter would come in at half time and say 'Its a tough game, if you pull this off I'll give X amount of money to each of you'," Sam recalls.

"I used to multiply it by the number of players and think 'Wow, this is amazing'. They install this sort of feeling in you that everything is possible. I used to think that if they all have a business, I can have a business too."

Sam Tarascio and his wife of half a century, Christine, have passed on that vision and work ethic to their own children, the eldest of whom, Sam, became managing director of Salta aged just 30, in 2005.

In 2014 their youngest son, David, quietly established a venture capital and funds management arm of Salta. Their only daughter, Lisa, now runs her own business with her husband. Collectively the family is worth a cool $1.43 billion.

But bridging the generation gap hasn't always been easy. "We have come across that little bit of difficulty where my aggression was maybe too great, or my expectation was too great. I don't know; we are from different worlds," the 75-year-old Sam senior told me in 2020, seated at a table with his two sons in Salta's suave Melbourne headquarters in an office tower at the Paris end of Collins Street.

"Do I agree with everything they do? No, of course I don't. Does that lead to debate? Yes. Does it occasionally lead to an argument? Yes," he added slowly, before his eldest son interjected with a single sentence, followed by a wry smile: "We have had some terrific conflicts!"

But his father continued, displaying a capacity for self-analysis rarely seen in family patriarchs, and one that has never been his forte.

"An entrepreneur who starts with nothing and creates a business sometimes struggles with the routine and the management system that is needed to run a business. I don't think entrepreneurs are good managers of businesses," Tarascio said bluntly. "They might be creative, but they are not good managers."

He joked that he once believed a fax machine was the best invention ever, and said for decades he never bothered to learn to use a computer because his personal assistants always knew how. "I could not get into the detail of running the business in the way Sam and David do it," he said.

His decision to let go has been seen a fundamental change in the structure and inner workings of the Salta empire and the Tarascio family, which they publicly revealed in this interview for the first time.

## EXTERNAL ADVICE

In 2015 the family agreed to bring in then PwC partner David Smorgon, himself a victim of the greatest family break-up in corporate history – the 1995 dismemberment of the $1.5 billion Smorgon Consolidated Industries empire.

"David would be one of the best people to have a view on this, having gone through a similar circumstance," Tarascio said. "I know he is very supportive of the way we are going and what we are going to be doing in maintaining the business as an intergenerational business."

In May 2018, Smorgon helped the Tarascios establish a formal business board, chaired by former Redflex CEO and Melbourne Water chairman Paul Clark. It replaced a loose and informal advisory board that had operated for many years. The two other external directors on the business board are former Aconex co-founder Leigh Jasper and Ted Yancken. The latter was for 20 years the group director of Melbourne builder Probuild Constructions, which most recently worked for billionaire John Gandel on the stunning glass-panelled roof at Chadstone Shopping Centre in Melbourne's southeast. Also on the business board are Sam senior, Sam and David Tarascio.

Smorgon also helped the Tarascios establish a family board, which he chairs, a family charter, and a set of values for Salta that took two years to formulate. The values are encapsulated in threes sentences: "The Tarascio Family values respect, trust and time for each other. We hold in high regard a strong worth ethic and commitment to the community, leading to success in our individual and collective objectives. We support each other through good and bad times, learn from them and humbly celebrate our successes, within a harmonious and united family."

Smorgon says Salta's values are living proof that wealth is never the glue that keeps a family together. "Shared values and principles, a willingness to learn and grow, together with genuine care, love and support for all family members, builds trust and respect, which in turn develops a healthy, harmonious and happy family," he says, before adding dryly: "It is not about the dollars."

Tarascio conceded that it was hard to let go and bring in external expertise at Salta. "It was fairly difficult, to the degree that you always have done what you wanted to do in the way and manner you wanted to do it," he said. But he doesn't regret it for a moment.

"The reality of life is that you are not here forever. If you don't make the provisions, then everything becomes a mess in the end. We have all seen heaps of examples of families suing each other. When there was a level of uncertainty as to where I was going, I thought it was appropriate and necessary."

He frankly acknowledged that giving his own children senior roles in his business carried an element of risk. "That risk is not a pure business risk, but it is a risk that would go through the whole family if things didn't work out," he said. "You have to be confident of the capabilities, and you have to accept there will be a level of conflict; it has to happen. As long as it is constructive, it is OK. It is the aspiration of most fathers that you have a family business, and to that degree it is fantastic."

Tarascio still controls the discretionary trust that owns all the Salta entities, and he regularly pays a so-called lifestyle dividend to his children that is flexible and correlates with the performance of the business. But under the family's succession plan, the Tarascio family board will become the successor appointee of all of the trusts on Sam senior's passing – meaning the business becomes effectively owned by the family shareholders.

"The business needs to be ongoing for multiple generations," his son Sam said. "We don't want it broken apart by family members and dispersed. We want it to be a long-term, sustainable family business. We wanted there to be no disruption to the business no argument at the time that [his father's passing] comes about, and that it be automatic – that there is total clarity."

Sam's sister Lisa, a former lawyer at Arnold Block Leibler, may have established her own successful conveyancing business with her husband Chris, but she still attends family board meetings and receives regular updates on the performance of the Salta businesses. In her father's autobiography, published in 2018 and titled My Way, she noted that Tarascio wouldn't allow her to work in the company warehouses during school holidays because of the foul language, and that he had always been very protective of his only daughter.

"I remember through the whole of my childhood sitting on my Dad's lap wrapped in his arms and feeling that all with the world was right," she said, before noting her father had always been "there to encourage and support Chris and me" through life's challenges.

Somewhat surprisingly, Salta flirted with the public markets for a time. In 2018, it engaged PwC and several investment banks to do the numbers for a potential float on the sharemarket. Tarascio said it got "very close", but maintained Salta's risk profile would never suit a public company. "I don't think it will ever be off the radar as the business continues to grow," he said, "but it is not something we are currently looking at."

## THE MATRIARCH

Tarascio's wife of 50 years in 2023, Christine, is also on the family board. "She fits in as the glue that keeps the family together, and that is very important," he said. In his book, he put it more eloquently: "There is no doubt in my mind that the family harmony we experience is a direct result of Christine's influence and loving ways, which have had such an effect on all of us. Christine is a saint in every respect." She has been the primary driver of the family's recent decision to establish the Tarascio Family Foundation after many years of working actively with charities.

David Tarascio, who turned 40 in 2020, is a key supporter of the foundation and of his mother's support for medical research after in

2021 suffering a life-threatening episode in his Melbourne apartment one evening.

It was 930pm when Christine received a call from her youngest son followed by a garbled message. He had collapsed after suffering a stroke but had been close enough to his phone to reach out and call her.

"We tried to get a doctor online and he was useless. All the ambulances were busy. When we got to his apartment, we couldn't lift him. The concierge helped with a wheelchair to get him into the car and we drove him over to the Epworth," his father recalls.

"They initially thought it was vertigo and the doctor didn't come to examine him until 2am. They initially said they would do an MRI at 8am the next morning but he didn't have it until 2pm that afternoon. Then all of a sudden, it was all systems go. They realised he'd had a stroke and the specialists and nurses came from everywhere. Yet he had gone around the clock with this clot lying around. It is a miracle he is still alive."

David spent 2022 in Queensland on long service leave from Salta. He has long been a keen tennis player and in recent years played tournaments on the international ITF tour in the 40-45 age bracket and other events run by Tennis Australia in the all-age category.

He is back on court playing after a lay-off.

"He has gone through a fairly rough patch. But he has come back very well," his father says.

David now says he wants to spend more time pursuing opportunities to support health related technology.

"There are amazing things beings done in stroke detection and many other areas of med tech, but not nearly enough," he says.

David also has bold ambitions for the family's venture capital arm, Salta Capital, which has an interest in companies across property development, technology, hotels and real estate, and a broad portfolio of shares. "It is a way of diversifying the business, born out of the fact that if you are in the same business and it is totally occupying your mind, it is hard to be open to other factors in the world that may impact the main business," he says.

In 2020 Salta Capital raised $50 million for a new venture capital fund known as Baton Ventures.

Meanwhile the core Salta Properties business is now managing an estimated $5 billion project pipeline spanning the construction, commercial, residential, hotel and build-to-rent sectors. Its flagship projects of the past two decades include the 150 Clarendon Street residential tower in East Melbourne and Richmond's Victoria Gardens Shopping Centre.

Tarascio and his sons still lunch together most days. The patriarch's title is now founding director, having changed last year from executive chairman. "We have been good in managing the transition, because in certain things Dad does recognise he is a fish out of water – some patriarchs don't," says Sam. "You have to recognise when the ways you have done things in the past are less relevant. It takes a pretty wise person to be able to recognise that themselves. We are lucky Dad has that skill and ability."

He says one of his prime objectives every day is to ensure his father remains involved in the business in the areas that interest him most, notably early-stage project management.

His brother has a slightly different take: "The way I'd summarise Dad, he is very tough, he is very hard, but I actually think he is quite fair. Whether it is family or business, he tries to see things from all angles, which is something I have tried to do as well. The best deals are win-wins for all. He is very good at knowing what is motivating people in deals on both sides. It is easy sometimes just to see things from your own point of view in business, in family and deal structuring, and it takes constant effort to see it from both sides. He is always doing that."

Tarascio senior took leave from the business for most of his 69th year to build a Hamptons-style house adjacent to the family's 2500-strong olive grove plantation at Point Leo on the Mornington Peninsula. He wanted it finished for his 70th birthday and it was, but not before he experienced the only workplace accident of his life: falling from the roof of the half-built home, injuring his head, bruising his ribs and snapping the tendon in his arm.

While Christine would happily spend the rest of her days at Shoreham, describing it as the "most beautiful place", her husband is not so sure.

After building their dream holiday home, plus the dam and water piping on the property, Sam is frustrated he can no longer keep up the pace on the tools.

"I find it difficult to work as I used to. I would love to work out there on the property with the guys. But I have a bit of calcification of the spine which makes it difficult to bend over. So when I come down here now, I just sit here," he says. "I can't work on (Microsoft) Teams."

What keeps him returning is spending time with his beloved grandchildren and his 2500-strong olive grove plantation.

His Italian family hails from olive oil processors in the Sicilian town of Vizzini in the 1930s.

He has always believed that his late grandfather would be proud of his grandson's hobby – producing Taralinga olive oil.

"It is not about making money really, it is about producing the very best," Sam says.

Taralinga Estate has now won four gold medals at the New York International Olive Oil Competition, known as the olive oil Olympics. It means Taralinga is on the official index of the world's best olive oils.

He says a big selling point of the product is its high level of antioxidants, which make it not only a delicacy, but a health alternative.

"The olive oil thing I am very passionate about. It is not a money-making thing. I can guarantee the level of antioxidants in our oil has the absolute maximum level," he says.

"We give it to all our customers and they love it. And the medals we have won prove its quality."

Asked about the most important thing he has taught his children and he momentarily rocks back in his chair before smiling proudly.

"I have always maintained that a lot of kids grow up having an expectation that relates to the parents' success. My kids have never had that. That is very, very important. While we now have a family charter and they now know where they are going, given all the work we have done, had we not done that, there was no expectation or feeling of entitlement. They would be just as happy being independent," he says. "The way I related to them through their formative years has contributed to that. That is something not many families are capable of instilling in their kids."

# NICOLA WAKEFIELD EVANS

Nicola Wakefield Evans was 18 years old in 1978 when she applied to be a pilot with the Royal Australian Air Force. She wanted to join the Australian Defence Force Academy in Canberra and learn to fly while studying for her degree.

To this day she will never forget that her application was denied because she was a woman.

"It never occurred to me I would be rejected. I would have loved to have been a pilot, either in the airforce or in commercial aviation. But that experience gave me a resilience and determination to succeed," she says.

Given her father was a magistrate, she turned to the law and forged a long legal career in mergers and acquisitions at law firm Stephen Jaques Stone James, now known as King & Wood Mallesons or KWM.

But ever since her Air Force experience, a fire has burned deep to be a passionate public advocate for the progression of women in society.

She now serves on the boards of the listed Macquarie Group, Lend Lease and Viva Energy, while in the non-listed world, she is a director of a number of entities including the Clean Energy Finance Corporation, MetLife Australia and the Takeovers Panel.

The younger of her two sisters, Romilly Madew, is the chief executive of the federal government's infrastructure adviser, Infrastructure Australia.

For years Wakefield Evans has been one of the few top corporate women prepared to consistently speak out on gender issues.

"I realised we needed to have a public discussion. Women have a nervousness about putting themselves out there. When something goes wrong, it is the women that bare the brunt of negative press," she asserts.

"I look at the example of how Catherine Brenner was treated (at AMP), compared to men in a similar role to hers. Her whole private life was put on public display."

Brenner and AMP CEO Craig Meller resigned from the company in 2018 after the Hayne royal commission sensationally revealed AMP had charged clients fees, despite providing no services.

Wakefield Evans describes the criticism and hounding of Brenner at the time as both "sexist and discriminatory", contrasting it with the treatment of the chairman of electronics retailer Dick Smith, when it collapsed in 2016.

"No one would know who he's married to. No one would know how many children he has. He didn't have the press camped outside his house, like Catherine did. Women tend to be held up, I think still, to a greater standard than men and if something goes wrong, you have a greater fall," she says.

Brenner has now returned to corporate life as a director of shopping centre giant Scentre Group and in spite of the AMP scandal, more women have risen in recent years to the head of the nation's top boardroom tables.

Some, like Debra Hazelton – also at AMP – Kathryn Fagg at Boral, Diane Smith-Gander at Zip and Elizabeth Bryan at IAG, have also faced significant headwinds. Anne Templeman-Jones at Blackmores was forced to stare down a recalcitrant founder and eventually stepped down from the role.

It was smoother sailing for the likes of Ilana Atlas at Coca-Cola, Kathleen Conlon at Lynas, Elana Rubin at Afterpay and Sally Pitkin at Super Retail, although the latter has stepped down as a director of the scandal-plagued Star Entertainment.

Wakefield Evans worries too many women have stepped up to be chairs during difficult times for their companies.

"Sometimes they are the last people standing. Look at Crown and David Jones in recent years. Often women are given more difficult jobs. Also because there is a belief we can get stuff done, we are not bound by long standing networks," she says.

But she is concerned the negative headlines associated with some high profile female chairman may scare more women off from taking on big chairmanships, even if the critics would say they were justified.

"I do worry it is going to have an impact. We don't have enough female chairs in the ASX," she says.

Wakefield Evans is also the local chairman of "The 30 per cent Club", a global group which champions increased gender diversity at board and senior management levels.

Its first mission was campaigning for women to make up 30 per cent of the directors on ASX 200 boards, which was achieved in 2019.

"I'm now confident we will get to 35 per cent by the end of this year. The goal going forward is to move to 40 per cent and beyond," she says.

She still believes there are not enough women in senior executive roles in public companies, despite female CEO's being appointed in recent years to the likes of Coca-Cola Amatil, CSR, Lynas, Woodside, Fortescue, Incitec, Optus and Telstra.

For the past eight years at Macquarie Group, Wakefield Evans has also had a ringside seat on the board to watch one of the nation's top female chief executives, Shemara Wikramanayake, in action.

Asked how the understated Macquarie boss is different as a CEO to the male chiefs she has worked with, Wakefield Evans replies: "I think women are different in the way we conduct ourselves, in the way we form relationships and in the way we lead. I do think there is a difference and it's a very positive difference. But I'm not saying one is worse than the other," she says, noting Wikramanayake has a "lovely personality" and style, but stresses she can also make tough decisions.

"She's very generous with her time and she's very respectful as well. I don't want anyone to think that her predecessors weren't. It's just that she just does it in a different style. She's got a great ability to form coalitions really well, she forms relationships well, but she also brings people together really well. That's always been a fantastic strength of hers."

## THE GONSKI EFFECT

Wakefield Evans was fortunate in the second half of the 1970's to attend the University of NSW Law School with Wikramanayake, where they were lectured by legendary businessman David Gonski.

He has since become an important mentor.

"In making big decisions about my career, I always talk to David. He has taught me to back myself and it is not something that comes naturally to women. He also taught me to make brave decisions," Wakefield Evans says, in reference to her second opportunity to work overseas in 2007, when she moved to Hong Kong as managing partner, international at KWM when she had four school-aged sons and a husband with his own legal career.

"David has also been very generous with sharing his connections."

It was Wakefield Evans' Asian experience that kicked off her career as a non-executive director when in May 2011 she was asked to join the board of transport company Toll Holdings by its chairman Ray Horsburgh. She says his guidance and mentoring was "invaluable".

"To be confident about the make-up of the boards you are on and having a chair you respect and is respected is vital. It is your reputation at stake.

"I have learned the chair is absolutely important. Ray was great for me at Toll," she says, before giving the same plaudits to former Lend Lease chair David Crawford at Macquarie chair Kevin McCann.

Between 2014 and 2020 Wakefield Evans was a director of the private directors club known as O'Connell Street Associates (OCA).

Ironically its darkened, nondescript offices on the sixth level of No 2 O'Connell Street in the heart of Sydney's CBD were long a bastion for the city's blue blood, exclusively male board members.

"It has changed remarkably over the past decade," she says.

"There are now more female associates and I was part of making that change.

"In leaving I wanted to make space for them to appoint more women to become members."

Over her 11 years on public company boards, Wakefield Evans has seen a huge evolution in the role of a director.

The clear message from the Hayne Royal Commission into the financial services sector was an expectation that directors understood their businesses better, including being prepared to make visits to the grass-roots operations.

More broadly the so-called directors club has come under fire in recent years for failing to take accountability where strategic or governance errors have cost shareholders dearly.

With her background in M&A and the capital markets, Wakefield Evans says she seen the "best and worst" of boards. But she rejects claims company directors are on a gravy train.

"We have to work hard. A lot of people think it is a bit of a cushy job. It is not cushy at all. No director I know thinks they are on the board for cushiness. It has taken time for public perception to catch up with reality of what we are doing," she says.

But still she worries the general public, corporate stakeholders, regulators and the media still don't understand the role of directors.

"When something goes wrong, the board is the first focus. But we don't run the company," she says.

"There is still that issue around the disconnect between expectations on directors and what we can do. We are not there full time managing the company's business."

## THE FAMILY LOGISTICS MANAGER

Wakefield Evans and her husband Kym Evans raised their boys with a strict no-weapons policy, which banned them playing with toy guns and swords.

"When they were children they thought that was a bit naff. Now that they are adults, I think they have really appreciated it because we worked really hard to make sure that they were great mates with each other. They have also got great relationships with women," she says.

She went back to work full time at KWM after her oldest son was born, and he has just turned 30. She long called herself the "family logistics manager", timetabling the family's activities on spreadsheets.

"I knew I needed to work through the guilt gene. There were times I couldn't go to a function when they wanted me to," she says.

"But I don't regret at all having a full-time working career and being a mother. Now I talk to younger women to say, 'You can do it and your children aren't going to end up monsters'."

In fact one of her sons, Riley, stood up at an International Women's Day function in March 2022 to publicly declare his appreciation for having a mother who had shown him leadership in working full-time, helping him frame how he would enter the workforce.

Two of her older sons now work for large organisations run by female CEOs and love it.

The family remain close and now sail regularly together on Sydney Harbour from the Royal Sydney Yacht Squadron in Kirribilli, the nation's oldest open boat sailing club, on their Seaquest RP36 called "Whistling Kite".

Wakefield Evans was in 2021 awarded the Squadron's Yachtswoman of the Year.

"It has been a very big part of my life. I am an advocate for women in sailing because you can compete equally with boys," she says.

"It also teaches you about resilience and risk at an early age."

Another of her greatest passions in life is to solve the scourge of domestic violence on society, after watching family members and friends in difficult relationships. She describes it as an ongoing "national emergency".

"It is not a socio-economic issue. It's a deep-seated cultural issue, and it can often just sneak up on you as well and that certainly happened to a very close family member of mine," she says.

"It is not a matter of throwing money at domestic violence. There's got to be significant change across a whole lot of structures in our society."

# KEN WARRINER

*Isis Downs station lies deep within the grazing country of Central Queensland, 20km east of the small township of Isisford and more than an hour south of Longreach, bordered by the Barcoo river.*

*The heritage-listed shearing shed on the site remains one of the biggest and most intact early twentieth century shearing complexes in Queensland, with its semi-circular, prefabricated design the only one of its type in Australia.*

*In early 2008 I made the long trek from my then home in Sydney to the property – which now runs only cattle – to interview Ken Warriner, one of the legends of the Australian cattle industry, for a feature story for The Australian Financial Review magazine.*

*When I arrived, we chatted at length on the shady veranda of the historic homestead overlooking its lush green lawn, which stood in stark contrast to the dusty surrounding landscape long an inspiration for many Australian poets, including Banjo Paterson.*

*In the evening we dined on freshly butchered beef from the property in the homestead's decorated main dining room, as Warriner regaled many stories – some of which were strictly off the record – of his decades-long association with the Packer family.*

*When I retired for the night to my room in the staff quarters a short stroll from the main house, I will never forget the clarity of the cloudless night sky. I have never again seen so many stars on an evening.*

*But the greatest thrill of my visit was standing with Warriner the next morning on top of a giant road train listening to the thundering roar as hundreds of Brahman cattle were loaded onto its trailers below us.*

*While he retired from CPC 2015, his family's legend will live long in the company. As will its association with the Packer's.*

Kerry Packer's good mate Ken Warriner became a business partner of Australia's richest man in 1983.

A country boy at heart, Warriner had just enjoyed a big night out in Sydney with his wife, Sally, and was badly hung-over.

Lying before him on a stainless steel table, in the intensive care unit at St Vincent's Private Hospital, dressed only in a pair of boxer shorts and wired up to a heart monitor, was Packer, cigarette in mouth.

He had summoned his mate to the hospital after being admitted for chest pains. But it was Warriner who was feeling the worse for wear.

"How are you going, son?" Packer asked.

"Kerry, I think I am crooker than you are. I haven't been to bed," Warriner replied gingerly.

"Have a beer," Packer boomed, as he pulled his monitors off, triggering a panicked visit from the duty nurse. "You'd better go and get this boy a six-pack," he told her.

By noon, adman John Singleton, the then Packer lieutenant Peter Baillieu and a few others had arrived with more beer. When Packer's heart surgeon Victor Chang came to check on his patient, he whispered to Warriner: "This will do him the world of good."

Warriner was then a co-owner of Ashburton Pastoral Company, which controlled some of the nation's heritage stations, including Newcastle Waters in the Northern Territory. Packer was keen to get a foothold in the industry.

That afternoon, between beers and beneath the cigarette smoke, a deal was agreed in principle that Packer would take a half-share in the Humbert River Station in the NT.

He subsequently bought the lot from Ashburton, along with Newcastle

Waters. And so the seeds of the evolution of the Packer family's cattle kingdom, the Consolidated Pastoral Company, were sown.

Warriner was the company's one constant over the decades before James Packer sold the business in 2009 to Terra Firma Capital Partners, the private equity firm founded by British buyout king Guy Hands. In 2020 Terra Firma offloaded CPC to Mr Hands' private family office.

Before James sold the business, the then 66 year old Warriner – long known in the industry as the Gecko and who to this day remains one of Australia's best-known cattlemen – granted me a rare interview.

Back then Consolidated Pastoral was one of an assortment of Kerry Packer's so-called "collectables".

They included a ski resort, a retail fashion chain and a skincare manufacturer managed as private equity investments by the family's private company Consolidated Press Holdings in the Consolidated Press capital portfolio.

Like his old mate Kerry, Warriner littered his conversation with the odd f-word and also admitted he has always loved a wager – he went to 24 Melbourne Cups in a row (and only watched one of them live because he was in the betting ring or the bar at the time). But Warriner also revealed that the ties that bound him to James Packer also ran deep.

When James finished his education at Sydney's prestigious Cranbrook School, he was sent up north by his father to be a jackaroo at Newcastle Waters, halfway between Darwin and Alice Springs in the cattle country of the Barkly Tableland.

Warriner was his boss.

Kerry's instructions to his mate were strict – treat him like everybody else!

"I said to James, 'this is going to come back on me' and James has reminded me of it a few times," Warriner told me with a grin.

When I asked how the young Packer coped with life at Newcastle

Waters, Warriner didn't mince words.

"He was good. It was very different to anything he had ever done in his life before. But he did do it bloody hard, as a lot of those young fellows do, and he was big. And the bigger they are, when they haven't done horsemanship and all that, the harder it is. But, oh shit, he stuck it out. He was a determined bloke. There were no refrigerators in the stock camps back then; they were bloody rough. They slept on the ground and had to crap under a tree for six months. But Kerry reckoned it was fantastic – the change in him."

While Kerry Packer only liked to venture to the outback to relax – his two favourite stations were Newcastle Waters and Carlton Hill on the Ord River in the East Kimberley – Warriner has loved working the land ever since his career began as a jackaroo near Blackall in central-western Queensland decades ago.

Three of his five sons, all to his ex-wife Sally, have worked in the business.

In August 2016 one of those sons, Jock Warriner, took me on an unforgettable aerial tour in his light aircraft of Newcastle Waters when I was visiting the properly for the annual Spellbore event, an annual competition run to identify the top stock camp in the north.

Nine months later Jock ended his 11-year association with CPC to join the Gulf Coast Agricultural Company, a premium group of properties located in the Gulf of Carpentaria.

Today he has his own aviation services company for the cattle industry, based at Kununurra in WA's East Kimberley region.

## ON THE GROUND

As Ken Warriner and I traversed the length and breadth of Isis Downs, bumping along in one of the station's four-wheel-drive vehicles on a clear, warm afternoon in April 2008, Warriner suddenly stopped the car and strolled into a paddock awash with different varieties of straw-coloured grass on land cleared only two years ago.

It had been a brilliant season for Isis Downs, following widespread flooding in December and January. As Warriner removed the Ray-Bans from under his broad-brimmed hat (which carries CPC's trademark wineglass branding), you could see the sparkle in his eyes.

"This is magnificent. There would be 20 to 30 different types of grass here and it is all seeded," he said. "Now we can work out how many cattle we will run on it."

Later in the day, as we stopped to admire a herd of stunning-looking Brahman cattle, Warriner fixed his eye on a perfectly formed calf in the corner of the paddock. "Look at that little calf. You can see the meat that would hang off that!" he said admiringly.

He told me Isis Downs would make $2 million to $3 million that year, after being in drought for five years. Spread over 2,327 square kilometres, it then comprised nine properties painstakingly put together since Consolidated Pastoral acquired the original station in 1987.

Like other cattle companies, Consolidated Pastoral has long reaped the rewards of the boom in agriculture in Australia's north, where reliable rainfall and cheap land supplies are providing a strong base from which to source beef for soaring Asian demand.

It has also played into the wider global soft commodities boom, which opened up new beef eating markets in China, Russia and Eastern Europe.

Companies such as Consolidated Pastoral have also reaped the benefits of vastly improved land values in the north.

But there was another extremely private side to Consolidated Pastoral – the properties were an integral part of the Packer family's social scene and, over the years, hosted some of the heavyweights of Australian and international business.

Allco's deputy chairman Bob Mansfield and former executive chairman David Coe were regular visitors to the historic fishing camp at Carlton Hill (it is legend that the idea to create Allco flowed from conversations beside the waters of the Ord River).

A regular visitor to Newcastle Waters in Kerry Packer's day was his good mate, former World Bank president James Wolfensohn and his high-flying international friends.

Warriner revealed Newcastle Waters had also hosted Fortescue Metals founder Andrew 'Twiggy' Forrest.

"He's a likeable bloke. He's a great family bloke," Warriner told me of Forrest. "He and his kids got a hell of a kick out of our stud stock at Newcastle Waters. They [the cattle] are very quiet and they'll come up and actually kiss you and his kids were having a ball with some of those little heifers."

For Kerry Packer, the properties were also a retreat from the daily grind of business – an opportunity to do a spot of fishing, pig shooting from a helicopter or just to be with people who were down-to-earth.

"It is one thing that Kerry really liked about it, compared to television," Warriner told me. "He said, 'you guys tell each other everything. You've got nothing to hide; it's all open.' He had a lot of time for the people in the north because they copped it pretty tough."

While Warriner talked to Kerry Packer almost every day, he says he didn't see him much on the properties, "particularly once the polo started."

He said he saw more of James out on the land, perhaps a "few times a year."

James was said to land his Global Express private jet at nearby towns such as Tennant Creek (the runway at Newcastle Waters could not handle the weight of the aircraft) and then he and his party were flown into the station in a light plane.

"When James is up there, he can be on the computer, on the phone, even though he is probably trying to let down a bit and not to get too hands-on. He was just up for two days and we went out on the property. He keeps you on the ball a bit because you know he can count," Warriner told me.

Also on that trip were James's wife Erica, his mother Ros, PBL Media chief executive Ian Law and his wife Roslyn. For many years Warriner accompanied the Wagga-born Ros Packer on an annual 'outback safari', touring all the stations in the north, sometimes staying on the road for two to three weeks at a time. She often dropped in on her good friends, the Paspaleys, the pearling family, and they have been sailing on the cruise ship MV Orion. Ros and Warriner are close. Immediately after arriving at Isis Downs for our interview, he made a phone call to her in New York. "She is good with the land. She knows cattle; she is a good judge of stock and she is really good with people," he told me.

Warriner attributed the success of the company to its aggregated nature. To try to replicate the portfolio today would be virtually impossible.

"We've got a string of properties that are strategically positioned across the top of Australia. We can take cattle from [Queensland] back to the Kimberley and vice versa because they will handle that country," he said. "We have bred a line of cattle that can handle all conditions."

John Underwood, a past president of the Northern Territory Cattlemen's Association, said Warriner and Consolidated Pastoral were highly respected in the industry.

"They aren't broken-arse cattlemen like us," he told me from his home at Riveren station on the Victoria River in the NT. "They've got the skills and they have had the vision to buy properties in all rainfall areas and soil types. They have got all bases covered."

Warriner also chaired two other CPC businesses, GRM and Austrex.

GRM international provides advisory and management services to 24 countries for government and private clients, and 28 bilateral and multilateral agencies in Australia and overseas. Austrex trades primarily in livestock from Australia to the Middle East, South-East Asia and China.

He was once a member of the committee advising the National Farmers Federation on Aboriginal issues and has long played a role in liaison with Aborigines in the NT and WA.

He was also previously a key figure in native title negotiations with the Miriuwung Gajerrong people of the East Kimberley.

"We've got a close liaison with a lot of Indigenous Australians," he said. "Our basic rule is they can go anywhere they like provided they abide by the law."

Warriner has long lived by a simple maxim – one that James Packer, given his extensive historical interests in the gaming industry, might relate to.

"The rural industry is a gamble. You think playing in a casino is gambling, but that's just heads or tails. Here you've got drought, floods, fires, bad handling, the dollar, you name it. And if you do everything right with your breeding, I still reckon you need 50 per cent luck."

## ENSURING REMOTE ACCESS

He didn't mean to but for half an hour in 1987, Ken Warriner thought he had cost Kerry Packer the deal of a lifetime. Packer had just agreed to arguably his best ever business deal, the $1 billion sale of his Nine television network to Perth tycoon Alan Bond. But Warriner had a problem.

He knew the deal covered Nine's flagship Sydney and Melbourne stations, but nothing had been said about Channel 8 in Darwin, which was also part of the Nine empire. Warriner was a director of the channel for many years and was keen that his friend keep control of it. And then there was the small matter of the satellite links that for years had delivered a live, commercial-free feed of the Nine, Seven and Ten networks to Newcastle Waters and other Packer properties; properties on which Warriner spent most of his time.

"We were down at Palm Beach and I asked Kerry about Channel 8 and the sat links. And Kerry said, 'Jesus, yeah, I want that too for Palm Beach [Sydney] and Ellerston [his property in the Hunter Valley],'" Warriner recalled. "He rang up [Bond's right-hand man] Peter Beckwith and said, 'In this deal, Channel 8 in Darwin is not in it, and the sat links . . . we need to keep those.' And I could hear the noise coming from Peter Beckwith. I couldn't hear what he said, [but] then Kerry's voice got louder. 'That is part of the deal,' he said. 'Talk to Alan, if he doesn't like it, well forget the deal.' "I'd discussed the deal with Kerry, where he felt he was a few hundred million in front. And I thought 'Christ this thing is only worth $12 million, that's a big risk.' And Kerry said, 'I'll bet you they'll ring back in half an hour to say there is no problem.'" It was a long half-hour for Warriner. But sure enough, the call came. "And he was spot on," Warriner said, laughing. "We were very close. He and my mother were two people I'd ring up when things were going wrong," he says quietly, before adding with a grin: "And they both pulled the pin at the same time."

For years Warriner and Packer went bull running and shooting in the Northern Territory, gambled at casinos and took the Channel Nine helicopter on holidays together. Warriner became a trusted lieutenant. He had first met Packer in the 1970s, years before the formation of Consolidated Pastoral, when Packer used to come up to the Kimberley cattle station, Mount House. Warriner was managing the property for the giant US-based King Ranch group.

Over the coming years, Warriner was exposed to every part of the

Packer empire and became close with many of the billionaire's crew of mates, including Lloyd Williams.

"Anyone who knows Kenny admires his loyalty. He's got tremendous loyalty. And that was something that was really valued by Kerry," Williams told me. "It's what countries are made of, people like Kenny."

Warriner also knew Packer's foot soldiers, including the legendary Nine network technicians.

"In 1984, they came up and installed the sat links for us at Newcastle Waters. I was sitting there with the techs, and one of the engineers on the ground asked his mate on the roof to put up something round to tune in on. And then there was this big brown-eye chucked by one of them. It was one of the first transmissions," he joked.

Warriner was with Packer a few weeks before he died.

"When I last saw him, Sally [Ford, Warriner's partner] and I went down and had coffee with him. And I think he knew the end was near ... He hung on like you wouldn't believe in those last three years. It was obviously very sad. We miss him enormously as a friend."

# ALAN WILSON

*I first met Alan Wilson in November 2015 in a non-descript meeting room in Abbottsford on the fringe of the Melbourne CBD. The occasion was the annual general meeting of the plumbing and bathroom products supplier he chaired known as Reece. The AGM was the only day each year that a journalist could ever talk to a member of the deeply private Wilson family. They would never return emails or phone calls.*

*That day I walked up to Alan after the meeting, turned on my tape recorder and asked him a few questions. He was very happy to chat, in his excitement even dropping an "f bomb" into his animated commentary on Woolworth's failed excursion into the hardware sector.*

*A year later I did the same with Alan's son Peter, from which I wrote a long feature article about the amazing Wilson family legacy at Reece. One of my long-time readers wrote to me afterwards describing them as "the Greta Garbo's of corporate Australia", in reference to one of the greatest screen actresses of all time.*

*Over the following years I have built a trusted relationship with Alan and Peter. So it was an honour and privilege to sit down with Alan in 2022 for the first wide-ranging interview of his life to mark his departure from the Reece chairmanship.*

*His son will now inherit the role, and in 2023 Peter granted me his only media interview to mark his succession. In my view, Reece is in very good hands.*

Alan Wilson's milestone 80th birthday celebration in October 2020 was a two-day affair, starting with a quiet picnic with family and friends in Melbourne's Canterbury Gardens on his birthday eve.

The next day the Reece annual meeting was held virtually for the first time due to the Covid-19 pandemic at the studios of CrocMedia in Southbank.

Afterwards Alan and his son Peter – Reece's managing director – celebrated with a cake, beers and champagne in the gardens outside, before heading to Peter's house where his wife cooked her father-in-law roast duck.

Peter opened a bottle of 1993 Grange, which marked the year he started at Reece.

It was an occasion upon which the family reflected not only on Alan's amazing milestone, but quietly contemplated the future.

That day Alan had been re-elected by shareholders as a Reece director for another three years, but in his mind he was beginning to wonder how long he could continue as chairman.

"The additional modern responsibilities of sustainability and governance I find difficult, simply because my focus has always been on the operations of the business and most importantly, its people. My strengths are not in those former areas, they are in the latter," Alan told me in August 2022 in the only media interview of his life.

"Over the last two years I have come to the view that Reece is now almost a $10bn company and it is time for someone else to chair the firm into its next era of growth."

The week of that interview, Wilson finally decided to relinquish his chairman's role at Reece and stay on the board as an executive director.

"A lot of these governance requirements, I don't believe I can do justice to them. I don't want to be responsible for things where I don't fully understand what is needed. I will be happy to give advice going forward in the areas I enjoy and can add value," Alan told me.

Reece's deputy chair, Tim Poole, stepped up to be acting chairman.

A year later Reece anointed Peter Wilson as the future executive chairman-elect but asked Poole to fill the void until the timing is deemed to be right in the future for a handover.

Most importantly Alan now continues doing what he does best – visiting stores – which became virtual via FaceTime during the worst months of the pandemic.

Since restrictions lifted, he has been physically back in the store network at least four times a week.

His decision to retire as chairman was a monumental one in the history of Reece, which traces its roots to 1919 when Harold Joseph Reece started selling hardware products from the back of a truck in Melbourne suburbia.

Reece was listed on the ASX in 1954 and a decade later the Wilson family became majority owners. Alan's father was involved in sheet metal manufacturing and his grandfather was a plumber.

Today, Alan and Peter Wilson know every facet and nuance of their customers and the industry in which they operate.

They have ignored calls from investors for short-term rewards at the expense of long-term growth and have become a unique example of a highly successful father-son team in business.

Peter came into the business in 1993 at an important point in its history and took Reece to another level by organising and professionalising the company while maintaining the values of his father and grandfather.

Tim Poole says it takes a certain type of entrepreneur to build something from basically nothing, which Alan did through hard work, empowering managers and exceptional trading skills.

"It takes a very different type of person to take what was a collection of 250-odd small businesses, bring them together as one group and turn it into a globally significant company in its industry which is what Peter did," Poole told me following Wilson's retirement announcement.

"Alan was the master entrepreneur that went from nothing to something significant and Peter was the exceptional CEO that took it to the next level. It is truly remarkable to think they are father and son and so different. Incredibly, their unique and different skills were so right for the time that each of them were running the business."

"The chairman-CEO relationship is very important but it is tough to get right and you overlay that with the father-son issue and the length of time they have worked together. It is quite unique and a special story in the history of Australian business."

## COMING TO AMERICA

It was code named Project Hamilton, Peter's long-held dream to take Reece to America, the biggest market in the world.

The name was chosen as a testament to his grandfather, Les, who was born in the Victorian town of the same name.

But the 2018 acquisition by Reece of MORSCO – one of America's biggest distributors of plumbing heating and cooling products – would be the largest and most difficult transaction in Reece's history, for which it undertook a mammoth capital raising.

Alan admitted in his interview with me that he had initial reservations about the deal.

"I was certainly apprehensive knowing the risks involved. But I was confident in our model, even if I knew it would take a long time to implement," he said.

After resuming travelling interstate in 2022, Alan visited North America later in the year to see the MORSCO business for the first time.

For years Reece has been criticised for its corporate governance practices and many have wondered why the company remains listed given it is 67.7 per cent owned by the Wilson family. But Alan was adamant Reece would not have grown to its current size if it had been private.

"Being listed has also given Reece an accountability to its shareholders and staff that has been to its benefit. We have been proud to pay our shareholders significant dividends over the decades," he said.

While Reece investors have long lauded the relationship between Alan and Peter Wilson, the former accepted he had found giving positive feedback to his son challenging at times.

"I suppose I am a bit like my father. He never gave praise. He would do it in an indirect way. He would never say 'Well done' but I would hear it from other people. But I knew he thought I was doing the right thing. It was implied," he said.

"I suppose I did have an expectation with Peter. But I am sure I would have said 'Well done' to him more than my father ever did to me. Peter is a very resilient character, which is a credit to him."

Asked what was the most important thing he has taught his son, Alan's response reflected the affection he held for his mother and Peter's grandmother, Ngaere, and for the business he has grown to love like a family.

"Doing the right thing by Reece," he said. "Look after Mother Reece and it will look after you. I would like to think that Peter has picked that up. We used to drink to that every year and I still say it on a regular basis and it is said to me back. My brothers understand it too. I would like to think he has picked that up and if he has, the journey will continue."

So, what has Peter taught him?

"That there is always a better way and if there is a better way, do it," Alan said. "I've often persevered with people who were not ideal for their roles but they were achieving goals for the company. I will turn the other cheek. In building the business, I would accept some different standards. Whereas Peter has always wanted a consistent, higher standard."

## THE SILENT TYPE

Peter has long lived by his father's one-liner mottos: Stick to your knitting. Make hay while the sun shines. It's not how you buy, it's how you sell. Keep it simple. We must make sure we are on the right horse. Through hard work you can achieve anything. Live within your means. Be humble.

"Most of these philosophies are now ingrained in the culture at Reece. Perhaps the greatest accolade to dad's leadership attributes is the huge number of people at Reece who see Dad as their father figure and their mentor," Alan said.

Asked why he has always eschewed publicity, Alan simply shrugged his shoulders and for a moment stared out the window of his corner office at Reece's high tech headquarters in the trendy inner-city Melbourne suburb of Cremorne.

It is a world away from its old office at Burwood.

"I was brought up not to talk about myself and I have followed that mantra all my life.

"I have a saying to let other people do the talking when it comes to yourself. I regularly say to people who are good, 'You don't have to talk about yourself, let others do it'," he eventually told me.

"I still enjoy the fact I can go anywhere and be incognito. I enjoy just being a normal person. I have always seen money as purely a tool to get from A to B. It has never been a driver for me. Achieving dreams has been my main driver."

Alan's wife Denise was diagnosed with Alzheimer's disease in 2017.

After battling for years to care for her, in 2022 it finally became too much for him and she was admitted to an aged-care home. Sadly, Denise passed away in June 2023.

The family, including Peter's younger siblings David and Claire, had celebrated Denise's 81st birthday in July 2022 with a small function in a private dining room at the home.

In our interview before his wife's passing, Alan had said he rationalised his situation knowing that compared to most people, he was still better off than many and had enjoyed a great life for all his 81 years.

"I have been able to do lots of things I like doing. It has been no good me fighting the reality of Denise's situation. I can't do anything about it. It has to be," he said.

For a moment you saw the pain in his eyes, of helplessly watching on as his wife slid towards a tragically inevitable fate.

"It is when you are in situations like this and you are tested that you realise that you love somebody," he said. "That is stronger than anything else. It is amazing how strong that can be. In the 50-year journey, when you've had your ups and downs, it is still there. It staggers you."

Alan is still up for his early morning walks and plays golf each Wednesday and Saturday afternoons with friends.

But he gets the greatest pleasure from continuing to engage with Reece's people.

He is immensely proud to have made the firm the nation's biggest – and most profitable – bathroom and plumbing-supply retailer and biggest trade supplier.

The Wilson family has still not sold a single share since it took control of Reece back in 1969.

"Mother Reece has been my love affair with this business," Alan told me.

"This place has given lots of everyday people a great career. I'm immensely proud of that."

# BEN WYATT

When Ben Wyatt announced his shock decision to quit politics in February 2020, it wasn't long before the then West Australian Treasurer – the first indigenous person to hold the role at state or federal level – received a phone call from Woodside Petroleum and Qantas chairman, Richard Goyder.

"I reached out to him when he first said he was going and told him 'If you want to have a chat, I'm prepared to be a sounding board,'" Goyder recalls.

Wyatt soon surprisingly reversed his retirement decision in a bid to see WA through the COVID pandemic, but by November 2020 and with a critical state budget under his belt, reiterated to the public that he would not contest the next state election to be held the following March.

"When he got serious about going again, I was a sounding board for him on the ins and outs of being a non-executive director versus taking an executive role. The more I got to know him, the sooner I was going to pop the question about him joining the Woodside board, subject to the views of my colleagues," Goyder says.

Wyatt again made history on June 2, 2022 when he became a Woodside director, in doing so becoming the first indigenous board member of an ASX200 company.

That same week it was announced he would be joining the board of Rio Tinto, which was still managing the fallout from its disastrous destruction of a 46,000-year-old sacred Indigenous site in WA's Pilbara region in May 2020. He took up his directorship in September last year.

What surprised Wyatt most about the early months of his non-executive director life was the loneliness. He reveals that he repeatedly asked himself a puzzling and provocative question.

"So where is everybody? Where are my Indigenous Australian colleagues? Because every chairman of every top 200 Australian listed company would say 'We need to have more Indigenous Australians on boards. But where are they?" he says.

"Even though it's unusual having an Indigenous Australian person join the board of a large, listed company, the concept itself is so well ventilated. So, I was surprised that I had come and there was just no one around. We've been talking about this for so long."

He believes there is now a solid group of Indigenous Australians with experience who can add value to large public company boards, not just in the executive ranks.

"Over the last 20 years you have seen the emergence of a cohort of Indigenous Australians with significant commercial and governance experience, particularly in the governance of service providers. That is not irrelevant to the experience and skill set of a commercial board. So, there are people around, you don't actually need affirmative action on this. Because if you look, you will find them," he says.

"All large companies that provide a service or a good to Australians should be thinking about how they might go about developing an Aboriginal person to join their board . . . I'd like to think five years from now, it will not be unusual."

The son of two school teachers who grew up regional WA, Wyatt studied at Duntroon Military College in Canberra and the London School of Economics before working as a barrister and solicitor with Minter Ellison in Perth and the WA Director of Public Prosecutions.

He then had a successful 15-year career in politics.

But now Australia's newest listed indigenous director, the nephew of Federal Minister for Indigenous Australians Ken Wyatt and son of the respected senior public servant Cedric Wyatt is adamant his transition to the boardroom should not be defined by the colour of his skin.

Richard Goyder acknowledges Wyatt was something of a "captain's pick" at Woodside, but reiterates his background in treasury and finance made him perfectly qualified to assist the company with its growth agenda.

"It goes back to the question of finding the right person and if they are indigenous, it is a big plus. At Woodside, we have lots of challenges and he will help us get through them," Goyder says.

"One of the really good things about Ben is that people know he is a pioneer but he doesn't play that card. (His heritage) doesn't play into my relationship with Ben other than I think he has a very good understanding of issues around indigenous Australians."

## JOINING RIO TINTO

Wyatt was Aboriginal affairs minister in the WA government when Rio Tinto sensationally blew up the ancient caves at Juukan Gorge in the Pilbara, triggering an international controversy and the eventual resignation of the chief executive and chairman.

The destruction of the caves was approved in a deal between Rio and the land's traditional owners – the Puutu Kunti Kurrama and Pinikura peoples – seven years earlier, before Wyatt became a minister.

Rio had also been criticised in a WA Parlimentary Inquiry for its workplace culture and last year commissioned an independent review by Elizabeth Broderick that found a systemic organisational culture of bullying, harassment and racism.

Wyatt was initially approached to join the Rio board by former chairman Simon Thompson and thought long and hard about being the director of company that had been rocked to its core by scandal.

"Once I accepted Woodside I kind of thought, 'Well, this is the direction I'm going now (onto boards). About the same time, the conversations with the now former chair of Rio began. I took a lot of advice on it," Wyatt says.

"I thought about it really deeply and took a fair bit of advice from some Aboriginal leaders whose opinions I value."

Richard Goyder reveals he counselled Wyatt to take the role if he felt the miner was committed to changing its approach to cultural heritage issues and restoring its reputation.

"I encouraged Ben when Rio reached out to him. I told him to do his own due diligence to ensure they were doing it for the right reasons, and of course he did that," Goyder says.

When he was eventually appointed to the board, Wyatt said publicly that he was "deeply saddened and disappointed" by the events at Juukan Gorge. But that didn't appease the critics.

Some believed that given his previous senior roles in government, he should have waited at least two years to join big corporate boards, especially Rio.

Senior indigenous leader Pat Dodson, who sat on the Juukan Gorge Senate inquiry, said Wyatt's appointment brought no credit to Rio and that it would do nothing to restore the firm's reputation after the disaster.

He claimed Aboriginal people, especially those whose sacred sites are endangered by mining, would "rightly be sceptical" about the appointment.

Wyatt says he and Dodson have known each other for many years and that he was somewhat taken aback by the criticism.

"We've talked at great length about the importance of Aboriginal voices and Aboriginal perspectives in corporate Australia, both in terms of the senior executive ranks and on boards. So, I was surprised because it was entirely consistent with what he'd been demanding of corporate Australia for a long period of time. I get that Pat was still angry and probably still is angry about what happened at Juukan, but my view is you have got to get in and make sure that Rio can regain a social licence that has some value. The rebuild of that social licence is something that I'm genuinely interested in," Wyatt says.

When in government Wyatt helped draft the Aboriginal Cultural Heritage Bill designed to better protect Indigenous sites of significance by compelling miners to consult early and meaningfully with traditional owners.

But the bill has been criticised by some traditional owners, who say it doesn't allow Aboriginal groups the final veto over what land is destroyed in a mining lease deal.

Wyatt says companies – especially miners – needed to develop a much stronger understanding of the Aboriginal decision-making process.

He argues what is important to a traditional owner group is often quite different to the commercial pressures of a publicly listed company and says indigenous governance practices can be employed by boards to balance environmental, social and governance issues with shareholder returns.

But more broadly he believes that in the wake of the Juukan Gorge disaster, it is possible to resolve the tensions between the agendas of mining companies and the preservation of Aboriginal culture and heritage across the nation.

For a start he believes that with the introduction native title legislation decades ago, there has been a much better and more equitable negotiating position between mining companies and Aboriginal groups.

"But also there are expectations now in corporate Australia around how you negotiate and partner with First Nations people. It's now really front and centre in what boards think about and what senior executives think about. I think there will always be a tension but it is resolvable," he says.

"The Aboriginal partners need to see value in a partnership with a mining company, whether that is value in the terms of the dollar sense or the broader corporate culture. That is, Aboriginal people actually are going to be part of the decision-making process, they are actually going to be important in how a mine is designed, implemented and run."

He says Rio's move in February this year to reached agreement with the Yinhawangka Aboriginal Corporation (YAC) on a co-designed management plan to ensure the protection of significant social and cultural heritage values as part of the proposed development of the Western Range iron-ore project in the Pilbara showed what was possible.

In November 2022 Rio also signed an agreement with the Yindjibarndi people – who have long been engaged in a bitter legal battle with Andrew Forrest's Fortescue Metals Group – to provide them with $20 million a year for at least the next 10 years in return for granting Rio continued rail access across their traditional lands to deliver iron ore to the ports at Cape Lambert and Dampier.

"I think the Aboriginal decision-making process values that kind of longer term consideration of the impacts on country and I think that is something that certainly when you speak to asset managers, they are now factoring into how they manage those sites. It's less transactional, basically," Wyatt says.

Speaking more broadly, he has long held the view that constitutional recognition is fundamentally important to First Nation peoples and believes corporate Australia has a role to come on board with the proposal to give Aboriginal Australians the right to be heard on legislation that affects them.

This is despite criticism from the likes of Northern Territory Senator Jacinta Price, a self-described Warlpiri-Celtic Australian, who calls "The Voice" another "virtue-signalling … gravy train".

"I think as a company you are going to be required to declare a position. That doesn't need to be contentious," Wyatt says.

"Because the point I keep making is, the idea that the federal parliament is required to speak to Aboriginal people about laws that might impact them, many state governments have been doing that for some time. So I think the Commonwealth proposition itself isn't that contentious."

However, the voice proposal was rejected by the Australian people in the 2023 Referendum.

When he was WA Treasurer in 2018 Wyatt also successfully legislated for the introduction of procurement policies which favoured Indigenous employment.

Prior to 2018, there was no policy in place to set targets to measure contracting outcomes for Aboriginal businesses in Western Australia,

The policies have since seen consistent year-on-year growth in WA government contracting with Aboriginal businesses.

The latest statistics show WA's state procurement policy has exceeded targets for Aboriginal goods, services and work contracts, with more growth in its third year of operation.

"They do work. They have an impact and they give Aboriginal businesses confidence to expand. I'm a big fan of the procurement policies of governments and corporations. All boards have to be alert to how they are perceived in the local communities where their companies operate," Wyatt says.

He is also supportive of Reconciliation Action Plans (RAPs), which since 2006 have enabled organisations to sustainably and strategically take meaningful action to advance reconciliation.

Hundreds of Australian corporations, governments and community organisations have since released RAPs that have been endorsed by Reconciliation Australia, the national organisation promoting reconciliation between Aboriginal and Torres Strait Islander peoples and the broader community.

"RAP's are important for companies to recognise how to employ more people and create more opportunities. There is a strong maturity in RAP's now, which is to be applauded," Wyatt says.

## RISK AND REPUTATION

Wyatt has long known and respected Gilbert & Tobin managing partner Danny Gilbert, the lawyer who in 2022 authored a landmark independent review into retailing giant Woolworth's flawed consultation process for a new big barn liquor store in Darwin.

The review found Woolworths prioritised commercial objectives over good relations with the community and was insensitive towards local Indigenous people.

Most significantly, it said Australia's largest retailer did not meet the standards expected of a leading corporate citizen when it pursued plans to open the store in the face of overwhelming community opposition.

"It's good. It's great, It's an amazing thing for a company to do because it wasn't a judicial thing or a parliamentary demand. Woolworths just did it. But it highlights that the legitimacy of what you do in a company has a lot more challenges to it now. Companies have come a long way. But I just think in the next decade, with more volatility globally and more government intervention, I suspect this social licence debate is going to be more intense on boards globally," Wyatt says.

"Publicly listed companies have higher expectations on them. But you've got to be aware that the social licence expectation evolve really quickly. You've got to be trying to predict the solution and be ready for it, because it sometimes changes really fast."

This plays into Wyatt's broader concerns about what he calls "growing hostility" in the Australian community towards traditional public company structures.

"The complexity I am seeing in the boardroom is the rapidly changing investment environment. What are appropriate ownership structures for that. For the first time public company structures are under challenge – private equity now has the scale to challenge. There are other options for how organisations are owned," he says.

"Whereas I still think companies that are really important to communities should be publicly listed, because of that level of transparency and public expectation and the ability of people to also share in the ownership of those firms."

While he says some companies have been the authors of their own reputational demise, he worries that public skepticism towards the motives of corporations has grown more hostile in the last five years.

"One of the biggest changes that humankind has had to grapple with is moving to eradicate carbon from our industrial system. Its a huge change. So that creates a lot of uncertainty and hostility. I think perhaps, as a result, people see corporations more as an avoider of local obligations. That's a real danger because companies that I'm involved with and others, are really important for the success of local communities," he says.

"Corporate Australia has to get back into the narrative around being part of why they are important to their local communities."

He says this also extends to business leaders being prepared to take public positions on important policy issues for the country.

"There are significant business leaders around the nation who I would like to see more and more engaged in some of this public debate around all sorts of different things. Whether it's around the global regulatory environment, climate change or whatever it happens to be. You do want to hear the perspectives of those who invest capital and what is important to them as they invest capital."

Looking ahead Wyatt is also concerned that the dynamic nature of the cyber security threat – especially in the wake of the attacks on Optus and Medibank – means that a comprehensive and long-term commitment to cyber resilience must be embedded within the culture of the nation's boardrooms.

"Cyber was a small part of my risk radar in government, but it is now large on my radar in th. corporate world. There is real risk you can have your corporate reputation ruined by a failure in a cyber event," he says.

Wyatt was respected during his time in government for being able to engage with all sides of politics in robust debates on policy issues, especially the then federal Coalition.

He believes the skills he honed from countless hours of cabinet meetings can now be successfully applied to the corporate world.

"So when you sit in a cabinet room, with every decision you make you are on a high alert to the impacts across a community. So a good government has its eyes and ears open to the community through mechanisms for feedback, input and opinions," he says.

"I think that is what politicians perhaps bring to boards, that perspective. They also bring the knowledge of how government operates."

Richard Goyder says Wyatt's political background has already added value to Woodside board discussions, especially his ability to think on his feet and have a good presence in the boardroom.

While the power of the Goyder network affect in Perth would seem to have been at work in Wyatt's new board roles, the Woodside chairman plays down its influence.

"Where it is helpful is in the mentoring and potentially being able to connect to people, and I certainly do that with people I think have value to add," he says.

"I know the perception might be a bit different but most board appointments now are through search firms, they come up with a list of candidates and recommend them to a board sub-committee, that recommends them to a board. The captains pick or so-called boys club appointments are largely a thing of the past. You can put people into a process now but do no more than that. Ben was obviously different. In the Woodside case he was a captains pick because I thought he was exceptional and he has proven to be so to anyone who has seen him the role."

Wyatt, who is also on the boards of the Telethon Kids Institute in Perth and the West Coast Eagles Football Club, believes he is already making an impact in his new public company roles.

"I think Rio is showing already the important signs about its own recovery in its relationship with traditional owners, its relationship with the community, and Australia more broadly. I'd like to think I've had an impact on that. And similarly with Woodside," he says.

But after graduating to public company life, he is determined to keep his feet firmly on the ground.

The week he was appointed to the Woodside and Rio boards, he had a telling conversation with his mother Janine. He recalls it regularly.

"My late father was a very high profile Aboriginal person from WA who was very engaged in Aboriginal and mainstream politics. So when it was announced that I was joining the boards, the immediate focus was on me being that first Aboriginal person etc, which was the same as when I became State Treasurer," he says,

"I said to Mum, "You know, dad would have liked this. He would have really liked it a lot. But dad would have also said to me, quite clearly, 'Don't become a wanker about it!. Seriously. He would have been very happy and proud of me. But he also would have told me. 'Make sure that you are there because you can do the job'."

# ABOUT THE AUTHOR

Damon Kitney, in his own words, was born with newspaper ink in his veins. Son of a pre-eminent Canberra Press Gallery journalist, Damon has spent nearly three decades in journalism including 16 years at *The Australian Financial Review*. He has been with *The Australian* since 2010 and writes a column in *The Weekend Australian* where he shares the stories, insights and wisdom of Australia's top business leaders.

Damon is so skilled in gaining the trust of our most successful (and often private) leaders that he had exclusive access to James Packer to tell his amazing personal story for the best selling book, *The Price of Fortune: The Untold Story of Being James Packer*, published in 2018.